The Bible:
The Word *of* God or the Word *about* God?

Published by :

Clear Faith Publishing
781 Caxambas Drive
Marco Island, FL 34145

Copyright © William J. Bausch

All Rights Reserved. No part of this book may be used or reproduced in any manner whatsoever, whether electronic, mechanical, photocopying, recording or otherwise, without the prior written permission of the publisher.

Unless otherwise indicated, all scripture citations are from the New Revised Standard Version Bible, copyright © 1989 National Council of the Churches of Christ in the United States of America. Used by permission. All rights reserved worldwide.

ISBN: 978-1-940414-31-7
Cover & Interior Design by Doug Cordes

The mission of Clear Faith Publishing is to spread joy, peace, and comfort through great writing about spirituality, religion, and faith that touches the reader and serves those who live on the margins. Portions of the proceeds from this book are donated to organizations that feed, shelter, and provide counsel for those in need.

For more information, please visit us at:
www.clearfaithpublishing.com.

THE BIBLE:

THE WORD *of* GOD
OR
THE WORD *about* GOD?

WILLIAM J. BAUSCH

It ain't those parts of the Bible that I can't understand that bother me; it is the parts that I do understand.

—*attributed to Mark Twain*

In memoriam

MAUREEN BERTODATTI NOWACKI

Acknowledgments

I would like to acknowledge several people who made this book possible. I want to thank my publisher, Jim Knipper, for believing in me and Shirin McArthur for her sharp editing. Then there is long-time friend Aiden Licari, PhD, who gave suggestions and support in equal measure. Fr. Victor Hoagland, CP, with his usual kindly and insightful comments, was most helpful. But most of my gratitude extends to Franciscan Fr. Bill Burton, professor of sacred scripture at St. Mary's Seminary and University in Baltimore. With freely given generosity and thorough and consistent interest, he went through the manuscript minutely, made sensible suggestions and corrections, and, overall, in the process, became a pleasant pen pal to someone he had never met. His encouragement to publish and his openheartedness were matched only by his extraordinary familiarity with sacred scripture. I add a grateful nod to Fr. Ed Griswold, who introduced me to him.

Needless to say, none of these people are responsible for the contents of this book, its judgments, or the not-infrequent zingers that punctuate some of its pages. Any folly is all my own.

CONTENTS

Foreword   xiii
Introduction   xvii

PART I:
WITNESSES FOR THE PROSECUTION   1

1. Period or Question Mark? (Part I)   3
2. Period or Question Mark? (Part II)   25
3. Back to the Future: An Excursus   41
4. History or His-Story?   51
5. Prophets and Problems   63
6. Old Skins, New Wine   75
7. Gods, God, and Holy Absence   91
8. Unfinished Business   109
9. Religious Visionaries and Violence   119
10. Be Aware of the Scribes and Pharisees   137
11. The Church to the Rescue (Part I)   145
12. The Church to the Rescue (Part II)   163

PART II:
WITNESSES FOR THE DEFENSE   175

13. The Lie that Tells the Truth   177
14. A Digression   195
15. Privileged but Not Unique   201
16. Befriending Science   215
17. The End: Suspending Belief, Embracing Faith   231

PART III:
WITNESS FOR THE ACCUSED   237

18. The Apology and the Council   239

Foreword

As a parish priest, I have always been struck by that incident in the gospel where, out of the corner of his eye, Jesus saw two of his future disciples staring at him as he went by. Jesus paused and said to them, "What are you looking for?" They answered, "Teacher, where are you staying?" He replied, "Come and see." The two went and they saw. They saw Jesus seeking the company of the excluded, the wretched, the sick, and the poor. They saw mercy, compassion, forgiveness, and a new life. And *so* they came to believe (John 1:36–39). When I read that, I knew what a parish must be about. I knew that people were looking for roots long before they were looking for beliefs. People were seeking a lived story long before its official formulations. People were forming relationships long before they embraced religion. In short, I learned this truth: Community comes before religion, belonging comes before believing, story comes before liturgy, and action comes before assent. The proper tactic of religion, I concluded, is not to push dogma, but to offer shared experiences.

No one can be argued into the faith. To fool people into thinking that they cannot enter faith unless they first wholeheartedly believe is getting things backward. In all the great religious traditions, the prophets and mystics spent little time telling people what to believe. Rather, people were first invited to trust that, despite all tragic events to the contrary, our lives have some ultimate meaning and value. Faith therefore is the fruit of discovery and experience, not something we must have at the beginning of the quest. Yes, the strategy must be community first and belief second. "Come and see."

It has struck me that today this is truer than ever. Religion, as we know, at least in the West, is in deep decline. We live in a post-religious society. Sociologists Rodney Stark and Roger Finke put the number of "unchurched" Americans at 83 percent. If this is true, it leaves just 17 percent of adult Americans as religiously committed.[1] Unapologetic unbelief is now the norm. The young have grown up in a time of endemic secularism, where the supporting staples of marriage, family, neighborhood, and church have frayed. The United States of America has taken a radical swing leftward and extreme liberalism has taken root in all of our institutions: in corporate life, in Silicon Valley, in the media, in Hollywood, in politics, and especially in our universities, which have abandoned the transcendent, the humanities, and the arts in favor of the hard sciences. There are only shallow jobs, mobility, speed, and plastic social platforms where virtual, not actual, people hang out. Sex has become as commonplace as sharing a latte at Starbucks: no commitments, no marriage, no family, and, above all, for the hookup couple, no children. "Individuality" is the totem word, the defining point of authenticity. The result of all this is that the young have lost the sense of place, of rootedness. They disdain organized religion, yet, in many ways, they are spiritual searchers.

We must appeal to them in the "come and see" sense of the "other" church. They and most people, thanks to the media, only know the official Church, the Church of the Vatican, the Church of the hierarchy, the Church of the sexual abuse scandals. But there is another church, the everyday church, the two-thousand-year-old church that continues to display quiet, persistent, daily heroism beyond the radar of the media. For over two thousand years, ordinary people have done deeds of love, forgiveness, charity, and compassion in the name of the

---

1 As cited in Kenneth L. Woodward, "Religion & Presidential Politics: From George Washington to Donald Trump," *Commonweal*, September 1, 2020, https://www.commonwealmagazine.org/religion-presidential-politics.

Risen Savior. Among them are the people who taught us how to read and write and preserved civilization during the dark ages, and the people who founded and, to this day, operate the hundreds of thousands of schools, leprosaria, hospitals, orphanages, and the largest AIDS support structure in the world.

People in our history include a deacon, Francis of Assisi; a widow, Catherine of Siena; a soldier named Ignatius of Loyola; and an archbishop from San Salvador, Oscar Romero, who, while celebrating Mass in his cathedral, was assassinated by the controlling powers because he spoke out against their oppression of the peasants—he fell onto the altar, his blood mingling with that of Jesus in the chalice. Closer to home, there is our contemporary, convert Dorothy Day of Staten Island, who founded the Catholic Worker Movement and whose cause is up for canonization, not because she once was a communist, a common-law wife, or had an abortion, but because she discovered in the Church the Risen Jesus and showed a heroic and profound concern for the poor. There is the church of Catholic Relief Services, the largest single private charitable organization in the world, given the highest marks by secular committees because almost all of its collected money goes to relief. There is the parish church of everyday care, worship, concern, and good deeds. I could go on, but columnist Nicholas Kristof sums it up well in a *New York Times* Op Ed piece. He wrote:

> In my travels around the world, I encounter two Catholic Churches. One is the rigid all-male Vatican hierarchy that seems out of touch .... Yet, there's another Catholic Church as well, one I admire intensely. This is the grass-roots Catholic Church that does far more good in the world than it ever gets credit for. This is the church that supports extraordinary aid organizations like Catholic Relief Services and Caritas, saving lives every day, and that operates superb schools that provide needy children an escalator out of poverty.
>
> This is the church of the nuns and priests [and lay people] in Congo, toiling in obscurity to feed and educate children. This is the church of the Brazilian priest fighting [disease].... This

is the church of the Maryknoll Sisters in Central America and the Cabrini Sisters in Africa [who risk their lives] in Swaziland to visit AIDS orphans. . . .

So when you read about the scandals, remember that the Vatican is not the same as the Catholic Church. Ordinary lepers, prostitutes and slum-dwellers may never see a cardinal, but they daily encounter a truly noble Catholic Church in the form of priests, nuns and lay workers toiling to make a difference.[2]

Where is all this leading us? It is leading us to consider, as I mentioned above, putting on the face of Christ for an unbelieving age by letting faith in action compel a second look without worrying about belief for the moment. Faith and belief are different, and faith can coexist with a shaky belief. But, in the long run, shaky belief is not to be downplayed or dismissed. As I have learned throughout the years, faithful people have doubts, particularly today, when Christian beliefs are mocked and ridiculed.

And so, here is the point of this foreword. I leave it to others to create witness parishes of community and service, and I appeal to the teachers to come up with a new apologetic for an educated people. This book on the Bible, with its eccentric viewpoint, is sometimes sarcastic, sometimes cynical, but nevertheless it constitutes a pastoral effort, for it aims, through the lens of biblical criticism, to expose the Church's vulnerable teachings and sometimes out-of-touch arrogance. My hope is that someone will address these tensions in pastoral and contemporary language. My yearning is for new apologists who someday will make books like this obsolete.

---

[2] Nicholas Kristof, "A Church Mary Can Love," *The New York Times*, April 17, 2010, https://www.nytimes.com/2010/04/18/opinion/18kristof.html?hp.

Introduction

> In Sacred Scripture, God speaks to man in a human way.
> —Catechism of the Catholic Church, 109

> The Bible is a huge, heterogeneous collection of material that can only be a unity by imposing some interpretative scheme on it.... Insisting that the Bible determines what we believe begs the question. It's the other way around. What we believe is foisted on the Bible.
> —R.W.L. Moberly

> Whenever we read the obscene stories, the voluptuous debaucheries, the cruel and tortuous executions, the unrelenting vindictiveness, with which more than half the Bible is filled, it would be more consistent that we called it the word of a demon than the Word of God. It is a history of wickedness that has served to corrupt and brutalize mankind.
> —Thomas Paine, The Age of Reason

In the last days of May 2020, a white policeman in Minneapolis, with three other cops looking on, pressed his knee on a Black man's neck to hold him down. The Black man, George Floyd, kept crying, "I can't breathe." His cries were ignored and he died. The story, caught on cell phone—as is everything these days—went viral and provoked outrage nationwide. People took to the streets across the country in protest of one more incident of endemic Black suppression. Protest marches and demonstrations, people holding placards with the rallying cry "I can't breathe," were found in every major city. As always, taking advantage of such public protests, anarchists, thugs, and gangs began devastating looting and destruction, burning cars and buildings and outright stealing. Other nations joined in sympathy. People chiseled "I can't breathe" into the Berlin Wall. Some said it was clearly God's punishment for the systemic persecution of Blacks.

All this was going on while, some five months earlier, the vicious coronavirus, COVID-19, was unleashed upon the world. As I write this in June 2020, it is still raging: some ten million plus cases worldwide, some 500,000 cases in the US, with massive isolation, businesses closing down, unemployment, the sick and dying overwhelming morgues, hospitals, and healthcare systems. Much collateral damage is disrupting lives, businesses, the economy, and worship. It's a pandemic we have never seen in our lifetimes. Once more, some people have said that God is reaping judgment on the country for its immorality, greed, racism, same-sex marriage, abortion, hedonism, materialism, loss of religion, blasphemy, or whatever one's poster-boy barbarism might be.

Religious leaders and commentators were quick to dispute this cause-and-effect scenario. In this, they were unknowingly echoing the ancient Athenian historian, Thucydides. Regarding the devastating epidemic that he witnessed, he wrote that there was neither metaphorical significance nor divine retribution in it. The plague, he wrote, was just a plague. So it is today. Our leaders say God doesn't do a moral tit for tat. One bishop insisted that Pope Francis and Jesus' own teachings in the gospels make it clear that God does *not* use punishment to judge humanity. God is not punishing us through the virus. God isn't like that.

Really?

> God saw that the earth was corrupt ... and God said to Noah, "I have determined to make an end of all flesh, for the earth is

filled with violence because of them; now I am going to destroy them along with the earth."

(Genesis 6:12–13)

[The two angels] said to Lot, ". . . we are about to destroy this place, because the outcry against its people has become great before the Lord, and the Lord has sent us to destroy it."

(Genesis 19:12–13)

The Lord said to Moses, "I have seen this people, how stiff-necked they are. Now let me alone, so that my wrath may burn hot against them and I may consume them."

(Exodus 32:9–10)

Now when the people complained in the hearing of the Lord about their misfortunes, the Lord heard it and his anger was kindled. Then the fire of the Lord burned against them, and consumed some outlying parts of the camp.

(Numbers 11:1)

While Israel was staying at Shittim, the people began to have sexual relations with the women of Moab. These invited the people to the sacrifices of their gods . . . and the Lord's anger was kindled against Israel. The Lord said to Moses, "Take all the chiefs of the people, and impale them in the sun before the Lord, in order that the fierce anger of the Lord may turn away from Israel."

(Numbers 25:1–4)

So, there you are, the bishop notwithstanding. There are many more Bible quotations that, in fact, make the case for a cause-and-effect deity—think Egypt and the ten plagues. So, "Do bad things and I will send terrible things upon you. Sin and I will punish you." It's all in the Bible, the Word of God contradicting the modern apologists who would be quick to reinterpret such incidents in creative ways—but on the surface, there it is: a dissonance, a tension, a contradiction.

The Bible apparently is not to be taken on its face value (except by fundamentalists) and, as this Introduction's epigraphs indicate, the judgments run the gamut, from literal to allegorical, from devoted belief to radical ridicule.

This book picks up on the tradition of the early and medieval questioners of the Bible, right up to its complete rejection by the Enlightenment philosophers, from Spinoza to Voltaire to Strauss to Hume to Paine to Feuerbach to Schopenhauer to the present-day noisy atheists who have had a field day challenging the Bible. So, nervously, I stand in that line—but, unlike them, I critique the Bible, not to discredit it, but to reset it. I will be expressing their issues in modern terms and in the light of more recent revelations they never dreamed of. More than that, I will boldly be suggesting the radical notion that the Bible is best read not as the Word *of* God but as the Word *about* God—that revelation is not a Deity speaking on high from its pages, but rather, revelation is to be found from the bottom up, in the people, uncertain and ever-recalculating, who wrote it.

This book, I reluctantly confess, is upsetting, deconstructing, and sometimes cynical. It presumes some scholarly background. Some of the material contains significant enlargements and expansions of ideas I wrote in previous books. In fact, this small book is a severe condensation of my 2015 book, *Sagas, Scholars, & Searchers*. It's quite a feat: downsizing a 450-page book to one under 250 pages! Even then, this book repeats (note the redundancies are for the purpose of emphasis), rambles a bit, and necessarily segues into the critical issues of the authority and credibility of the Church.

This book is divided into three parts. The first part, "Witnesses for the Prosecution" (shades of Agatha Christie!), is where, so to speak, I make my case. The second part, "Witnesses for the Defense," is where I examine how modern scholars, chastened by archeological, philological, and evolutionary findings, offer a new interpretation of "what the Church has always taught." I end with a chapter on science and the Bible. The third part, "Witness for the Accused," offers a brief apology for my writing of this book in the first place.

Part I:

WITNESSES FOR THE PROSECUTION

Chapter 1

PERIOD OR QUESTION MARK? (PART I)

> Christ Jesus is knocking at our door in the words of Sacred Scripture. If we hear his voice and open the doors of our minds and hearts, then he will enter our lives and remains ever with us.
>
> —*Pope Francis*

In 2019, in order to promote the reading of the Bible, Pope Francis named the Third Sunday of Ordinary Time as "Word of God Sunday." The following year, 2020, marked 1600 years since the death of St. Jerome. Born in Dalmatia (modern Croatia), Jerome lived in Rome, where he translated the New Testament from Greek into popular or "vulgar" Latin (as opposed to literary or standard Latin), and then he moved to Bethlehem, where he translated the Hebrew Old Testament into Latin. Together, these translations became known as the Vulgate. The Roman Catholic Church adopted it as its official Bible until recent times (though it contains too many flaws and some really egregious errors).

Coincidentally, in 2019, Richard Dawkins, one of the Four Horsemen of New Atheism,[1] published his book *Outgrowing God: A*

---

1 See Christopher Hitchens, Richard Dawkins, Sam Harris, and Daniel Dennett, *The Four Horsemen: The Conversation That Sparked an Atheist Revolution* (New York: Penguin Random House, 2019).

THE BIBLE: THE WORD *OF* GOD OR THE WORD *ABOUT* GOD?

Beginner's Guide. One of the chapters was titled with the question, "The Good Book?"—note the question mark.

So, which is it: The Bible as the Word of the Lord with a period or the Bible as the Word of the Lord with a question mark? Fundamentalists and conservatives on the one side, atheists and liberals on the other, have definite convictions as to the correct answer. For the former, the Bible is God-inspired and literally or metaphorically true if you make allowances for the genre of each book. For the latter, it is man-inspired, either as iron-age myth, worthy of contempt, or revered as noble in vision and foundational for Western civilization.

Then, in between, there are people like me: loyal, confused, and loaded with objections, puzzlements, and a touch of skepticism, which has provoked the subtitle of this book: Is the Bible the word *of* God or the word *about* God? I don't believe the former and lean toward the latter. If someone starts telling me, "The Bible says," I tighten up, bracing for what's coming. This makes me a conflicted Christian, but there it is.

You can be the judge as I make my case for "about" rather than "of." My premise maintains that the phrase, "the word *of* God" has no content, no really viable meaning. Nor does the use of the word "inspiration." These words imply a dictation model: God literally spoke and the recipient copied down the dialogue precisely and accurately—though officialdom, to cover the tensions, quickly adds, "using his own human words, cultural outlook, and anthropological limitations." Or the word used is God's "influence," but that influence seems so thin and subtle that it can't be captured.

If this distinction between "of" and "about" is too awkward (and, I admit, it is), let me state it this way—and I'll restate this theme several times throughout the book. From now on, instead of calling the biblical anthology "The Bible," let's drop that appellation entirely and start using the phrases "sacred scripture" or "sacred writings" in our teaching and preaching. "Sacred scripture says" rather than "the Bible says" will cut the Gordian knot of verbal contortions every time "God" says or does something outrageous or awkward. Again, the phrase "the Bible" conjures up God and God's static word. "Sacred writings," on the other hand, conjures up the writers, their times, and their living writings. The use of "sacred scripture" is a deliberate shift *away* from God and *to* the authors and their interpreters. This gives us more leeway in explaining its words, for it has more built-in fluidity than the word "Bible" does.

"Sacred scripture," moreover, is truer to history. It means that the Hebrews had sacred writings they respected but did not enshrine. Those writings were revered, but not idolized. The faithful casually stuck their sacred scrolls in a closet in the Temple and took them out to be studied, commented on, and reworked to fit the times, then put them back. The process was, to quote a phrase we will use again, "a work in progress." It was dynamic; the term "sacred scripture" implies that dynamism and prepares our minds for an evolutionary word rather than a fixed word.

I know this is not entirely satisfactory: sacred scripture or the word about God. I'm trying to make a point. Obviously, a firm catechesis is needed, till the people catch the original Hebrew notion of "a work in progress," that sacred scripture is a loaded word, a moveable feast, always ready to move on. In church, I don't know what to say after the liturgical readings. "This is the word of the prophet" or "This is the sacred pilgrim's word" are clumsy phrases. I'm just trying to avoid the chiseled-in-stone, "this is the word of the Lord" pronouncement when we just read, "Wives, be subject to your husbands in all things."

With this long preamble, let me list eight reasons for my choice of "about" over "of."

1. AUTOGRAPHS AND COPIES

First reason: There are no autographs, no original manuscripts of the Bible. There are no agreed-upon texts. There are only copies of copies, translations of translations, and they not only frequently disagree with one another but also, over time, have been endlessly edited, redacted, updated, and shaped by the agendas, interests, and politics of the editors. The Old Testament notion, for example, that Judah was more important than Israel is a partisan rather than historical judgment. It is clear that many of the words of the prophets

Isaiah, Amos, Hosea, and Micah have been overlaid with later additions. Two versions of the book of Jeremiah eventually appeared. One could also think of Tyndale's translation of the New Testament, where he used the word "congregation" instead of "church," "senior" instead of "priest"—because these were both too popish for his tastes. Of course, modern translations have their own subtle cultural biases as they bow to political correctness; using, for example, "my child" instead of "my son" in Proverbs 1:8, in spite of the fact that the wisdom literature—indeed, the whole Bible itself—is addressed to young men. The Ten Commandments are written in the second person masculine.

Along these same lines, scholars often refer to the "Deuteronomistic History," meaning that an editor took the books from Joshua through 2 Kings, and perhaps the book of Jeremiah, to be a Deuteronomistic historical work and rewrote them to fit his agenda. The so-called Priestly party has its hands all over the Pentateuch, with all of its muddled and contradictory versions of the Adam and Eve and Noah sagas.

Bottom line: All copies contain variations, some minor, some very significant. The Bible you hold in your hand, in other words, includes some editor's many decisions, with footnotes citing other variations. As Kaltner and McKenzie summarize it,

> There are no originals ("autographs") of any of the books of the Bible but only generations of handmade copies. Accidental errors and occasional deliberate changes by scribes crept in with every copy, and copies made from copies only compounded the problem. Not all manuscripts are of equal value. Biblical scholars use techniques of textual analysis and comparison to try to reconstruct the original text or at least get as close to it as possible. While many textual variants are minor and insignificant, some are quite important and involve large portions of a book or even a whole book. Such variants can alter a book's content and message. Even small variants can sometimes change the meaning of a passage.[2]

---

2 John Kaltner and Steven L. McKenzie, *Sleuthing the Bible: Clues that Unlock the Mysteries of the Text* (Grand Rapids: Eerdmans, 2019), 241.

Thus, to talk of the Bible as the static, unalterable, monolithic "word of God" is misplaced, to say the least. To see the Bible as examples of how to live rather than stories of the human condition, as a source of ethical guidance and timeless instruction rather than providing a template against which to measure life, is to make claims that do not hold up.

A Work in Progress

In any case, logically having no original text certainly compromises any notion of divine inspiration, sending the scholars to search for the best-guess translations. In fact, the earliest complete Bible we have dates to the 900s CE, the earliest complete New Testament dates to the 300s CE, and a lot of altering went on in all that time.

That stunning discovery of the Dead Sea Scrolls in 1948, for example, revealed several versions of the Great Isaiah Scroll. As the editors of the volume *Discoveries in the Judean Desert* (2011) put it, "the biblical text was pluriform and still developing prior to the Jewish Revolts [in 66 CE and 132 CE].... *It is full of isolated interpretive insertions.*"[3] Right up almost to the New Testament era, then, interpreters were tinkering with the Hebrew scriptures, leaving us multiple versions. The great literary scholar Robert Alter, when asked to put together a critical edition of Genesis, said he would have to do his own translation first, since the existing ones were so inadequate. (His translation of the Hebrew Bible is a masterpiece.) How do we know which one is valid, which one is *God's* Word? In short, the biblical collection slowly acquired the status of "sacred," but hardly one with Divine authority.

Nor do we have the whole picture. The Bible twice mentions the Book of Jasher, in Joshua and 2 Samuel. It cites the Books of the Wars of the Lord, the Books of the Chronicles of the Kings of Israel, the Books of the Chronicles of the Kings of Judah, and others that we do not possess. So how can the Bible be the Word of God when we don't always know what that (original) word is, when the words sometimes

---

3   As quoted in Hershel Shanks, "Isaiah Among the Scrolls," *Biblical Archaeology Review* 37:4, July/August 2011; italics mine.

conflict, or when subsequent scholarship, as we shall see, overturns a long-held and long-cherished authoritative "word of God"? No definitive, stable Bible appears till well into the Christian era. Not to mention that the trouble with the Bible is the avalanche of interpretations that wildly contradict each other and defy each other with no credible referee to sort them out. Distinguished scholars disagree. Traditional churches, early or late, dogmatize and later reverse meanings. It's a veritable free-for-all, and we're supposed to discern the word of God from this cacophony? As Mother Superior sang in *The Sound of Music*, it's like trying to hold a moonbeam in your hands.

2. SAY WHAT?

Second, to this day there are opaque and nigh untranslatable passages in the Bible. The punning and wordplay are often beyond us. How can the Bible reveal God's word when the word is very difficult to read or understand, thereby making "revelation" an oxymoron? Some manuscripts are still impossible to read with certainty. They are dense, full of contradictions and puzzling and unexplained statements. Understandably, there is always the natural tendency for words, clear at one time or in one social context, to become puzzling to a later generation. There are the shifting meanings of words that render the text no longer clear. Then there are the *hapax* words; that is, words that occur only once in the entire Bible or elsewhere, so there are no other places to make comparisons with which to detect their real meaning. The Book of Job, for example, is full of them.

Worth noting, too, is that copyists of the Torah are obliged to copy not just every letter but every character, every mark. Over the years, fallible copyists have inscribed enlarged or shrunken characters; backward, upside-down, or fractured letters; and yet all these must, by law, be faithfully included in order for the Torah to be considered kosher and usable. Like a virus, these notations and subsequent changes keep replicating themselves over the centuries.

Also, given the fact that Hebrew has no capital letters, periods, commas, or spaces (letters run together), it is difficult to know where one sentence ends and another begins. Meanings can change dramatically depending on how one punctuates it. Recall the famous definition of a panda as a passive vegetarian: an animal who eats shoots and leaves, or a panda as a cold-hearted killer: an animal who eats, shoots, and leaves. Meaning depends on where one puts the commas.

Also, Hebrew has no vowels. The little signs that indicate them were added much, much later, which means that the people who added the vowels had to make choices as to which vowels they chose and where they put them. So, for example, if you had just the consonants "l" and "v," you could add the vowels of your choice and come up with "love," "alive," "olive," "lava," and others—and so alter the meaning. In the sixteenth century, Erasmus, the great Dutch humanist (and the illegitimate son of a priest), dared to find mistakes in Jerome's Vulgate translation. One of the most famous of these is found in Matthew 3:2, where Jerome translates John the Baptist's cry, "*Metanoeite!*" as "Do penance," which, as a proof text, fitted in nicely with the medieval Catholic system of confession and penance. Erasmus (and Luther) correctly pointed out that the word actually meant "Repent!" and had nothing to do with confession.

If you want an amusing example of an Old Testament gaffe, here's one from the Hebrew biblical scholar James Kugel:

> Some of the things that people had always believed about words in the Bible—including, prominently, verses in the Psalms—turned out to be wrong. For example, the most common Hebrew word for soul, *nefesh*, means something a little less spiritual elsewhere in the Semitic world: throat or neck.... Thus, when the Psalmist cries out (to quote the old King James translation), "Save me, O God; for the waters are come in unto my soul" (Ps. 69:2), it turns out what he really meant was: the water is up to my neck![4]

Modern translations have made the correction, but for centuries "soul" was the word used and "soul" was the "word of God."

---

[4] James Kugel, *How to Read the Bible: A Guide to Scripture, Then and Now* (New York: Free Press, 2007), 469.

Ferreting out *the* Word of God from such misinterpretations and misunderstandings is a shifting challenge.

3. THE BIBLICAL YIN AND YANG

Third, all scholars admit that the Bible is shaped by orthodoxy (tradition) and orthodoxy in turn is shaped by the Bible, so you're not sure if you're hearing the word of God or the word of the partisan author. There is an ongoing circular, symbiotic relationship between the two. The orthodoxy interprets the Bible and the Bible then "proves" the orthodoxy. It happens over and over. Church orthodoxy is read into the biblical text, which in turn is often made to confirm the orthodoxy, usually by way of allegory or "creative" exegesis. So, for example, even though there are "teachings" showing that our hierarchical structure and church order come right out of the New Testament, there is no way to reconcile the various types of actual ministry in the New Testament with the later pattern of bishops, priests, and deacons. There is no way one can "prove" that the apostles were ordained "priests" at the Last Supper, although the Church cites the Bible that it is so. There is simply no literary or historical evidence for this tradition.

Regarding the infancy narratives of Matthew and Luke, the renowned New Testament scholar Raymond Brown makes a simple remark that the two accounts "are contrary to each other." In the beloved Christmas gospel (Matthew 1:22–23), we have this translation: "All this took place to fulfill what had been spoken by the Lord through the prophet: 'Look, the virgin shall conceive and bear a son, and they shall name him Emmanuel.'" The word for "virgin" is a mistranslation; the word really means any unmarried young woman. In Isaiah 7:14, it is translated correctly: "Look, the *young woman* is with child and shall bear a son." Matthew knows the story about Isaiah telling King Ahaz that either he (Isaiah) or the King will have a remarkable son; no more, no less. But Matthew has taken it as a prophecy meant for his time and applied it to Jesus. The prophecy "proves" the fact and the fact confirms the prophecy. A modern writer does the same when, reflecting on Joseph, she writes, "growing up as an obedient Jew, Joseph must have known about Isaiah's *prophecy* of the virgin birth."[5] Such a statement reflects imposed orthodoxy at work to prove Mary's virginity.

Matthew also says that Judas, in tossing his thirty pieces of silver into the Temple and hanging himself, was fulfilling Jeremiah: "Then was fulfilled what had been spoken through the prophet Jeremiah, 'And they took the thirty pieces of silver, the price of the one on whom a price had been set, on whom some of the people of Israel had set a price, and they gave them for the potter's field, as the Lord commanded me'" (27:9–10). First of all, the quotation is from Zechariah, and secondly, it literally has nothing to do with the matter at hand. (By the way, the Book of Acts [1:18] says Judas died by falling in a field.)

A more esoteric example is to be found in 1 John 5:7–8, where a few versions expand on this passage to say: "There are three that testify in heaven, the Father, the Word, and the Holy Spirit, and these three are one. And there are three that testify on earth: the Spirit and the water and the blood, and these three agree." If this passage, once assumed to be written by John the beloved disciple, was genuine, it would be a clear reference to the Trinity, and so we would have the Bible "proving" a teaching. Instead, it was found to be a Christian orthodoxy that likely came from the second century and was imposed on the text. Today, in current Bible translations, this passage has accordingly been corrected: "There are three that testify: the Spirit and the water and the blood, and these three agree." The point is that, in earlier times, the old anachronistic assertion was considered inspired as the "Word of God" when clearly it wasn't. The same is true with John's gospel where, in 1:13, "who *were* born" was changed to "who *was* born" as a way of smuggling in the doctrine of Jesus' virginal conception. In chapter 7, we'll see how Protestant orthodoxy forced an egregious misinterpretation on St. Paul.

---

5   Judy Coode, *The Presence of God: Reflections for Advent 2010* (Washington, DC: Pax Christi USA, 2010).

Sidebar

While we're on the subject of partisanship, we might mention the apologetic given by the evangelists, especially Luke. It's an understandable one; Christians were being persecuted by the Roman Empire and the evangelists wanted the empire to know that they, as a sect, were not only harmless, but loyal. Early Roman authorities like Pilate found Jesus innocent, just as the Roman magistrates found Paul innocent. The Christians, in short, were careful to distance themselves from any sign of resistance to the Romans, such as the Jewish revolt of 66–70 CE. Notice that Matthew, for example, creates the incident of Pilate's wife's dream declaring Jesus as innocent. He also, like Mark, famously makes sure that the Jews take the blame for Jesus' death. He was quick to quote Jesus as teaching the payment of taxes and even his phrase "the Kingdom of heaven" is meant to suggest an otherworldly kingdom, not a rival political one. This placating of the Romans is also strong in the Gospel of Luke. None of this equates to classic anti-Semitism as we know it, but we do get an unmistakable, if unintentional, inflation of the "exonerate the Romans, blame the Jews" motif. On this subject, here's as good a contemporary commentary as any. It's from a column by Karen Sue Smith:

> At the Harvard Club recently I attended a lecture by Elaine Pagels, the well-known author of *The Gnostic Gospels* and winner of many prestigious awards including a MacArthur fellowship, a.k.a. "the genius award." Her presentation revolved around an important scriptural question: Why did the author of Mark's Gospel let the Romans off the hook so easily but come down so hard on the Jews as the people guilty of condemning Jesus to death? At the level of history Pontius Pilate appears to have been legally responsible for Jesus' death. Crucifixion was a punishment typically used by the Romans on political rebels and slaves. *It appears that Mark has deliberately exaggerated the power and responsibility of the Jewish leaders in Jerusalem and played down the legal responsibility of the Romans.* He presents Jesus as undergoing several "trials" and as being condemned by Jewish leaders. Pilate seems reluctant to sentence Jesus at

the hearing. When I asked Daniel Harrington S.J. about Mark he said that Pagels' view is plausible adding that *"Matthew and Luke go even further in exculpating the Romans and blaming the Jews for Jesus' death."*

Why? Pagels' answer, in a word, is that it was a matter of Christian *survival*. Jewish resistance to Rome boiled over into revolt in Israel (66–74 A.D.) about the time that Mark wrote his Gospel. "In this context," Harrington says, "it seemed to be in the best interests of early Christians to distance themselves from the Jewish leaders and their followers." But what may be *understandable and even shrewd* in the first century can appear morally disappointing and even embarrassing in the twenty-first century.[6]

Admittedly, from a purely human point of view, the evangelists were absolutely right and politically savvy. They were trying to save their own necks. Who can blame them? Garry Wills, in his book on St. Paul, *What Paul Meant*, agrees with Krister Stendahl's argument that Luke, for example, *omits* material, *misinterprets* facts, and *rearranges* the Pauline story for a purpose of his own, which was to cozy up to the Roman Empire.[7] So Paul, writing prior to the Jewish war, urges making peace with Rome: "Let every person be subject to the governing authorities; for there is no authority except from God, and those authorities that exist have been instituted by God" (Romans 13:1). Notice those italicized *omits*, *misinterprets*, and *rearranges* and tell me this is the Word of God.

All this backs up my case that the Bible isn't the inspired Word of God, but the human word about him. Furthermore, it shows that orthodoxy, even political orthodoxy, gets read into the text and the text supports the orthodoxy. In this instance, what a sad history resulted: "Blame the Jews for the death of Jesus." Of course, we might mention

---

6   Karen Sue Smith, *Church*, Winter 2002, 64. Italics mine except for book title and the word "survival."

7   As discussed in John M. Buchanan, "Heavy Lifting: Reading Theology," *Christian Century*, September 18, 2007, https://www.christiancentury.org/article/2007-09/heavy-lifting.

the further persecution of the Christians by the Jews as extenuating circumstances.

A necessary sidebar within the sidebar. There was mention of Pontius Pilate in the paragraphs above. It is worth mentioning here that Jesus' encounter with Pilate is probably a literary invention that strikingly makes the evangelists' point: There are two kingdoms, the kingdom of Man and the Kingdom of God, and you must decide. I maintain that this is a powerful revelatory story and not a factual one because, if you think about it, it is most unlikely (though remotely possible) that Jesus and Pilate would ever have met. Pilate was a vicious, cruel, inept tyrant, eventually sacked by Rome. During the Passover period, he would have routinely crucified hundreds and hundreds of people to show Rome's might and its intolerance of any resistance or rebellion, which was common enough among these "obstinate" people.

Jesus was of the peasant class, another anonymous pawn in the occupation, another minor so-called political rabble-rouser. He would have simply been routinely killed in the usual roundup with others like him. There is no way an insignificant minor peasant and the mighty Governor of Judea would meet, much less engage in a one-on-one theological conversation. Like the nativity narratives, the Jesus-Pilate encounter is marvelous storytelling, one of those fictions that tell the truth which we will explore in chapter 13. Their power lies in the fact that they still rightly engage and challenge us today. Again, the only trouble with the Pilate story has been its unintended legacy: Pilate is not guilty of the death of Jesus; Caiaphas is. Rome is not guilty of the death of Jesus; the Jews are. And if there were any doubt about it, one could point to the God-inspired gospels, where the evidence was unimpeachable: The Jews actually accepted responsibility for the death of the Christ: "His blood be on us and on our children" (Matthew 27:25).

This may not be one of those truths that "God wanted to be put into the sacred writings for the sake of salvation" (Pontifical Biblical Commission's words, see the next chapter), but it has made its pernicious impact as if it were.

Before I move on, I hasten to add that if the encounter between Pilate and Jesus was unlikely, the political context it depicts was definitely not. When Jesus the Jew was born, there were strife and combat everywhere. Israel was a constant battleground, with core despair over the Roman occupation. Over and over again, questions were raised: "What happened? How do we survive?" All was in tension. Revolution was always in the air. There were seven separate revolts between the years 26 and 36. Jesus witnessed most of them. Galilee was a notorious hotspot for revolutionary movements and Jesus, remember, was a Galilean. There were extreme partisanship, factions, hatred, infighting, and Jewish intellectual foment.

Jesus the Jew was born into this moral and political cauldron and bore its burden and scars. His modern, scrubbed persona—serenely walking the peaceful fields like an early Francis of Assisi or the calm, majestic Aslan-like lion, fully in charge—is far from reality. What in fact makes him remarkable is that, in the midst of the toxic political and religious strife, he rose above it all, bringing the kingdom of God directly to the poor. He touched untouchables, dined with outcasts, and offered faith in place of despair, beauty in the midst of muck, and forgiveness where revenge raged on every corner. In the great, foundational Beatitudes, he offered humankind another path. In the great judgment scene (Matthew 25:31–46), he offered a criterion for connection and wholeness:

> I was hungry and you gave me food, I was thirsty and you gave me something to drink, I was a stranger and you welcomed me, I was naked and you gave me clothing, I was sick and you took care of me, I was in prison and you visited me. . . . Truly I tell you, just as you did it to one of the least these who are members of my family, you did it to me.

We have to rethink our concept of Jesus in a context like that and, today, in our own fractious and unmoored times, with clenched teeth, try to hold onto the faith he offered.

The Parables

If you want more detailed but more recognizable examples of yin and yang, it will pay you to take an extended look at Jesus' parables. To begin with, the parables contain—unsurprisingly, since they were told by an early first-century Aramaic-speaking Jew to other early first-century Aramaic-speaking Jews—echoes of the Hebrew Scriptures. For example, "A man had two sons" resonates with Jacob and Esau. Jesus' meeting the Samaritan woman at the well recalls Abraham's servant and Rebekah, Jacob and Rachel, Moses and Zipporah, and so on.

More to the point, scholars remind us that when the Jesus parables got passed around and eventually written down by the four evangelists, a lot of decades had gone by and the evangelists, writing outside of Palestine, didn't always understand or like the original Aramaic interpretation that came with the story. It didn't fit their times, their agenda, or their orthodoxy, so they changed it. The result was twofold: (1) we never do learn Jesus' original point; and (2) the evangelists' interpretations, now written down and eventually canonized, became the only ones we know—and were sometimes erroneous, but we're stuck with them. In other words, when we now read Jesus' parables in the gospels, we are getting them not necessarily as Jesus told them, but as the evangelists interpreted them. Sometimes Jesus' parables and their later interpretations are not the same and we wind up interpreting the interpreters, because sometimes their interpretations rub *us* the wrong way.

Take Matthew 22:1–14. These verses tell the story of a king's wedding banquet for his son and the shocking indifference of the invited guests, some of whom beat up and kill the king's messengers. The king in turn sends out his hit men to take care of them and has his servants go to highways and alleys to invite others. Scripture scholar John R. Donahue, SJ gives this commentary (the italics are mine in the quotations that follow):

> Matthew, Luke and the second-century Gospel of Thomas recount this parable with *very different applications*. In Luke the substitute guests are "the poor, the crippled, the blind and the

lame," an epitome of the Lukan Jesus' good news for the poor. In Thomas there is a simple dinner, and the guests refuse because the invitation conflicts with their business interests. Matthew is unique in *allegorizing* the punishment of the refusing guests into the destruction of Jerusalem, ("burnt their city") and adding the expulsion of the man without the wedding garment.

Matthew's interpretation of this parable has unfortunately *provided fuel for anti-Semitism*. The guests who refuse to come are equated with the Jewish people who first heard the invitation of Jesus but failed to respond. The consequence of this rejection was the destruction of the Jewish Temple. The guests who came to the feast in their place are taken to represent converts to Matthew's community, both Jews and Greeks. Such a view was unfortunately *part of the "blame game,"* as it was played in the first century.[8]

Here's another parable. Amy-Jill Levine reminds us that Luke 18:2–5 is a parable concerning a widow and a judge. Luke tells us that the parables were told to the disciples about "their need to pray always and not to lose heart," that the parable is informative about God's providing swift justice to those who remain faithful, and that the judge is a negative allegorical image of God. She says,

> Luke's opening contextualization and concluding lesson are not necessary, or even necessarily logical, readings of the parable. For Luke's readers in antiquity or for readers today, a tenacious widow who threatens to give a judge a black eye is not an image of fervent prayer; divine justice has not been swift, for we are still waiting for that kingdom to come; and the judge is in no way an image for the divine. Luke turns the parable into an allegory, and so platitude replaces provocation.[9]

---

8   John R. Donahue, "What Shall I Wear?" *America*, October 7, 2002, https://www.americamagazine.org/faith/2002/10/07/what-shall-i-wear. Italics mine.

9   Amy-Jill Levine, *Short Stories by Jesus: The Enigmatic Parables of a Controversial Rabbi* (New York: HarperCollins, 2014), 18.

All this is a lot to take in, but it makes my point. All those italicized words above are meant to ask: Before Mark got hold of the original parable, was it the inerrant "word of God," the word of Jesus, the Revelation of the Father, with its distinct message? If so, did it "lose" its inerrancy and divine inspiration when Mark took it over, added his own interpretation, and moved it into the official canon? When Matthew, in turn, took over Mark and, in his own personal extended allegory that he "placed on the lips" of Jesus, added even more material—never included nor intended in the original parable—did *that* become the inspired Word of God, and did it abrogate Mark's, and especially the non-canonical Thomas? Does all this reworking, which strays considerably from the original meaning, come under new divine inspiration? Do we have a multiple choice of inspired interpretations? Does the original utterance of Jesus, now no longer known by ordinary people—or the scholars, for that matter—have nothing to say to us anymore? In all this, how will we ever discern the "word *of* God"?

The Puzzled Disciples

Let's be frank. It seems clear that the disciples themselves likely didn't understand Jesus' parables, given their record of consistently misunderstanding him and his rebukes of their lack of understanding. Not only that, they doubt Jesus' healing powers, question his mission, deny him, betray him, flee him in time of need, and all the rest. Jesus often seems to be out of their comfort zone—so often, in fact, that they just didn't "get it." (In his gospel, Matthew deletes such negatives about the disciples—a sign of a work in progress, like all the books of the Bible.) So, once more, it's likely they didn't always catch the point of Jesus' parables and he had to explain some of them in private. If *they* didn't get it, the next generation fared no better. Immediately, in fact, the evangelists who became the first interpreters of the parables domesticated and allegorized them. In so doing, they started a trend that the Church Fathers (who never met an allegory they didn't like) picked up, one that has continued to this day.

The result has been that Jesus' parables, which by definition are open-ended and historically specific, not only lost their original impact but, sad to say, eventually devolved into a virulent anti-Judaism that, in turn, by the time of the Church Fathers, turned into anti-Semitism. Jesus is made to look good by making the Jews look bad. The narrow, legalistic, elitist, self-righteous Pharisees and scribes are equated with "hypocrites," in contrast to the humble, pure, charismatic publicans and tax collectors; the priest and the Levite in the Good Samaritan parable represent the Law and the Prophets and the Samaritan represents Jesus; the original vineyard owners (Israel) forfeit their heritage to newcomers (Christians); Jewish narrowness is contrasted with Christian universalism; the stern, capricious, punishing God of Israel versus the gentle, forgiving God of Jesus—all are allegorized themes derived from Luke's and Matthew's treatment of the parables. Even when we compare some of the parables (such as Luke 14:21) with the Gospel of Thomas 64, it becomes clear that the interpretation and domestication of Jesus' words has already begun. I make my case. The circular dance between orthodoxy and text goes on and finding the word *of* God in these human machinations is futile.

4. THE TALMUD LENS

Fourth is what I call the Talmudic lens. You don't see things as *they* are. You see things as *you* are. And, when it comes to the Bible, nothing could be truer. The ancient rabbis, modern Christian commentators, and the Four Horsemen of New Atheism all see the Bible from their cultural perspective. The first two, the rabbis and Christian commentators, as James Kugel reminds us,[10] see the Bible this way: (1) The Bible is cryptic; the words said one thing, but really meant another. You just had to unlock the meaning. Respected scholars, for example, say that there is absolutely nothing in the Bible about a Messiah who must suffer, yet, if you bring that conviction to the Bible, you will "find" it in Isaiah. (2) The Bible was a collection for all

---

10   Kugel, *How to Read the Bible*, 14–15.

times and seasons, a book of instructions on how to live. It was always relevant, and you just had to sift through it to discover how it is. (3) The Bible contains no errors or contradictions. If there appeared to be any, it was just that—an appearance—and you had to reroute your interpretation. (4) The Bible is a divinely given text.

If you approach the Bible with a fourfold faith stance like that, then it's a whole different story. What if you don't have faith? The catch is that, according to Church teaching, you can't "earn" it, only predispose yourself to it. It's a gift of God. If you're not given that gift, then, as regards the Bible, you can either be one of the antagonistic atheists or a reluctant unbeliever like physician-author Richard Selzer, who laments:

> My entire life has been one long search for faith. I haven't found it. I do not believe in God. Having said that, which should lift an eyebrow or two, I want you to know that I love the idea of God. I love piety. Without it, you lead your life unmoored, in a state of isolation. You are a tiny speck in a vast universe. I'm jealous, frankly. I feel as though I have missed out on the greatest thing that can happen to a person—faith in God. It must be wonderful.[11]

If we go back to the first way of Talmudic "seeing"—the Bible is cryptic—then naturally we're going to get exotic allegorical interpretations like these examples from the epistle of Barnabas: When Moses broke the tablets in anger, that was a sign that the old Covenant with Israel had been broken (4:8b); the biblical prohibition against eating pork means to avoid people who only pray when they're in trouble, just as pigs only snort when they are hungry (10:3). The prohibition against eating rabbits, hyenas, and weasels really warns against deviant sexual practices. When Abraham circumcised 318 men, it really is a symbol of Jesus' redemptive work, for the number 318 in Greek is the first two letters of Jesus' name, just as the first letters in Greek of

---

11   Richard Selzer, in *Wittenburg Door*, Summer 1989, 27, as quoted in Brian McLaren, *Finding Faith—A Search for What Makes Sense* (Grand Rapids: Zondervan, 2007), 115.

the names Jesus and Christ, when placed one on top of another, form the outline of the cross.

If you take this kind of allegorizing to the extreme, you get this sort of howler from, of all people, a liberal Baptist minister who supports gay marriage by appealing to the Bible: "If two lie down together, they keep warm; but how can one keep warm alone?" (Ecclesiastes 4:11) And how about the prohibition of eating meat and dairy at the same meal deriving from Exodus 23:19 ("You shall not boil a kid in its mother's milk.")—a prohibition, generally acknowledged by Judaism, that goes way beyond anything that the text itself requires? Then too, the first Christians, like St. Paul and the early Church Fathers, "saw" the Old Testament solely in terms of prophecy—that is, every page "naturally" announces Jesus. *Of course* the famous Christmas-time refrain from Isaiah 9:6 in our Advent liturgy is "clearly" a mighty prophecy about Jesus:

> For a child has been born for us,
> a son given to us;
> authority rests upon his shoulders;
> and he is named
> Wonderful Counselor, Mighty God,
> Everlasting Father, Prince of Peace.

Again, the truth is that, despite Handel's glorious *Messiah*, the words refer either to the coronation of a king, probably Hezekiah, or the birth of Isaiah's son, but have been coopted into prophecy. Unfortunately, a lot of vile anti-Semitism depends on the canard that the Jews were deliberately obtuse not to see this "obvious" fact. It all depends on what you bring to the Bible.

Here's another example of creative interpretation, this time from Jesus. It was within the popular lore that one day God would send a descendent from the line of David to restore the kingdom. So foretold Nathan. One day, Jesus, the messiah and the Davidic king, got into a debate with the Pharisees. He asks his opponents just how it is possible that the messiah should actually be descended from David by quoting Psalm 110, which reads:

> *The Lord* [God] says to my lord,
> "Sit at my right hand,
> until I make your enemies your footstool."

But Jesus gets creative (see Matthew 22:44). He makes *David* say the first line. Now we have a different ballgame. *David* is calling one of his descendants "lord," his superior. In other words, Jesus is saying, this Davidic descendant is not just an ordinary person, but "Lord," and who is that Lord but Jesus himself? Jesus makes the psalm say what it doesn't say. This manipulating of the Bible was standard in Jesus' time, but it niggles at us: With a bit of creativity, it seems you can make the Bible say whatever you want.

What I am trying to say is that it escapes us how the biblical writers, like, say, Matthew or the author of the Epistle to the Hebrews, can segue so easily from citations that seemingly have nothing whatsoever to do with what they are claiming and make them fit. It's a form of exegesis that baffles the modern mind. If, for example, St. Paul writes that "Christ died for our sins in accordance with the scriptures" (1 Corinthians 15:3) and the scholars prove that no such scriptures exist, how do I manage that? It's like the biblical writers hit the search button for, say, the word "mountain" and then, no matter how uncontextualized the word, they apply whatever they find to what they're working on, force it into relevance, and make "predictions" out of it. I call this the chameleon school of exegesis.

A quotation from scripture scholar Felix Just, SJ, defines this. Commenting on the Epistle to the Hebrews with its vast number of Old Testament quotations, he makes this observation (emphasis mine):

> Most biblical quotations in Hebrews are fairly short and used *without much regard for their original historical or literary contexts,* since they are mostly interpreted as speaking about or referring to Jesus.[12]

---

12   Felix Just, "The 'Epistle' to the 'Hebrews,'" *Catholic Resources for Bible, Liturgy, Art, and Theology,* https://catholic-resources.org/Bible/Epistles-Hebrews.htm.

See what I mean? Maybe people did things like that—take words totally out of context and rework them to fit their agendas—but, if so, it's a stretch and raises the suspicion that there's no criteria beyond the orthodoxy the writer is pushing. But, once you fool around like that, it's anybody's game and, as Shakespeare noted, "the devil can cite Scripture for his purpose." The allegories of some of the Church Fathers are really pretty far out. It all seems so subjective. To make the Bible work as a religious source, you have to bring a prior faith to it.

5. A BROTHERS GRIMM'S ECHO

Fifth, a picayune objection, or at least a wink and a nod to the use of the "Word *of* God." It concerns Matthew 17:24, where the issue is paying the Temple tax. The theological point in context is, as Jesus pointed out, that the sons of the king are exempt—that is, himself, presumably, as "Son of God," the true Temple—and, by association, the disciples, as sons of the kingdom. However, Jesus says, "To avoid scandal, let's pay it." So far, so good. Then he continues with this instruction: So that we do not give offense to the Temple's caregivers, "go to the sea and cast a hook; take the first fish that comes up; and when you open its mouth, you will find a coin; take that and give it to them for you and me." I don't know. This story looks like it could come straight from the Brothers Grimm's repertoire or one of the weirder gnostic gospels. Jesus dabbling in magic tricks? It somehow doesn't fit. Did it really happen that way, or is it an insertion—and, if so, are there other such "tricks" like changing water into wine? This is the "word *of* God"? I don't mean to be disrespectful, but the episode is so uncharacteristic of the gospels that it makes you wonder.

Chapter 2

PERIOD OR QUESTION MARK? (PART II)

> Very few books on the New Testament start where they should: with the statement that there is no direct evidence outside the New Testament that Jesus ever existed.... It seems more probable that such a figure did exist than was invented.... The real question is whether such a Jesus is accurately portrayed in the gospels.
> —*Philip R. Davies*, THE BIBLE FOR THE CURIOUS: A BRIEF ENCOUNTER

6. STORIES RECYCLED

Sixth, this thought. Though we've heard it before, it is easy to forget that the writers of the seventy-two books of the Bible were, as we say, children of their times, just as we are of our times. That is, they used the language, concepts, and symbols of the culture they knew to tell their stories. And they constantly borrowed and recycled old stories from the surrounding cultures and adapted them as their own. *There are few biblical stories whose storylines, metaphors, and local lore are original.* As is fitting for the context of their times, they all have very human antecedents. Books like James Hoffmeier's *Israel in Egypt* and *Ancient Israel in Sinai* give plenty of evidence that the biblical books contain texts that go very, very far back in history, way beyond what the Bible's compilers could have remembered. Still, the Pontifical Biblical Commission insists that although God is the author of the Bible, it was in fact written by humans and therefore is subject to all the historical, cultural, and literary limitations of their times. Let's take time to realize just how much the biblical writers *were* children of their times and how unoriginal their human stories are.

This realization all started in the nineteenth century, which saw an explosion of electrifying finds as the science of archaeology came of age. Scientists were uncovering troves of ancient chiseled, painted, or written material and they were learning how to decipher such messages. What amazed the scholarly world of Bible readers was how many of the biblical stories, beliefs, and cultural attitudes were not original, but borrowed, although with a "Yahweh" twist. For example, most people today probably know about the Epic of Gilgamesh from the Early Bronze Age. Long before the Bible, it told a Noah and the Ark story almost exactly as portrayed in the Bible.

> On day seven, I released a dove which flew away but returned.
> There was no place for it to rest.
> I released a swallow, which flew away, but it also returned.
> There was no place for it to rest.
> I released a raven, which saw that the flood had subsided.
> It ate, circled, and flew away.[1]

People fail to realize how many other borrowings and reworkings there are in God's "authored" book collection. From the Buddha, for example, we get one of the earliest expressions of the Golden Rule. If Jesus said, "Do to others as you would have them do to you," Buddha said, "Consider others as yourself." The Judeo-Christian faiths did not have a lock on wisdom and virtue, nor were Jesus' teachings entirely novel. For example, the Confucians' book *Great Learning* opens with, "The Way of the Great Learning lies in illuminating virtue, treating the

---

1   Victor Harold Matthews and Don C. Benjamin, *Old Testament Parallels: Laws and Stories from the Ancient Near East*, 4th ed. (Mahwah, NJ: Paulist, 2016), "Gilgamesh and Utnapishtim."

people with affection, and resting in perfect goodness.... Like a tree, rooted in the mysterious earth, the man of *ren* [human-heartedness] aspires to Heaven but, at the same time, he reaches out compassionately to the people."[2] Confucianism has long set the tone for the modern-day renewed sense of interconnectedness. Here is the famous "Western Inscription" inscribed in the western wall of Confucius' study:

> Heaven is my father and Earth is my mother, and even such a small creature as I finds a place in their midst.
>
> Therefore, that which extends through the universe I regard as my body and that which directs the universe I consider as my nature.
>
> All people are my brothers and sisters, and all things are my companions.
>
> The great ruler [the emperor] is the eldest son of my parents [Heaven and Earth], and the great ministers are his stewards. Respect the aged—this is the way to treat them as elders should be treated. Show affection toward the orphaned and weak—this is the way to treat them as the young should be treated.... Even those who are tired and infirm, crippled and sick, those who have no brothers and sisters, wives or husbands, are all my brothers who are in distress and have no one to turn to.[3]

That's "biblical" to the core. The Bible, I repeat, has no originality, no uniqueness, concerning the care of the poor. In fact, Mesopotamian influence is all over the Hebrew scripture. As Karen Armstrong reminds us,

> The preoccupation with social justice and equity... was neither peculiar to Israel nor the result of a special divine revelation.... The protection of the weak and vulnerable was a common preoccupation in the ancient Near East. The

---

2 As quoted in Karen Armstrong, *The Lost Art of Scripture: Rescuing the Sacred Texts* (New York: Alfred A. Knopf, 2019), 284.

3 Ibid., 287.

> Sumerian kings had insisted that justice for the poor, the orphan and the widow was a sacred duty decreed by the sun god Shamash.... The Code of King Hammurabi... decreed that the sun would shine over the people only if the king and his aristocracy did not oppress their subjects.... The theme of a divine covenant... pervaded the Near East.[4]

In other words, caring for the widow and the orphan is not a peculiar Christian practice or revelation. When Jesus taught what we call the Lord's Prayer, asking God to "forgive us our debts, as we also have forgiven our debtors" (Matthew 6:12), he is reflecting the Book of Sirach (28:2), where it its written, "Forgive your neighbor the wrong he has done, and then your sins will be pardoned when you pray."

Parallels

One can find other similarities and derivatives in books like *Old Testament Parallels: Laws and Stories from the Ancient Near East*. Let me share some examples.

A hymn to the Egyptian god Ptah has this line: "The *ka*-souls of all the living were created in the image of Ptah." This is not far from Genesis 1:26, that says, "Then God said, 'Let us make humankind in our image.'"[5]

"Having done all these things, Ptah rested and was content with his work." Genesis 2:2: "And on the seventh day God finished the work that he had done, and he rested on the seventh day."[6]

Of the Egyptian god Atum, one papyrus says, "When the almighty speaks, all else comes to life. There were no heavens and no earth. There was no dry land, there were no reptiles... in the land." Yahweh is not the only deity who creates by a simple word from his mouth.[7]

---

[4] Ibid., 21–22.

[5] *The Hymn to Ptah* as cited in "Ancient Egyptian Parallels in the Bible," *ProjectAugustine.com*, https://projectaugustine.com/biblical-studies/ancient-near-east-studies/ancient-egyptian-parallels-in-the-bible/.

[6] Ibid.

[7] Matthews and Benjamin, *Old Testament Parallels*.

An Assyrian tablet tells of the priest Adapa, who duels with the wind just as Jesus did on Lake Tiberius. His story also contains a talking snake. The legal dealings of Abraham and Rachel in the Bible reflect very old Assyrian traditions. The stories of Abraham and Sarah, Jacob and Leah and Rachel, Moses—all have parallels in ancient sources prior to the Bible.

Here's an old story from Ugarit that has a son scolding his father. Note the motifs we usually associate with the Hebrew prophets:

> Your illness made you derelict.
> You did not hear the cases of widows.
> You did not hear the cases of the poor.
> You did not drive out oppressors.
> You did not feed orphans in the city.
> You did not feed widows in the country.[8]

The stories of Baal and Anat portray El [who is referred to as El, the Merciful] and Baal in much the same way as the Bible portrays Yahweh. The divine patrons of both Ugarit and Israel share many of the same titles and govern the cosmos with the help of a divine assembly; both battle with raging seas and with death itself; both build magnificent temples and both are enthroned in the heavens.

Stories of twins or brothers are consistently found in many pre-biblical accounts such as the Egyptian story of Anubis and Bata and are reflected in the biblical story of Cain and Abel. The Jacob and Esau saga corresponds to the Egyptian gods Horus and Set who also struggled in the womb and who fought over who would lead the nation. To top it off, Set even had red hair, just like Esau. The Joseph story of being propositioned by his master's wife is an old one as well. Talking animals find a home in the biblical stories of Eden's snake (Genesis 3:1–7) and Balaam's donkey (Numbers 22:28–39).

Everyone knows that Moses was rescued from the water by a princess of the Egyptian court. How many know that it's an almost exact copy of the story of Sargon, whose mother, after his birth, hid

---

8   Ibid.

him in a basket woven from rushes, sealed it with tar, and set it afloat in the river Euphrates, where he was found by a royal gardener? We might also remember that Moses is an Egyptian name. As we shall note again, the Exodus story, as found in the Bible, comes from around the sixth century BCE, which makes it about six hundred years after the events described—although recently some scholars, finding evidence of greater literacy before that, surmise that an earlier date might be possible. Still, whatever the case, Tel Aviv University's Israel Finkelstein reminds us that the biblical texts were written to promote the "ideological messages of the time."[9]

The flight of some slaves gradually came to resemble a Cecil B. DeMille production. Further, the Bible's rendition of some four million people traipsing across the continent, leaving no physical trace and no record elsewhere of such a stupendous event, is beyond belief. The Exodus is more a theological statement, claiming that the God of Israel is on the side of the oppressed and will liberate them. Yearning for and accounts of liberation are common to all ancient cultures.

The Hittites invented the Covenant and treaty form found in Genesis and Leviticus. The book of Joshua is a mirror of Assyrian conquest accounts. The various codes, like the well-known Code of Hammurabi, are found in the early books of the Bible. The Covenant Code, the Holiness Code, the Deuteronomic Code—all really contain nothing new. They are copies of other people's ancient codes, often just lifting them verbatim.

The famous Egyptian Book of the Dead has parallels in the book of Job. Check out these words:

> Do justice and live.
> Does the handscale lie? Is the standscale tilted?
> Do not be tempted by corruption.

---

[9] American Friends of Tel Aviv University, "Study Confirms Widespread Literacy in Biblical-Period Kingdom of Judah: Texts Dating Back to around 600 BCE Were Written by 12 Different Authors," *ScienceDaily*, September 10, 2020, www.sciencedaily.com/releases/2020/09/200910110828.htm.

> Do not return evil for good.
> Do not speak falsely.
> Do not steal.[10]

The Teachings of Ptah-Hotep and Amen-em-ope appear everywhere in the Hebrew Bible, often verbatim, especially in books such as the New Testament Epistle of James and the Old Testament books of Proverbs, Sirach, and Ecclesiastes—books that, like modern advice columns, deal in good manners and offer homespun advice about which fork to use. Samples include:

> Do not take counsel with fools.
> Do not covet the goods of the poor.
> Do not bear false witness against your neighbor.
> Do not go to bed worrying and wondering, "What will tomorrow bring?"
> No one knows what tomorrow brings.

They all sound like they're from the Bible, but they are not. The last line sounds very much like Jesus' teaching in Matthew 6:34, "So do not worry about tomorrow, for tomorrow will bring worries of its own."

If you didn't know better, you would guess these sayings are from the Hebrew prophets instead of old Egyptian writings. The lamentations found in the books of Lamentations, Jeremiah, Ezekiel, and the Psalms have parallels in the Lamentations for Ur.

Here's a representative commentary about Jacob's blessing of his sons in Genesis 49:

> Jacob's final words to his sons are from an archaic poetic composition *inserted* into the narratives of Jacob's last instructions and blessings. *Much of the Hebrew text is difficult, and many of the images are obscure;* but some of the later realities of the Israelite tribes and of their relationship with one another are reflected in these brief statements about Jacob's sons. Here, as elsewhere

---

10 Matthews and Benjamin, *Old Testament Parallels*.

in Genesis, Jacob's sons represent the *later* Israelite tribes that bear their names. *Thus the fortune of the sons described here are in fact the fortunes of their tribal descendants.* Since Judah is given the preeminent role among his brothers (v. 8), this composition reflects the period of the monarchy, when the family of David, from the tribe of Judah, established dynastic rule over Israel in Jerusalem.[11]

A common example of vested interests at work—and this is the Word of God?

We might nod to the similarity of Elijah being whisked up to heaven in a fiery chariot, Jesus being taken to the top of the Temple and to a very high mountain by the devil (by what means we are not told), and Muhammad being whisked to Jerusalem by Allah.

Let's compare the annunciation to Mary by the archangel Gabriel to the angel of the Lord who appeared to Manoah, wife of Zoram, and said to her, "Although you are barren, having borne no children, you shall conceive and bear a son" (Judges 13:3) and Mary's song of praise to the song of infertile Hannah in 1 Samuel 2:1–10, who also miraculously conceived:

> "My heart exults in the Lord....
> My mouth derides my enemies,
> because I rejoice in my victory....
> The bows of the mighty are broken,
> but the feeble gird on strength.
> Those who were full have hired themselves out for bread,
> but those who were hungry are fat with spoil....
> The Lord makes poor and makes rich;
> he brings low, he also exalts.
> He raises up the poor from the dust;
> he lifts the needy from the ash heap.

Compare this to Mary's *Magnificat* (Luke 1:46–55). It is almost a word-for-word copy.

---

11   Walter Harrelson, *The New Interpreter's Study Bible: New Revised Standard Version with the Apocrypha* (Nashville: Abingdon, 2003), 81; my emphasis.

Well, enough. You get the picture. The Bible surely has its own unique genius and distinctive traditions. Still, much of the Bible, as befits the writings of a small, minority community, is borrowed and recycled material—which is legitimate; how else could they express themselves except in the common idioms, metaphors, symbols, and shared stories of their milieu? Still, we must ask: When the ancient epics and stories of Israel's neighbors and forebears, when the sayings of Amen-em-ope are dropped, sometimes verbatim, into the Bible, when these uninspired stories and sayings of ordinary wisdom were taken wholesale into the Bible and "baptized," as it were, did these (so many of them "pagan") antecedents then instantly become the inspired "word of God"? While they hung out as ordinary fare for the regular folk, were they merely human words, but instantly became *God's* words upon their inclusion in the Bible? Again, in the light of these reflections, how valid is the Bible as the Word *of* God and not the word *about* God, about bending and recasting these stories in the context of Yahweh?

7. THE RADICAL WORD

Seventh—hold onto your hat for this one—some modern liberal apologists of many denominations are consistently making the case for a revered and respected Bible, yes, but one that is woefully obsolete and *superseded* by modern science and contemporary experience. We'll get his full words in chapter 11, but here let me quote this much from Catholic scripture scholar Luke Timothy Johnson: "We are fully aware of the weight of *scriptural evidence pointing away from our position* [the approval of gay and lesbian lifestyles], yet place our trust in the power of the loving God to reveal as powerfully through personal experience and testimony as through written texts."[12] Then there's the Episcopal theologian, the Rev. David P. Jones, who said, concerning the consecration of a gay man as bishop, "Ten years ago I would not have been happy about this because I would have felt it's *clearly contrary*

---

12   Luke Timothy Johnson, "Homosexuality & the Church: Scripture & Experience," *Commonweal*, June 11, 2007, https://www.commonweal-magazine.org/homosexuality-church-0.

to the Bible, contrary to the traditions of the church. It's all because I've experienced the ministry of this man and a couple of others that I think I was mistaken."[13] And that gay bishop himself, Gene Robinson, declared, "Just because Scripture and tradition say something is wrong, that doesn't necessarily mean it's wrong."[14] Think that one over.

Let's turn to the popular Methodist scholar Walter Wink, who advocates same-sex marriage:

> Where the Bible mentions [same-sex sexual] behavior at all, *it clearly condemns it. I freely grant that. The issue is precisely whether the biblical judgment is correct.* The Bible sanctioned slavery as well and nowhere attacked it as unjust. Are we prepared to argue today that slavery is biblically justified? ... In the same way, fifty years from now people will look back in wonder that the churches could be so obtuse and so resistant to the new thing the Holy Spirit was doing among us regarding [sexuality].
>
> What happened to bring about such a monumental shift on the issue of slavery was that the churches were finally driven to penetrate beyond the legal tenor of Scripture to an even deeper tenor ... [embodied] in Jesus' identification with harlots, tax collectors, the diseased and maimed and outcast and poor....
>
> [Regarding sexism and patriarchies] The way out, however, is not to deny the sexism in Scripture, but to develop an interpretative theory that judges even Scripture in the light of the revelation in Jesus. What Jesus gives us is a critique of domination in all its forms, a critique that can be turned on the Bible itself. The Bible thus contains the principles of its own correction. We are freed from bibliolatry, the worship of the Bible.[15]

---

13 As quoted in Laurie Goodstein, "New Hampshire Episcopalians Choose Gay Bishop, and Conflict," *The New York Times*, June 8, 2003, https://www.nytimes.com/2003/06/08/us/new-hampshire-episcopalians-choose-gay-bishop-and-conflict.html.

14 As quoted in Bob Harvey, "The Power of Culture: Homosexuality and the Church," *Faith Today*, March/April 2004, https://bbnc.evangelicalfellowship.ca/page.aspx?pid=1946.

15 Walter Wink, *Homosexuality and Christian Faith: Questions of Conscience for the Churches* (Minneapolis: Fortress, 1999), 47–48. All italicized words in the above quotations are mine.

Franciscan Richard Rohr adds:

> The number of violent, dualistic, imperialistic, sexist, clannish, patriarchal, homophobic, fully contradictory, and historically entrapped texts in the Bible are just too many to be contradicted or roundly dismissed. Now, when anyone calls such a Bible 'inerrant,' most modern and postmodern people just discount the honesty or thoughtfulness of the speaker.[16]

Current gender issues—with the full implication that Leviticus, St. Paul, official church teaching, and deep non-church traditions were wrong for twenty centuries—have catalyzed such modern dismissal of the Bible as normative. Those quotations surely undermine any notion of the Bible's infallibility, inspiration, or authorship. The biblical judgments are and have been "incorrect," the Holy Spirit notwithstanding. The word of God is faulty—or, let's say, "incomplete"—if not obsolete and uneven. If the Bible that contains God's words has promoted social justice and compassion, it has also justified contempt, discrimination, torture, and murder. How do you sort them out? We need therefore to develop new interpretative theories and get free of the "bibliolatry," the worship of the Bible as the Word *of* God.

8. WHICH BIBLE?

Finally, we may ask, *which* Bible is the Word of God? Is it the not-yet-canonized but sacred writings (Bible) *before* Ezra or the revised Bible *after* him? Is it the Bible after the Babylonian captivity, when the scribes rewrote it, or the Bible after the Roman destruction of the Temple, when the Pharisees reworked and rewrote it? As Karen Armstrong put it (italics mine):

> The *newly edited* history, now dominated by the theme of exile and return ... [gave] the biblical narrative—for perhaps the first time—a strong, internal coherence.... [The editors] had

---

16 Richard Rohr, *What Do We Do with the Bible?* (Albuquerque, NM: CAC Publishing, 2018), 27.

> no qualms about giving these old tales a new twist. Whatever the original story of Abraham may have been, the editors now focused on the fact that when God commanded him to leave his home in Mesopotamia, he went willingly into a self-imposed exile—and that was why Yahweh favored him ... [and] as soon as Abraham arrives in Canaan, the editors made Yahweh promise to give the entire Land to his descendants.[17]

Or again,

> The stories of Moses were already well developed by the sixth century BCE, but during the exile, the editors seem to have *introduced new elements*. Hitherto, the oral traditions had focused on the crossing of the Sea of Reeds, the Sinai revelation and the years in the wilderness. But the exiled Judahites seem to have added new details about the Israelites' enslavement in Egypt which closely mirrored their own experience in Babylon.[18]

In short, the scribes rewrote the Exodus story to fit their times, even adding totally new elements, as when Ezra, who was inventing and giving commentary on the old traditions (*midrash*), said that Yahweh had instructed Moses that during the seventh month, Israelites should live in leafy shelters (*sukkoth*) in memory of their ancestors' years in the wilderness. This was a complete innovation and Israel had never done such a thing from the days of Joshua to Ezra's day. Again, it is clear that during the post-exilic period,

> Several of the old cultural texts were rewritten so that they could address the contemporary situation. Jeremiah's letters were altered to reflect Jerusalem's destruction and the ensuing exile. The two books of Chronicles, composed by priestly authors, glossed passages of Genesis, Samuel and Kings, giving them new meaning.... The authors were reading between the

---

17 Armstrong, *Lost Art of Scripture*, 100–101.
18 Ibid., 104. My emphasis.

lines of the old texts and adding new reflections.... Ezra would be remembered as a creator of scripture as well as an exegete.[19]

Speaking of creativity, how about the differing canons? It's a fact that no patristic Old Testament canon is identical. There was no complete unanimity about which books belong in the Bible until the canon was settled much later. Today, the Protestant canon contains sixty-six books, the Catholic seventy-two. The Protestant Bible discards, for example, 1 and 2 Maccabees as not belonging in the Bible. Yet the Protestant compilers are faced with the embarrassment that both St. Augustine and Origen cite 2 Maccabees as the scriptural basis for the doctrines of prayers for the dead and creation "out of nothing." How about Luther's famous rewriting of sacred scripture? Romans 3:28 reads, "For we hold that a person is justified by faith apart from works prescribed by the law." Luther's translation: "So we now maintain that man becomes justified without the work of the Law through faith *alone*." He freely tinkered with the sacred word—just like Ezra. Moreover, Luther wanted to delete the Book of Esther; banished Hebrews, Jude, and Revelation to the back of the New Testament; and famously called the Epistle of James an "epistle of straw " because it contradicted his thesis of salvation by faith alone. (For a complete undermining of Luther, see chapter 7.)

How about the Bible Augustine used, or Luther used, or today's Bible, whether it be Tyndale's Bible, Zwingli's Bible, or the Jerusalem Bible? Clearly, depending on the epoch in which you lived, the "Bible" meant very different things to different people at different times. That "Word of God" turns out to be in the eye of the beholder. How can we announce with confidence, "*This* is the Word of God" today, when tomorrow may offer another version? Whose canon do we honor? The word *about* God covers the ground better and more accurately gives us the dynamic of revelation.

So, it's been a little dense, but these are my eight reasons for not taking the Bible literally as the Word *of* God when the "Word *about* God" covers it better: People circling the mysteries of life's big

---

19 Ibid., 109.

questions, seeking answers, searching for God, forever parsing the words, embracing the epics, listening intently to and interpreting the ancient, revered stories for the sounds of silence—and leaving room for a change of heart, a change of direction, with each new insight, and ultimately revealing God in the process.

Let me end this chapter appropriately with a teaser or two.

THE BIBLE TELLS ME SO

Before the world opened up and geography, anthropology, and archeology expanded our knowledge, these kinds of statements had some traction:

> The Bible is the word of God.
> How do you know that?
> Because the Bible tells me so.

> The Jews are God's Chosen People.
> How do you know that?
> Because the Bible tells me so.
> Who wrote the Bible?
> The Jews.

> God gave the land to the Jews in perpetuity.
> How do you know that?
> Because the Bible tells me so.
> Who wrote the Bible?
> The Jews.

As I said, given our global width and depth today, this common circularity doesn't cut it anymore.

A CHOSEN PEOPLE, A NATION SET APART

On the subject of being chosen, the Hebrews were not the only ones in history to make that claim. The reason we believe them and not the others is an accident of history—namely, the sweep of a globalized Christianity and the book it brought with it. For example, the eighth-century Franks, especially after they stopped the Muslims at Poitiers under Charles Martel, were certain that God had appointed them as a chosen people. That's why the pope could say of Charles' father, Pepin, "The name of your people has been raised up above all the other nations"[20]—just like Israel.

In fact, the conviction of being a "chosen people" is found among many ethnic communities and nations across the ages. It's where people believe they stand in a privileged relationship with the deity, but of course, like the Israelites, only insofar as they adhere to a strict moral and ritual code of duties. Certainly the Church and many European nations made the claim. The conviction of closeness can also be found, for example, in Iran, Burma, and Japan. The idea of ethnic election has been vital to the cohesion and persistence of many ethnic communities down through the ages and continues to underpin the sense of national identity in many national states today.

One could think of the United States of America, when the Mayflower pilgrims, settling into their new country, were quite conscious, as preacher John Winthrop reminded them, that they were a chosen people. In 1845, the notion that the United States was specifically destined by God to expand its dominion and spread democracy and capitalism across the entire North American continent as its Manifest Destiny was a biblical type of claim. We catch another example of this when, after defeating the Spanish in the Battle of Manila Bay in 1898, President William McKinley sought to annex the Philippines by declaring that, after much prayer, he understood that almighty God had led him to see that the United States was called to "educate the Filipinos, and uplift and civilize and Christianize them, and by God's grace do the very best we could by them, as our fellow-men for whom Christ died."[21] (Never mind that the Filipinos had been Catholic for more than three hundred years.)

---

20   Tom Holland, *Dominion: How the Christian Revolution Remade the World* (New York: Hachette, 2019), 195.

21   As quoted in Woodward, "Religion & Presidential Politics."

Just as the Israelites had wrested Canaan from the native heathen, the white Dutch Calvinists or Afrikaners, originators of *apartheid* (separateness), considered themselves a chosen people that had been brought to the promised land of Africa to carve out a homeland. So, just as Esau asked Isaac after Jacob stole his birthright, "Have you only one blessing, father?" (Genesis 27:38), we ask, "Have you only one chosen people?"

So, once more, "the Bible tells me so" and "Chosen People" were good catch phrases in a pre-modern world whose context was small. In a global world, these phrases don't hold up so well today.

Chapter 3

BACK TO THE FUTURE: AN EXCURSUS

> Biblical storytellers invented and augmented dialogue, characters, and scenes to turn past moments into a flowing story.... They shifted and arranged the past, or wove together discrete moments, all for the purpose of telling *their* story for *their* audience.
>
> —*Peter Enns,* THE BIBLE TELLS ME SO

Reread and digest that epigraph and you have the content of this brief hinge chapter that spells out what went before and what will come after.

BACKGROUND

The starting points of this chapter are the stories of the monarchy, the five hundred years (more or less) from Saul and David to the Babylonian sack of Jerusalem. These stories are all about the kings of the period: the good, the bad, and the indifferent. The majority of the Old Testament books, some 80 percent, deal with some aspects of the monarchy—the rare time when, at last, Israel had a kingdom and land of its own. Most of the material is found in the books of

1 and 2 Samuel, 1 and 2 Kings, and 1 and 2 Chronicles, with this latter originally placed at the end of the Old Testament and then unfortunately placed right after Samuel/Kings. I say unfortunately because Chronicles tells the story of David and the monarchy all over again, but completely changes things and whitewashes David almost beyond recognition. Samuel/Kings was written during the exile, when the question was, "What did we do to deserve this?" Chronicles was written after the return to the Holy Land, when the questions were, "What's our future? Do we have one?" 1 and 2 Kings deals with both.

Chronicles bowdlerizes Samuel and Kings and rewrites it like the Communists rewrote Russian history or the Nazis German history. For one thing, Chronicles totally omits the northern kings in its account. That's because, as memories of the northern kingdom faded, all that was left was Judah, the people who returned from the Babylonian exile. Judah was clearly the future. And although David and his dynasty had disappeared, upending God's promise that his throne would be established forever, Chronicles does the usual face-saving end run and changes the promise to *"my* (meaning God's) throne will be established forever." To the returned exiles, this meant, "Hang in there. God will prevail even if David didn't." And as far as David goes, you would never know the Samuel/Kings David and the Chronicles David were the same person. David gets a total whitewash: no Bathsheba adultery, no despicable killing of her husband Uriah, no rebellious sons and their coups and murders, no fight for the throne. Chronicles even gives David a major role in the building of the Temple, a conceit that out and out contradicts Samuel/Kings. No way can you match the two stories, which reminds us again that the Bible is the (partisan) word *about* God. By the way, the stories of the kings and exile, however spun, are some of the few things in the Bible that are verifiable by history. Records and sources back up the general outline of this period.

Anyway, as I said, that's all background. The point is that, at this moment of history, when you had an identifiable people with memories of a past "golden age" where the monarchy had land (lost and regained)—this was the period when much of the Bible was written. It was the Omega point from which everything, from the past to the future, from origins to prophecy, was processed.

ORIGIN STORIES

The origin stories found in the Pentateuch, then, are the product of the later monarchy-exile period. This means that the scribes, to justify the present, were judging, maneuvering, and manipulating the past from where they were standing. As we have seen, they modeled their creation account on the Babylonians'—with the spin, of course, that Yahweh is superior to any of their gods. And to be sure, we know the Babylonians (the nasties who sent the Jews into exile) are the bad guys, the arrogant ones who, way back when, tried to build stepping stones to heaven and brought upon humanity a babble of languages. Esau, ancestor of the Edomites, is a stupid dolt. The Canaanites get their comeuppance in the Flood story. The monarchy's neighbors to the east, the Moabites and Ammonites, are the offspring of incest. In short, the authors who wrote the origin stories already branded their current enemies as wicked from day one. Abraham's trek to Egypt mirrors the Exodus. God's covenant with him is God's covenant with David. As Peter Ends understates it, "The overlap between Israel's ancestors and the political realities of the monarchy is not a coincidence.... Israel's later political realities find their way into the origins story ... [its enemies are] being introduced *and already evaluated*."[1]

THE LAST SHALL BE FIRST

If you will recall, the Kingdom of Judea was not only small—about the size of Vermont—but politically outgunned, outnumbered, and overshadowed by the major powers during all its career. It was the Cinderella of its times. It was last. So, the authors of the Bible once

---

1   Peter Enns, *The Bible Tells Me So: Why Defending Scripture Has Made Us Unable to Read It* (New York: HarperOne, 2014), 109, 108. His italics.

more had to reach back and invent a history that spelled out clearly what another Jew, Jesus, would proclaim, namely that "the last shall be first"—meaning themselves, of course. From the (invented) start, the younger and firstborn roles are subverted. In Genesis, God favors Abel over his older brother, Cain. Jacob, the younger, is chosen over his older brother Esau. Joseph of the multicolored coat is the youngest of the twelve siblings, yet winds up ruling over them. David is the youngest of his brothers, who are all passed over. Solomon is made king over the rightful heir, his elder half-brother. And here comes the kicker: Judah was fourth in line, but here we find David as the iconic king and Judah as his kingdom. Its split-off rival kingdom, Israel, was conquered, leaving Judah. Once more, the "younger brother," surviving the exile, came out on top. Israel's deepest past was made to speak to the present. The last wound up first, thanks to Yahweh's power.

There are more clever parallels. Adam disobeyed Yahweh. He was expelled from the Garden. He was sent into exile. He should have obeyed and stayed. Instead, he disobeyed, but wound up on the outside. Sound familiar? The Exodus story, where Yahweh is stronger than the Egyptian gods that Israel was flirting with, are part of the same coming attractions. Noah floats to safety on the ark, Moses floats to safety on the reed raft, and Israel "floats" to safety through the waters of the Red Sea. All this was the work of Yahweh, who was still with them, exile and all. Again, the Judean scribes did not rewrite the stories of origin. Rather, they invented them. They invented a past from scraps of lore to support and validate who they were in the present, not who they were or what had happened in the past.

You can catch a minor example of this kind of time warp in the gospels. In Mark 7, the Pharisees castigate Jesus and his disciples for eating with defiled hands. Jesus replies that "It's not what goes into one that defiles, but what comes out of one"—theft, adultery, murder, and so on. Mark thereby has Jesus declare that *all* the Old Testament food laws were now null and void. Hold it! The scholars step in and say that Jesus didn't say this back in the 30s. It's an anachronism. It's Mark's own creative gloss, written for the later Gentile Christians, reminding them they needn't keep those laws.

PROPAGANDA

Let me now repeat the same general thought from a different perspective, the perspective of propaganda. The Hebrews began as Canaanites (and Lord knows what other mix of peoples) before they became an identifiable people. The first thing to recall is that, from the beginning, Israel, to use an anachronistic phrase, was a minor, third-rate people, politically and culturally. It was perpetually defeated, invaded, dominated, exiled, and dispersed. It was the underdog. To this extent, we saw that other nations had prophets decrying inequality, but none as vibrant and vocal as the Hebrew prophets. That's because they were always on the lower side of any inequality. Andrew Carnegie and the Robber Barons did not sing soulful songs of deliverance; the people they exploited did.

The second thing to remember is that conflicts were not just nation against nation, but also gods against gods. Whoever's god was greater and more powerful garnered the most victories, so it was necessary to placate them, to be on their good side. The power of the gods was shown by mighty victories and the subjugation, if not the annihilation, of one's enemies. The chronicles of Egypt, Babylon, and Assyria, chiseled in stone, exalt the stupendous deeds and awesome power of the gods. Elaborate stories and exaggerated feats were part and parcel of the propaganda machine. It was only natural in the book of Nahum for Yahweh to gloat over the destruction of Nineveh.

Enter the Hebrews. They needed to get a foothold among the nations, however faint. So, they necessarily began to tell their stories, for it is a nation's shared stories that hold it together. The stories needed to be attractive and compelling to match the best of those of the Big Guys. Thus, in keeping with the standard practice of its neighbors, of the culture, exotic lore springs up. Mighty fictional leaders are invented. Minor skirmishes are expanded into awesome victories. Small victories are ballooned into fearsome feats. Guided by their god, a small group of slaves who fled Egypt becomes the Exodus saga of millions seeking freedom. Scraps of legends and incidents of courage are patched together and inflated and, most of all, this nation's god is formidable, matching and exceeding the deeds of his rivals.

So, as the people of Israel slowly got their act together and, as we have amply seen, wrote and rewrote their story, they followed normal protocol. They wrote propaganda. And they wrote it in language and ideas that were familiar to them, for we must remember that they were children of their culture, which means that they were an ancient tribal people with all the limitations that this implies. They saw the world, and saw their tribal warrior God, through a tribal mentality. That means we are getting the view of a people from a certain time and place in history, described in their cultural language. What we're getting is Israel's stories, not an historical account of who God was or what he did.

Once you grasp this, it makes all the difference. Reading Genesis, Joshua, and Judges, for example, not as history but as propaganda, not as literal but as a people fighting to get its place in the sun, puts a different spin on them. A petulant, cruel, exterminating Yahweh ordering genocide *is not to be taken literally, but as standard puffing.* Got it? "Don't mess with us. God is on our side and he's stronger than your god." The many borrowings from the contemporary lore, symbols, and literature of its neighbors is a nod to Israel's need to be current, to be as good as or better than those "pagans." So, the extermination of the Canaanites, the inflation of David and his magical kingdom—actually its supposedly golden age was quite tiny and short-lived—all are grist for the propaganda machine. Not that there isn't some history, but it's history with a big asterisk.

But, all the while, Israel is refining its relationship to God, moving from polytheism to monotheism, from a disposable deity to one who actually cares for them, has chosen them, and sticks with them through thick and thin.

As they grew and years went by, circumstances changed and different ways of looking at things became common enough. We have already seen how the Hebrews came to different conclusions and were quite creative in letting disagreements and contradictions stand.

BEING "CREATIVE"

The whole enterprise of going back to the future and masking propaganda as history is suspect to the modern mind. To learn that those foundational stories of origin, so well-known and beloved, are self-serving flashbacks of another time (and they *are* that) worthy of a good movie, is disturbing to many. It reeks of propaganda because it is.

Anyway, note the word "creative" used above. "Creative" will turn out to be the recurring talisman in the rest of the Bible and its interpretations. Like the magic word that opens up secret caves and treasure troves, whenever a scripture verse is twisted beyond recognition into a novel interpretation, apologists will call it "creative." It's a win-win situation. Scripture is not to be contradicted, only "creatively" read. In the example above, when Jesus altered sacred scripture, the brilliant scribes in the audience apparently had no comeback. Of course, we're getting only one side of the story. A well-educated scribe, one supposes, would have jumped in with, "Wait a minute! You just misquoted scripture." But since he did not, "creative" must cut it, though it's a mystery to us how subjective arguments can carry the day.

So be on the alert. The rest of this book is full of examples of creative scripture interpretations.

A TRIFLE

The following distraction doesn't add much to the preceding but, for what it's worth, I thought I'd toss in a little Shakespeare. Shakespeare was famous for borrowing and reconfiguring, a point expressed by the noted Shakespearean scholar Stanley Wells, who writes:

> Almost all of [Shakespeare's] plays are based on tales that had already been told and had found literary expression. He drew on classical poets such as Ovid and Virgil; on Chaucer's *Canterbury Tales* and Spenser's *Faerie Queene*; on prose fictions such as Boccaccio's *Decameron* and Sidney's *Arcadia*; on histories such as Plutarch's *Lives of the Noble Grecians and Romans* and the

English chronicles of Edward Hall and Raphael Holinshed. He refashioned already existing plays, such as Plautus' *Menaechmi* (for *The Comedy of Errors*), the anonymous *King Leir*, and George Whetstone's unacted *Promos and Cassandra* (for *Measure for Measure*).[2]

Mutatis Mutandus—adjustments being made—you've got the dynamics of the biblical authors.

Sidebar 1

A recent column in the *Wall Street Journal* tells how the ruling Communist Party in China sees religion as an enemy and continues its terrible persecutions. Religious minorities are threatened, but especially Christianity, the fastest growing religion in China. To counteract this, China has set out on a unique, massive project to rewrite the scriptures, purging passages deemed incompatible with "core socialist values."[3] The yin and yang goes on.

Sidebar 2

In the late 1990s, three books written by a Jewish atheist, Michael Drosnin, made the best-seller lists, the first two reaching third on the *New York Times* best-seller list. They were *The Bible Code*, *Bible Code II*, and *Bible Code III*. The books were all the rage. As befits the times, the story started with the computer. An Israeli mathematician had laid out the words of the Torah and did a computer search, turning up such eye-openers as references to Kennedy and Dallas, Hitler's name written upside down not far from Nazi written backward, and so on. Drosnin picked up on this and wrote his books, claiming such things as the 2001 World Trade Center attack being predicted and there being only three years left until Armageddon, a

---

2   Stanley Wells, ed., *An Oxford Anthology of Shakespeare* (Oxford: Oxford University Press, 1987), xv.

3   Matthew Taylor King, "The Gospel According to Xi," *The Wall Street Journal*, June 4, 2020, https://www.wsj.com/articles/the-gospel-according-to-xi-11591310956.

never-ending trope. Skeptics dismissed his work, claiming you could do the same thing with the phone book or *The Last of the Mohicans*. Nevertheless, nonsense that it was, Drosnin was obviously tapping into the human need we all have to know; to know there's some meaning to life, that all isn't just chance or a cosmic joke, that's there's a purpose somewhere, a Being who has Personality and feels and loves. He was tapping into our need to have some control in a chaotic world.

To this extent, misguided as he was, Drosnin stood in a long line of consistent traditions, from the ancient rabbis to the early church allegorists to the modern commentators who seek to mine the Bible for answers, all of whom have advanced our understanding and, as history has shown, have sometimes compounded the nonsense.

Chapter 4

HISTORY OR HIS-STORY?

> If there is any history in the Bible, it's there by accident.
> —*Northrop Frye*

THE PROLOGUE

The epigraph above is by a renowned biblical scholar and translator of the Hebrew Bible, so he knows what he's talking about. And we're going to unpack his statement in this chapter.

The first point is that scientific findings, as we have noted before, have challenged the historicity of many of the Old Testament stories. Michael D. Coogan sums up the results:

> With regard to Abraham and Sarah, Isaac and Rebekah, and Jacob and his family, we are for the most part in the realm of legend, and it is extremely difficult to determine if any of the traditions concerning them in Genesis 12–50 have a historical basis. An analogy from British history is King Arthur, who may have been an actual historical figure, but the repeatedly retold legends about him are our only sources, making historical judgment difficult.

> The quest for historicity is complicated by several factors. First, biblical chronology itself is essentially unreliable, given the ages attributed to the ancestors, and has its own internal inconsistencies. Second, because so many stages of composition and editing have shaped the narratives, they are often anachronistic, since each generation of storytellers, writers and editors added elements from their own times. Third, because of the use of different sources in the final form of the narrative, many inconsistencies are found.[1]

Yes, it is clear from geography, language, text, and culture that the biblical stories, supposedly occurring around the twelfth century BCE, were in fact composed in the sixth century BCE. There is overwhelming evidence to support this. What the scholars have found is that the anonymous writers,[2] editors, and redactors who operated until the early part of the Christian era drew upon old legends, sagas, epics, and myths to tell a story that supposedly happened six hundred years before.

Moreover, since the authors all necessarily came from a specific place in history, most of their writing reveals *their* background, politics, and special agendas, and they produce not a few anachronisms. They also definitely had their partisan agendas and imposed them on the text. All this explains the many errors and bloopers in the Bible. In addition, most of the time, the overriding motivations of these unknown writers were (1) the power struggle over leadership when the Jews returned to Jerusalem and (2) the theodicy question: How could Yahweh allow his chosen ones to suffer such grief and how do we get back in his favor? How do we get back to the golden age?

As for the gospels, they too were written in exceedingly troubled and politically unsettled times. There were the tensions between the "Jesus Jews" and the "Moses Jews," the mounting antagonisms

---

1   Michael D. Coogan, *The Old Testament: A Historical and Literary Introduction to the Hebrew Scriptures* (Oxford: Oxford University Press, 2006), 79.

2   Despite labels, outside of St. Paul's seven authentic epistles, we really don't know who wrote the other sixty-six books of the Bible.

between Jerusalem's high priests and the Roman rulers, the frequent Jewish rebellions against Roman authority, and the traumatic destruction of the Temple. Jesus and early Christians lived in an atmosphere where there was talk of a new pattern, another kingdom, the Kingdom of God, which seemed to be just around the corner. St. Paul firmly believed and preached about an *immediate* end of the world and the immediate establishment of God's kingdom (perhaps in his lifetime), whereas, some fifty years later, the evangelists tended to talk about an *impending* end, mostly because the "immediate" end didn't happen.[3]

After the destruction of Jerusalem and the Temple, the first Christians, like the traditional Jews, had to struggle for survival and identity. How would they handle Gentile converts? What was their relationship to Judaism? And who and what was Jesus? It's not easy for us to tell at this remove. After all, we get him secondhand in Greek and not in the Aramaic Jesus knew and with which he taught. Jesus was profoundly a Jew of his time, named after Joshua, Moses' successor and military hero. He spoke Aramaic, knew some biblical Hebrew, and likely, as an artisan, understood enough colloquial Greek to do business—especially since just four miles from his hometown of Nazareth was the influential Greek-influenced town called Sepphoris, the capital of the younger King Herod.

Oddly, this town is never mentioned in the gospels, reflecting the fact that Jesus' life was fully lived in a non-Greek culture. Jesus may well have worked in Sepphoris for many years in his youth and was probably no less Hellenized than most of the Jewish Palestinian tradesmen of his day. The earliest surviving pieces of Christian literature, St. Paul's epistles, written just two decades after Jesus' death and resurrection, are not written in Aramaic, but in Greek, reflecting a radical shift in the cult of Jesus as it quickly moved from Judaism to Hellenism. Also, like with the writers of the Old Testament, there was a lot of projection backward. Depending on the agendas and theology of the writers, various gospel portraits of Jesus emerged that were not compatible. Bottom line: as Kaltner and McKenzie put it,

---

[3] A good read here is Paula Fredriksen's *When Christians Were Jews: The First Generation* (New Haven, CT: Yale University Press, 2018).

"When we read the Bible, we can never know for sure what, if anything, really happened."[4]

That's the prologue. For some, there is scandal and shock to learn that all the Torah's stories are not historical or that the literal gospel stories are likewise called into question. It all seems to undermine any concept of the "Word of God" or "Gospel Truth." Whom can you trust? Where does that leave us?

FACT OR FICTION?

As I write this, I realize that some people may be scandalized, but all that I have written so far does reflect the best of modern scholarship. Yes, despite all the centuries of feverish searching with the Bible in one hand and cutting-edge technology in the other, evidence backing the Bible as literally true remains fragile, indeed difficult to hold onto. As scholars read the archaeological data, they find disagreement about almost everything, but there is no doubt that the preponderance of evidence, which grows each year, supports the conclusion of the "minimalists": namely, that overall, there's no real history in the Bible. Again, Northrop Frye's words: "If there is any history in the Bible, it is there by accident."[5] Even the ancients saw this. For example, there was the recent discovery of the earliest extant Latin interpretation of the gospels, probably written around 800 CE. It was lost for 1500 years and is the work of a fourth-century bishop who interprets the gospels outright as a series of allegories. The gospels, according to this ancient bishop, were written with symbolism in mind. They are not literally true.

All this might not set well with the more fundamentalist groups that interpret the Bible literally, insisting it is not open to interpretation,

---

4   Kaltner and McKenzie, *Sleuthing the Bible*, 75.
5   As quoted by Tom Harpur in Anthony Wile, "Tom Harpur on Bible Mythology and Why He Says Jesus Christ Never Lived Historically," *The Daily Bell*, March 13, 2011, https://www.thedailybell.com/all-articles/exclusive-interviews/anthony-wile-tom-harpur-on-bible-mythology-and-why-he-says-jesus-christ-never-lived-historically/.

but they are a minority. And it is offensive to certain politicians who have vested interests. For example, at an event marking fifty years of settlement, Prime Minister Benjamin Netanyahu (currently under indictment for fraud and bribery in 2019) proclaimed: "What has enchanted me more than anything was the simple, clear and distinct fact that we are walking in the paths of the Bible. Here, right here, the fathers of our nation trod the paths from Hebron to Jerusalem. Near here, in Bethlehem, King David was born. There he was anointed king, and not far from here David fought Goliath, the Hasmoneans fought the Greeks and Bar Kochba—the Romans."[6] Archaeologists' response? Maybe David did—but it's not likely.

THE RELIGIOUS AND POLITICAL CONTEXT

To suggest that the Pentateuch is a fabrication does not mean it is fraudulent or cut from whole cloth, but that it is the literary product of a beleaguered people, led by the Jewish literate elite from Yehud—later called Judea (a portion of Palestine portioned off for the Jews by the Persian conquerors in the sixth century BCE)—desperately needing to regroup and redefine themselves after a series of profound tragedies. Again, the biblical writers did not record the past as much as they created it and reshaped it from pieces of traditions, legends, and stories.

This is not just conjecture. As suggested above, the latest archeological and scientific findings convincingly show that there is no historical support for the traditional stories of Abraham, Isaac, Jacob, Moses, or Joshua. Did they exist at all? Are they, as some scholars think, fictional characters? Egypt, for example, has no memory of Moses, the plagues, or the parting of the Red Sea. No wonder one scholar says of Moses that he was a "figure of memory but not of history." The stories

---

6   Nir Hasson, "Is the Bible a True Story?" *Haaretz*, November 1, 2017, https://www.haaretz.com/israel-news/MAGAZINE-is-the-bible-a-true-story-latest-archaeological-finds-yield-surprises-1.5626647.

were invented on the rebound. Recall that in 586 BCE, Jerusalem was conquered by the Babylonians, who destroyed the Temple, left the city a ghost town, and exiled the elites. The Persians came and conquered the Babylonians and created Yehud. Eventually, the Temple was rebuilt (nothing like the original) and some exiles returned (not the inflated numbers the Bible would indicate). Emboldened by this, the Jews set about constructing and inventing a past not centered on king or prophet or priest, but on God. Meanwhile, Alexander the Great came along and the Greeks displaced the Persians and were in turn displaced by the Romans who destroyed the second Temple. All through this, little Palestine was occupied or overseen by the victors.

So here was the problem. By the sixth century BCE, the monarchy was gone, the king is gone, the Temple (till its reconstruction) was gone, animal sacrifice was gone, and the priesthood was an off-again and on-again rivalry. All this left the Jews searching for a new rallying point, new meaning, a new identity. Long polytheistic, as we have noted—the archaeological evidence is strong on this point—they regrouped around the God Yahweh, as recycled Canaanites, for that is what the Jews once were. Now they became monotheists, a stance firmly cemented only by the time of Second Isaiah. They believed there was this one, universal God who had called them and destined them to greatness.

But, at this point, they were confronted with the age-old, unsolvable problem we have seen before: the theodicy challenge. If they were indeed the chosen ones, God's special people, a covenanted tribe, then how could all this have happened to them? The narrative that finally emerged was that God, because of their sins, punished them. He did not abandon them. He allowed Jerusalem to be destroyed. But, in time, he punished the destroyers and sent in the Persians with their leader, Cyrus, to set the Israelites free to rebuild the city.

God could do this now, *would* do this now, because, after all, he did care for them, and had cared in the past: for example, the escape from Egypt. A kingdom could be established once again, along the lines of the mythical kingdoms of David and Solomon. So, behind all their sufferings was a deity who was always there, who loved them, and who would restore them to the greatness of old. Moreover, he gave them the gift of the land—Israel—and they were bound to claim it. This last fiction, by the way, is a most sensitive one, the most sacred of sacred cows. It says that present day Israel's claims to its country turn out to be based on stories that are not true. As John van Hagen sums it up:

> One problematic meaning-making effort has to do with the status of Jerusalem, the supposed heart of God's coming kingdom. Modern scholarship has both questioned Jerusalem's historical accuracy as the center of a united kingdom and undermined Jewish claims to that city. Finkelstein and Silberman [renowned Jewish archaeologists] argue persuasively that David was a legendary tribal chief and that Jerusalem was the center of a small city-state inhabited by various tribes. Present-day Israel has chosen to ignore the reality-based, 10,000-year-old history of Jerusalem and has instead focused on a biblical tradition that identifies the city as belonging rightfully and exclusively to the Jews. The reality is that Jerusalem was inhabited some 2,000 years before David's supposed conquest and for almost the same amount of time by other peoples after Jews were forbidden to enter the city following the Bar Kochba revolt in 135 BCE.[7]

To resume: In order to claim Yahweh's favor, the people would have to remain faithful, to remake themselves. They would be a people "set apart." Separation from foreigners, study of the Torah, ritual, purity laws (all 613 of them), liturgy (the role of the high priest grew considerably), right living, moral behavior, and justice (the "widow and orphan" refrain) were required to keep the relationship intact. So, this creative period produced the books that purportedly told what happened some 600 years prior (and could happen again) and invented ancestors, heroes, and sagas that confirmed God's special

---

7   John Van Hagen, *Rescuing Religion: How Faith Can Survive Its Encounter with Science* (Salem, OR: Polebridge, 2012), 62. See also Rashid Khalidi, *The Hundred Years' War on Palestine: A History of Settler Colonial Conquest and Resistance, 1917–2017* (New York: Metropolitan, 2020).

choice, plus the poetry, song, and practices that, in addition to a newly embraced monotheism, would mark them off forever as different. All this wasn't easy. It was a very long, checkered, and bitter history of jockeying, factions, and internecine warfare until Israel finally settled into the identifiable religion we know today.

CHRISTIANITY

Christianity was born during the last of the invasions—that is, in the time of the Roman occupation. We have a greatly idealized picture of the beginning of Christianity. St. Luke's Acts of the Apostles is hardly an unbiased, nonpartisan resource. The fact is that there were, at the beginning—from the first to the third centuries—many Christianities with no central authority. It started with Jesus, the first-century observant Jew in an occupied territory, a Jew who, like his contemporaries, was struggling with the dissonance of God's promises and present-day reality. Jesus was a follower of the apocalyptic prophet we know as John the Baptist, who warned of the final days to come: "Even now the ax is lying at the root of the trees" (Luke 3:9). Jesus seemed to believe that God's kingdom, as it had been united at one time under the Hasmoneans, was possible. It was going to break into the world at any moment and all would be fulfilled. His ministry evoked a sign that it was about to happen—"Thy kingdom come on earth as it is in heaven"—but, once again conquered and now under Roman rule, that kingdom seemed as far away as ever. Still, he held on to his trust in the Father and held on to that trust to the end.

When Jesus died, his followers were bewildered. They were Jews and continued to follow Judaism and Temple observance. They gathered in little groups in Jerusalem and in the villages of present-day Syria and Turkey. They met in house churches, each with different memories and sometimes different beliefs, leadership styles, and approaches. Recent discoveries, such as the early Christian documents at Nag Hammadi in 1945, provide evidence of the diversity of the various Christian communities.

There was no central authority, not even that of the "pope" or bishop of Rome, because when Peter went to Rome, there was no diocese there for him to be bishop of. That is why the Roman Church's claim of tracing a succession of bishops back to Peter as Rome's first bishop is not sustainable. The institution of one bishop overseeing all the Christians from a single locality is a second-century development, long after the deaths of Peter and Paul. To put it bluntly, as historian Diarmaid MacCulloch writes, "The early succession of Roman bishops is actually historical fiction."[8] In any case, there were diverse Christian communities with diverse forms of leadership, beliefs, and literature with the usual liberal-conservative divide. There was even some nasty rivalry among them (as evidenced in the short, one-page letter known as 3 John). These communities could not even agree on Jesus' identity, who he was, or when he was coming back. St. Paul certainly thought it would be in his lifetime.

Before the Romans razed Jerusalem and destroyed the Temple, Paul had already begun to widen the concept of Jesus, to make him more "cosmic," to link, as it were, the divinely anointed One—the Messiah or "Christ"—to Jesus. About half the references to Christ in the New Testament can be found in Paul's letters. Then came the disaster: the destruction of the centralizing icon of the religion, the Temple. Add to this trauma the growing influx of Gentile converts and the death of the original apostles and you have the makings of massive disorientation and confusion. The "orthodox" Jews, as we have seen, regrouped around the Torah, the "portable" Temple. The "Jesus" Jews didn't know what to do, but they knew they had to follow a different path. Being Jews, they kept much of their Jewish heritage: the "Bible" as they knew it, its moral teachings, plus the letters of Paul. Other teachers formed little communities imbued with the sense of the Risen Christ among them.

The Eucharist, Last Supper-like commemorations, the rites of baptism, and the widening Gentile membership eventually brought

---

8   Diarmaid MacCulloch, review of *The Eastern Orthodox Church: A New History* by John Anthony McGuckin, *The New York Review of Books*, July 2, 2020, https://www.pressreader.com/usa/the-new-york-review-of-books/20200611/282020444520501.

a Hellenistic lens to the story of Jesus and added to the complexity. Later, in the second and third centuries, the nigh universal acceptance of the four gospels gave them some common ground—although, as we have seen, the gospels continuously morphed into an ever-escalating "orthodoxy" about Jesus. Even though there was, by that time, a political attempt to keep an organic connection with the parent religion—the gospels are clearly full of references and allusions to the Old Testament—Christianity was also on its way toward separating from the mother religion. It wasn't long before an inter-family squabble became an "us against them" situation. Already in the fourth gospel, Jesus the Jew would wind up addressing his audience as "you" Jews. Jesus had become Greek. He began to be universalized.

Ironically, Jesus the Jew wanted to reform Judaism, to transcend the legalisms that suffocated it. He challenged people to break through conventional thinking. There is no evidence he wanted to extend his influence beyond Israel and therefore to start a worldwide church. He left no instructions, no program, no plan, but it happened. The ever-growing church gained ground as the Jewish revolts against the Romans in 115 and 133 depleted and scattered the Jews. Christianity increasingly entered a Hellenistic world with its Greek philosophical framework (Plato and Aristotle framed its doctrines) and it eventually adopted the Roman system of government, all the while becoming more a part of the Roman world and less a witness against it.

SOME JEOPARDY-LIKE TRIVIA

Let's end this "deconstruction" chapter with a nod to the engaging work of John Kaltner and Steven L. McKenzie, as they offer a litany of biblical put-downs and anachronisms.

God has different names in the Pentateuch, attesting to different traditions. There is this little smear job: Noah's three sons were Shem, Ham, and Japheth, whose duty was to repopulate the earth after the flood (Genesis 9:18–19). Noah gets drunk and lies naked in his tent. Ham comes in and looks and tells his brothers. They come

HISTORY OR HIS-STORY?

in but, out of respect, avert their eyes. When Noah awakes, he blesses Japheth and Shem but curses Ham, saying he shall be a slave to his brothers. But there's a hidden zinger here in this etiological story. Ham represents Canaan, Israel's enemy. His curse explains why Israel conquered Canaan (neat, if not true), not to mention a nasty side effect of this story: Ham is pictured as the ancestor of black-skinned people, so you get the biblically approved justification of racism.

In one version of the ark story, Noah takes in one pair of each animal species, while, in another, seven pairs. The flood is alternately from ground water or rainwater. It lasted for 40 or 150 days, depending on which part of the story you read. Does Noah release a raven or a dove? We're not even mentioning again the whole idea that the Noah story is a replay of a much older Sumerian story, the Epic of Gilgamesh.

Lot and his daughters are escaping the Sodom and Gomorrah conflagration. They think they are the only people left alive, so the daughters get their father drunk, have sex with him, and produce Moab and Ben-ammi, founding fathers of Moab and the Ammonites, Israel's bitter enemies and lowdown good-for-nothings. But, after all, given their incestuous beginnings—the fictional story implies—what can you expect? Notice how the biblical text skewers them: "Thus both the daughters of Lot became pregnant by their father. The firstborn bore a son, and named him Moab; he is the ancestor of the Moabites to this day. The younger also bore a son and named him Ben-ammi; he is the ancestor of the Ammonites to this day" (Genesis 19: 36–38).

In case you don't get it, the later book of Deuteronomy (23:3) nails it down: "No Ammonite or Moabite shall be admitted to the assembly of the Lord. Even to the tenth generation." It's another putdown story. By the way, on the way out, Lot spots a salt pillar that, if you look at it quickly, looks like a woman. Result? Lot's wife has paid the price for disobeying the angel's orders not to look back (Genesis 19:26). History? No. Etiological myth? Yes.

We move next to the Jacob-Rachel-Leah saga (Genesis 29–30), where Jacob loves lovely Rachel, is tricked into marrying plain Leah, and from the two women we get the origin story of the twelve sons who become the Twelve Tribes of Israel. These are the twelve sons who sneakily avenged the rape of their sister Dinah by a guy named Shechem (Genesis 34). The sons told Shechem's family that they would intermarry and pool their wealth with their clan if the men were circumcised. They agreed, and while they were still in recovery from the procedure the brothers attacked and murdered them.

Moses' father-in-law gets three different names—Reul, Jethro, and Hobab—pointing to multiple traditions behind the story of Moses' father-in-law.

Genesis mentions camels quite a bit. The problem is that domesticated camels were way down the road in the future; they were not introduced into the land of Israel till the tenth century BCE. Then there are the Philistines, who are mentioned in Genesis. Same thing; they came much later.

The laws Moses gave to the people—the Torah—could not have come from his hand, but from a much later time. They deal with a settled, agricultural society: oxen, donkeys, livestock, real estate, doorposts, and so on—in short, a settled farming society, not a bunch of nomadic wanderers slogging through the desert with their backpacks.

The book of Job is a stich job of prose and poetry, indicating that at some point the two were joined together. In the Book of Judges, twelve judges are mentioned, plus the number of years they served. Add them all up and you get over four centuries! That's more than twice the timespan between former slaves entering the Promised Land and establishment of the monarchy. Clearly, we've got pure mythology here.

Everything in this chapter, and indeed in this book, points to the intent of the narrators of the biblical books. Convinced of their closeness to God, they are intrusive, interpretative, partisan, contradictory, and manipulative, all in the interest of creating a national myth, of giving an identity to what became the Hebrews that would help them endure and survive as a people. In the process, they have left us, not the word of God, but lasting words about God.

Chapter 5

PROPHETS AND PROBLEMS

> There is no doubt that behind the prophetic literature were powerful, generative personalities called prophets. About some of the prophets (as, for instance, Jeremiah) we know a great deal. About many others we know nothing.
>
> —*Introduction to the prophetic books in the*
> New Oxford Annotated Bible

Think of the Hebrew Scriptures and most people are apt to think of the prophets. Prophets were an institution everywhere in the Mideast, including among the Canaanites, and prophecy is well attested to in Mesopotamia, Phoenicia, and other places. These foreign prophets are recorded as also receiving messages in a dream or at their temples, like Samuel did. They all seem to use the same devices as Israel. They were closely connected to the kings and used divination, including consulting the dead (remember Saul calling up Samuel?), checking out the liver of sacrificed animals, shaking arrows, casting lots, using sacred objects such as the *urim* and *thummim* (parts of the vestment of the priests), music, ecstasy, and so on.

Cities were arising five thousand years ago and social stratification and inequalities were rising. Egyptian sages developed a concern for justice, and the kings of Mesopotamia proclaimed the establishment of "righteousness" or "justice" or "equality." In Persia, the prophet Zarathustra (or Zoroaster) taught that the one supreme God, Ahura Mazda, had created all good things and wanted people to practice truth and kindness. Some scholars (but not all) think he lived around the time of the Hebrew prophets and may have influenced them, but there are, in any case, similarities between them.

On the other hand, other nations seem to have nothing as well-drawn as the Israelite prophets, who advised and reproached kings alternately—prophets and kings were the yin and yang of the monarchy; one did not exist without the other—and who penned those powerful and colorful words we associate with their books (although, as we shall see, whether the books we have reflect their actual words is problematic). No other nation had such a great collection of prophetic writings and such strikingly poetic cries for justice as the Israelites.

Still, all was not smooth on the prophetic front. Perhaps John Collins gives us the best summary about the state of the prophets and prophecy (italics are my emphasis):

> It is of the essence of prophecy that the prophets addressed specific situations in highly concrete terms.... Nonetheless, like many of the Assyrian prophecies, the biblical oracles come to us embedded in collections that were made for later generations. Moreover, the biblical prophetic books *are often edited with later situations in mind.* There is, then, an inevitable tension between the words of the prophets in their original context and the "canonical shape" given to their oracles by later editors.... The historical prophets whose oracles are preserved in these books were often highly critical of the political and religious establishments of their day. The scribes who edited their books, however, were part of the establishment of later generations.[1]

In other words, as so often happens, we have a conflict of interest. The prophetic books, like all the other books in the Bible, are hindsight productions. This means that they are heavily edited, reworked,

---

1 John J. Collins, *Introduction to the Hebrew Bible* (Minneapolis: Augsburg Fortress, 2004), 286.

and readjusted books made to conform to current ideology and to support current propaganda needs. Those doing the editing and adjusting often had very different attitudes and agendas from the prophets themselves, so we're not sure whose words we have, the prophets' or the partisan editors'.

THE PROPHETS' SCORECARD

The prophets of Israel, who wielded great influence, were not immune to the law of averages and after the exile they declined and fell into disrepute. Maybe one reason for this disdain is the fact that, after the exile, the words of the great prophets of old had become canonized scripture, and latter-day prophets began to quote *them*, for God's word was increasingly considered as written for all time, to be interpreted throughout the ages.

Besides that, there were no more kings around for prophets to be the conscience of. But there may be another, more basic reason the prophets went out of style: credibility. What they foretold, what they prophesied, simply didn't come true. They kept on saying, "Thus says the LORD," and, whether or not those words were actually and truly the genuine communications of the LORD himself or simply their own words wrapped in the authority of the LORD, they failed to pass the acid test: They were wrong.

One thinks, for example, of Amos, who predicted that King Jeroboam would die by the sword (7:11). It never happened. Or the prophet Huldah, who predicted that King Josiah would die in peace (2 Kings 22:20). She was wrong. Josiah did not die from old age or "in peace," but was violently killed by the Egyptian pharaoh Neco in the battle at Megiddo. Or how about Ezekiel? In 26:7–21, he predicted as a word from the LORD that Nebuchadnezzar of Babylon would destroy the city of Tyre so thoroughly that it would never be rebuilt. It never happened. Ezekiel appears to have realized his gaffe, so he makes a second prediction, saying that since Nebuchadnezzar did not seize and conquer Tyre, Yahweh would give him Egypt as a consolation prize (29:18–20). This didn't come true either, although, some three hundred years later, Tyre was conquered by Alexander. The city of Tyre was later rebuilt—contrary to Yahweh and his prophet—and to this day is thriving as Lebanon's fourth largest city.

Then there is Yahweh's promise via the prophet Hosea (11:9), "I will not again destroy Ephraim; for I am God and no mortal, the Holy One in your midst, and I will not come in wrath." But Ephraim was destroyed again and, two chapters later, we get an outright contradiction of the previous promise: "I will destroy you, O Israel; who can help you?" (13:9). Assyria conquered the northern kingdom of Israel in 722 BCE and in turn was defeated in 612 BCE by a coalition of Medes and Babylonians. The prophet Nahum exulted in Assyria's comeuppance and, after saying, "So there, take that!" to defeated Assyria, prophesied of Israel, "Nevermore shall you be invaded" (1:15). Fifteen years later, it was overrun by the Babylonians.

Ex-Jesuit, ex-Catholic Jack Miles sums it up in his prize-winning book *God, a Biography*:

> True, most of the marvels that Isaiah and the other prophets predicted for an Israel returned from exile never came to pass. The failure of prophecy, a fact of massive importance in the history of Israelite and then of Jewish religion, is a personal failure in the life of God.... The promises God made through Isaiah and the earlier prophets have clearly not been kept.... The reason why prophecy is passed over in silence [in the Psalms] is almost surely also the reason why it died out and why the prophet Zechariah himself looked forward to its dying out—namely, that what the prophets prophesied had, in very large measure, not come true.[2]

PROBLEMATIC TIDBITS

The books of Samuel have clear indications of various traditions being sewn together, and not too cleverly at that. The famous account about King Solomon resolving the dispute between two

---

2   Jack Miles, *God: A Biography* (New York: Vintage, 1995), 230, 268, 278.

women who claim to be the mother of a child is an evident addition from some other source—evident because Solomon's name is never even mentioned. And what's this? David is organizing priests and Levites, gatekeepers and musicians for proper temple worship (1 Chronicles 23–26) and the Temple isn't even built yet? David will never see it. His son Solomon is the one who builds it—not to mention that, anachronistically, all those Davidic directions belong to the Second Temple.

David is also quite versatile. In an unclear and complicated biblical text, he kills Goliath twice: once with a sling and again with Goliath's own sword. Goliath himself undergoes massive height shifting. He is 6 feet 2 inches tall or, in another translation, 9 feet 6 inches. Incidentally, the Goliath story seems to be introducing David for the first time, but he's actually been around quite a bit before that. The evidence seems to point to a mixture of different traditions, not to mention, again, muddled texts.

Speaking of temples, King Jeroboam built temples in the northern kingdom of Israel. But according to 1 Kings 12:26–33, this was a no-no because it took away from the centralizing Temple at Jerusalem in the kingdom of Judah. Therefore, Jeroboam and all the kings of the northern kingdom of Israel were guilty of idolatry. The Bible, written by the Judeans, has nothing good to say about any Israeli king. They are all rotten, from top to bottom, and mercilessly slandered even if, historically, there were some good ones among them. But the biblical story doesn't wash because there was no centralization of worship at the Jerusalem Temple at the time of Jeroboam. That emphasis on the centrality of the Jerusalem Temple came much later, under the southern King Josiah, who faked finding an old book of Deuteronomy, which he forged, showing laws that "clearly" said all sacrifices, to be valid, must take place at the Jerusalem Temple. All other shrines were illegal. Pretty contrived, all the way around.

It is clear that sections of one biblical book are lifted and inserted into other books. For example, Isaiah 36–39 is straight from 2 Kings 18–20. Jeremiah 52 steals from 2 Kings 24 and all of 2 Kings 25. Psalm 18 is essentially the same as 2 Samuel 22. The Elijah and Elisha stories of the widow and the raising of her son and the jar that never empties are so identical that it's clear that one borrowed from the other.

Concerning the psalms, hardly any of them were written by David, and they are full of anachronisms. Some psalms are ascribed to Korahites, Asaph, or Moses. The headings and the contents seldom match. A quickie: a psalm (51) attributed to David reads:

> Do good to Zion in your good pleasure;
> Rebuild the walls of Jerusalem.

Which would be a neat trick since Jerusalem didn't need rebuilding until the Babylonians came and leveled it; that was left to Nehemiah, hundreds of years later.

We find common motifs in the Bible, echoes of one another. Meeting at the well is one of them: Isaac and Rebecca, Jacob and Rachel, Moses and his wife, Jesus and the Samaritan woman. Miraculous births are also common motifs: Sarah; Samson's mother; Hannah; John the Baptist's mother; Mary, the mother of Jesus.

As we have seen, the Bible functions as propaganda. The priestly caste, for example, had a large influence on the Bible—being big into ceremonies and pageantry, purity laws and institutionalized religion—and you'll find their influence all over the books of Genesis, Exodus, Leviticus, and Numbers—and, of course, the Temple always has pride of place as the one center to worship Yahweh. The fact is that most of those many laws, practices, and religious instructions, touted as coming directly from Yahweh in the distant past, came from far later periods. The claim of early Yahweh origin was meant to give them legitimacy.

Then there's the Deuteronomy slant, with its interest in legal matters and the law in general. The phrase, "If you heed these ordinances" is all over the place because the Law was a sign of fidelity to Yahweh. Those who follow it will be rewarded. Those who do not will be punished. Following the law and worshipping Yahweh alone became the motifs of much of the Bible. Again, these vested interests are the basis of much of the biblical propaganda that tweaked the Bible's message. Even where there are actual historical events, they are presented through the lenses and convictions of the various parties.

THE NEW TESTAMENT

Before we venture into the New Testament books, we must remind ourselves that they were not the only early Christian writings. There are contemporary manuscripts that never made it into the canon, such as the Shepherd of Hermas, the Didache or Teaching of the Twelve, the pseudonymous epistles, and the Gnostic gospels. Those that made it into the canon have an interesting history and some, like the book of Jude, should not really be included—except that the leaders at the time thought that the apostle Jude actually wrote it. Some books were hotly contested, like John's gospel and the book of Revelation.

Turning to the New Testament, we have two accounts of Paul's conversion: his own and Luke's in the Acts of the Apostles. Paul is anxious to let it be known that he received his mandate straight from the Lord. There was no bright light, no being made blind. He went straight to Arabia and never went near Jerusalem for three years. Luke, always anxious for the centrality of authority to be at Jerusalem, from which the church radiated, would have none of that. Sooner or later, he had to have Paul come to Jerusalem.

According to some scholars, Paul's orders in 1 Corinthians 14:34–35 that women should be subordinate and silent in church have all the earmarks of somebody else's insertion.

We have two "Whoops!" in the gospels. Matthew is intent on having Jesus as the Messiah, who traditionally comes from the line of David. David is one of Joseph's ancestors, but Jesus isn't his biological child, so that breaks the line. Solution? Matthew has Joseph name Jesus, which is tantamount to adoption, and that saves the day. In his gospel, Luke calculates that Jesus was born during the reigns of Octavius Augustus Caesar and King Herod the Great (the latter around 6 or 7 BCE) *and* during Quirinius' census, which occurred in 6 CE. The figures won't work. That's ten years after Herod's death in 4 BCE. Luke messed up on this one.

The iconic Christmas crèche we all venerate doesn't exist in the New Testament. It's a pastiche of pieces from Matthew and Luke. Matthew has no manger and the holy family flees from

Bethlehem to Egypt and back to Nazareth to duck Herod's wrath. Luke has the opposite trip: The Holy Family starts in Nazareth, skips Egypt, and ends up in Bethlehem. Of course, for both, Jesus being the Messiah means he *must* be born in David's town of Bethlehem. Still, this focus on Bethlehem is curious. I mean, read the New Testament, from the gospels through Acts, and you'll find that Jesus is never identified that way. He is always Jesus of Nazareth or a Galilean (some twenty-two references). He's never, ever called Jesus of Judea or Jesus of Bethlehem, titles that would have given him Davidic credentials.

Noticeably, his followers are called Christians three times in the New Testament: "It was in Antioch that the disciples were first called 'Christians'" (Acts 11:26); King Agrippa, questioning Paul, says, "Quickly you will persuade me to play the Christian" (Acts 26:28); and in the first letter of Peter we find, "Yet if any of you suffers as a Christian, do not consider it a disgrace, but glorify God because you bear this name" (4:16). Also notice this: In Acts 24:5, some Jews accuse Paul, saying he is "an agitator among all the Jews throughout the world, and a ringleader of the sect of the Nazoreans."

Bethlehem is never attached to the adult Jesus. On the other hand, some commentators, cloning Jesus as David who had to flee in exile, say that Jesus was mimicking him. Nazareth was Jesus' Davidic "exile." Matthew gives Jesus' long genealogy and concludes, "So all the generations from Abraham to David are fourteen generations; and from David to the deportation to Babylon, fourteen generations." Actually, if you go back and count them up, there is one more generation in the middle section, giving Matthew an "F" in math.

Remember the story of Jesus sailing on the Sea of Tiberius to the town of Gerasa, where, as Mark says, a man with an unclean spirit *immediately* ran up to him (Mark 5:1–13)? Well, seeing that Gerasa is some thirty miles away, that "immediately" is a bit of overstatement. It gets worse. Jesus expels the legion of unclean spirits from the man and, upon request, they enter the swine, all two thousand of them, and they rush into the sea and are drowned—some thirty miles away? That must have been some sight!

One can't help but notice that in the famous Beatitudes discourse (Matthew 5:1–12), all sayings employ the third person—"Blessed are *those* who...*"*—but switches to "Blessed are *you* when people revile you and persecute you" in verse 11. This one seems to be directed to Matthew's community, which was undergoing persecution at the time the gospel was written.

The first three gospel writers all identity the "Last Supper" as the Passover, but John insists it was *before* Passover and that, in fact, Jesus died the day before Passover. John has an agenda in mind. Having dubbed Jesus early on as the "Lamb of God," Jesus, as the Lamb, simply had to die on the day before Passover, at the exact same time the Passover lambs were being slaughtered. To be sure we don't miss the point, only John mentions that the soldiers did not break Jesus' legs, just as the bones of the Passover lambs were not to be broken. So, we have a contrived scene, contradicting the other three gospel writers, to make a theological point—which may be valid, but that's not the issue. The issue is that, once again, the biblical writers with an agenda feel free to alter the text and push their point.

Speaking of John, he's the only one to have the story of the woman caught in adultery (8:3–11). The most reliable manuscripts don't have the story at all, and it very much looks like a popular story inserted later into John's gospel. One of my personal disappointments was to learn that one of the New Testament's most powerfully moving and challenging phrases, "Father, forgive them; for they do not know what they are doing," is found only in Luke (23:34) and, more to the point, is missing from most manuscripts.

BOTTOM LINE

At this point, a simple but obvious summary is in order. In our world, the average person's concept of the Bible is that it is authored, in one way or another, by God. The Bible is considered almost "dropped from heaven" and is traditionally a very sacred book. We kiss it with reverence. It is incensed during liturgy. The deacon parades it, holding it high as he places it on the lectern. The cover may be of gold and the artwork inside striking. Devotees are urged to read it daily. It is quoted as the Final Word and resourced for divine truth. In a word, the Bible is now canonized scripture, which means that it may never be altered, subtracted from, or added to. It is a holy, immutable, inviolable icon that we have inherited like some revered treasure, forever solemnly handed on from generation to generation. All well and good.

Still, to make a "it really doesn't matter" point, from all this theatrical reverence, one would never learn that this single hallowed book, ensconced on a platform like a tabernacle, is in fact a collection of seventy-two books of varied lengths and quality; that many started out as occasional literature, revered but not sacrosanct; that the books, at times, contradict each other; that they were endlessly rewritten and reinterpreted; and that some are largely irrelevant today. The beatified Bible, in reality, is more like a revered, weathered national flag, torn in places and with blood and bullet holes on it. It held the country together, at a price. It's a symbol of pride.

All this is not to slight the Bible—not at all. It is right and proper that we should honor it. I'm simply noting that all this spiritual glamor tends to hide a very dramatic and contentious history that leaves the people emotionally unprepared for criticism of the holy hodgepodge that it is.

So, to repeat my theme: The scriptures, before their very late canonization, were indeed revered as sacred, but hardly untouchable. They were often considered raw material, to be shaped as circumstances demanded. They were constantly "a work in progress." The ancients felt completely free to alter, change, rework, and contradict the scriptures. For them, the sacred writings were there to be bent to address ever-changing circumstances and, often as not, they were utterly transformed in the process. Accepting that truth may be difficult for modern folk to grasp, but it may help to lessen any sense of scandal and betrayal. Taking on its own terms a Bible that has upheld patriarchy, warfare, slavery, absolute monarchy, and racism is challenging, but essential.

The Church today freely admits this history, freely admits all these inaccuracies and contradictions—though at one time it accepted them as literal truth—but still insists that "the books of Scripture must be acknowledged as teaching solidly, faithfully and without error that truth which God wanted put into sacred writings for the sake of salvation."[3] Accordingly, it parses them to conform to orthodoxy. The average person reads those words and may even obediently accept them, but they can be forgiven for scratching their head a bit when they try to figure out *which* scriptures are "taught faithfully without error," as those writings existed, in different eras of history, with many, many different stages of corrections, revisions, rewritings, reinterpretations, and reworkings.

---

3   Pope Paul VI, *Dei Verbum*, 11.

Chapter 6

OLD SKINS, NEW WINE

> All scripture is inspired by God and is useful for teaching, for reproof, for correction, and for training in righteousness.
> —*2 Timothy 3:16*

With some apology, let's continue the theme of the last chapter, a kind of "beating them to death" because they figure so prominently in today's climate of doubt. For starters, we note that those words in the epigraph above (and they obviously refer to the Hebrew Bible) were not likely written by St. Paul, though they have a very Pauline slant. Does the word "inspired" mean what we take it to mean, that the Bible is truly the divine, breathed-upon Word of God? Can we hold this belief in the light of our knowledge of the Bible's recycled borrowings from its surrounding culture? Can we reconcile this while remembering the many mistakes and contradictions; a very partisan human authorship; the subordination of women, the rightness of slavery, and so on—all this is inspired? And if we hold that the entire Bible is inspired, then we have to read every part of it—all seventy-two books (by Catholic reckoning)—as true, when clearly not every part is. In this chapter, let us examine how the Roman Catholic Church officially explains the tension.

In 2014, the Pontifical Biblical Commission, following up on Vatican II's document *Dei Verbum* (the "Word of God"), published a statement entitled, *The Inspiration and Truth of Sacred Scripture.*[1] It begins by firmly stating that no matter what limitations we find in the Bible, it still remains God's inspired word. *Dei Verbum* insists that the Bible is truly God's word, even though this divine word is composed of human words by human authors. God didn't directly dictate the scriptures, but rather worked through the human authors who, it hastens to add, being human, were subject to limitations. "In composing the sacred books, God chose men [no women, notice], and while employed by him they made use of their powers and abilities, so that with him acting in them and through them, they, as true authors, consigned to writing everything and only those things which he wanted."[2] The Commission quickly adds, "not every dimension of truth is present but only that truth which God wanted put into the sacred writings for the sake of our salvation."

Ah, there's precisely the issue: Who decides what is "for the sake of our salvation"? There are some 34,000 Christian denominations in the world and many variations of the Reform-Reconstructionist-Conservative-Orthodox Jews, all reading the same Hebrew Scriptures. They have different, sometimes contradictory notions of what constitutes "for the sake of our salvation." So, again, who decides? In passing, we must mention that the answer used to be one of the great selling points of Catholicism. Let everyone else flounder in their errors, but the One, Holy, Catholic and Apostolic Church possessed eternal, unalterable, never-changing truth, guaranteed by an infallible pope and a Spirit-guided magisterium. (Chapters 11 and 12 will take a second look at that.)

The Biblical Commission warns us not to be put off by those many admitted inaccuracies in history, geography, or science that fill the pages of the Bible. These errors don't affect the authentic truth in relation to the message of salvation. Nor should we be put off by

---

1   Pontifical Biblical Commission, *The Inspiration and Truth of Sacred Scripture: The Word that Comes from God and Speaks of God for the Salvation of the World,* trans. from the Italian (Collegeville, MN: Liturgical Press, 2014).

2   Paul VI, *Dei Verbum,* 11.

the cultural, social, and partisan perspectives of the human composers, nor the very complex transmission, composition, and ultimate and somewhat contorted canonization process of the biblical books.

Why we shouldn't be put off isn't made clear. God acting "in" and "through" the human authors, who were allowed their idiosyncrasies, is perplexing. How did God "act" on the human authors and leave them free at the same time? (This reflects the old "grace and free will" controversy.) How do we tease out and disentangle what is for "the sake of our salvation" from commands to slaughter a people or proclaim "happy" those who take Babylonian infants and dash them against a rock (Psalm 137:9) without a lot of clearing-the-throat commentary, such as "Psalm 137 is a 'rage' cry, born in understandable frustration at being so defeated and beaten, and so is not to be taken literally"?

If it's any comfort, tradition tells us that when Mahatma Gandhi, the nonviolent Hindu, came across the *Bhagavad Gita* passage where the god Krishna encouraged believers to slaughter an enemy, even their own kin, he was quick to pronounce such passages as metaphor, meaning that we should "strike at our darker side"—a tactic we employ. Consider this great understatement of the Commission:

> The objections—raised in the past and still current today—because of inaccuracies and contradictions of a geographical, historical, and scientific nature, which are rather frequent in the Bible, purport to call into question the reliability of the sacred text and hence its divine origin. These, however, are rejected by the Church in the affirmation that "the books of Scripture must be acknowledged as teaching firmly, faithfully, and without error that truth which God wanted put into the sacred writings for the sake of our salvation" (*DV*, n. 11). It is this truth which gives full meaning to human existence, and it is this which God wanted to be made known to all peoples.[3]

One Catholic scripture scholar adds that the Biblical Commission says that the Church has not endorsed any particular

---

3   Pontifical Biblical Commission, *The Inspiration and Truth*, 163.

explanation of exactly how the Holy Spirit moved the biblical authors and that, in fact, inspiration cannot be conceived of in terms of *individual* authors, but rather, biblical inspiration must encompasses the entirety of the complex process that produced the books of the Bible as we now have them. So, the individual books are not necessarily inspired—that gets the inconsistencies, errors, and nasty things off the hook—but the "entirety" is. Talk about fudging the case. How the "whole" is inspired but not its "parts" is mystifying. And when the Church does ascribe the inspired Word of God to this or that passage, which is compatible with orthodoxy and current sensitivities and, as we shall see later, reverses its "imprimatur," does that eat away at the "entirety"?

It is difficult to find real meaning in any of these rather gratuitous words. You get a sense of trying to square the circle. They're just words that don't seem to really say anything or give us good answers. They remain, as one can readily see, basically faith words—the old Talmudic principle we visited previously is very much at work: seeing things as *you* are, not as *they* are. And if you're coming from a faith perspective, then everything you see and say is all right and cannot be disputed.

Think of the ramifications of this: Defenders of the Qur'an or the Book of Mormon (their "Word of God") could make the very same statements. Just replace the word "Bible" with "Qur'an" or "Book of Mormon" and go back and re-read the words of the Commission and you'll get the idea. And who are we to counter them, just because we don't see, don't believe, as they do? Reconciling all these errors, all the mistakes, all these biblically approved horrors (slavery, cruelty, subordination of women) as the fault of the human authors or the context of the times, but not the God who "acted through them," is a challenge. It is surely a distinction without a difference.

This quotation about sums it up: "The Bible's authority stems from the Church's belief that, while *we do not know* how biblical inspiration works, the Bible, under the guidance of the Holy Spirit, can guide our lives in ways of faith and morals."[4] It is clear that, in reference

---

4   Ronald D. Witherup, "The Use and Abuse of the Bible," *Scripture from Scratch* no. 899 (August 1999).

to or defense of the Bible, we must first enter the area of faith—as do the Muslims and the Mormons.

Bruce Feiler, author of *Walking the Bible,* mines the same sentiment. Of his mentor, a man named Gabi, he writes:

> "How does proving the Bible help faith?" I said. "I'm a local Jew," he said, "I don't care whether this or that detail is incorrect in the Bible. It doesn't change my attitude toward the Bible, toward religion, toward God. Or toward myself." ... "Look," Gabi said, "Serious people know that some parts of the Bible go well with archaeology, others do not. So what? I'm not going to find in archaeology, ever, a business card that says 'Abraham, son of Terah.' But it doesn't matter. It's not a book of history. It's a book of faith."[5]

Ah, yes, faith. Again and again, this sentiment occurs: The biblical stories may or may not be literally true, but what counts is the message, the feeling one gets from them, the inspiration one takes from them, the faith one brings to them. This comes very close to the old bromide that it doesn't matter what you believe as long as you're sincere. More: "What is vital is only that what happened [in the Bible] was experienced, while it happened, as the act of God."[6] Thus claims Martin Buber. You could say the same about Mormon founder Joseph Smith and his purported visions from the archangel Gabriel that were experienced by him "as an act of God."

Again, Feiler, quoting a conversation:

> "From my point of view, there are three possibilities about the stories in the Bible," Doron said. It was late afternoon now and we were sitting on the edge of the sentry post with our feet dangling over the side. The bright white heat of midday had diminished. Our conversation had grown more personal. These were the moments I once avoided; now they were the ones I most craved.

---

5   Bruce Feiler, *Walking the Bible: A Journey by Land Through the Five Books of Moses* (New York: William Morrow, 2001), 106–107.

6   Martin Buber, *Moses* (Atlantic Highlands, NJ: Humanities Press, 1946), 77.

> "First, things happened as they are told in the stories. Second, some things happened as they are told; others were made up. And third, a very, very clever man made the stories up. So which one do you believe?" I asked.
>
> "In some ways it's my personality to believe the religious way of thinking. In other ways it's my personality to believe that someone made it up. I don't have a concrete opinion. And that's the nice thing about the Bible. You can take it however you want. What really matters are the clues within the stories about how to believe. So, one, two, or three, in the end they're all the same. The basic message is the same. It's solid truth."
>
> Arriving back to the campsite, I thought about Doron's comments. Here was a man as dry and scientific as any I had met who viewed the Bible as offering him some higher meaning. In many ways Doron's attachment meant more to me now than that of the people I had met during our earlier stops in Israel. It seemed to confirm my own evolution, my embracing the story for its emotional resonance, regardless of its factuality. I could accept the story for its moral code even as I struggled to identify its grounding in reality.[7]

These last two sentences surely express what most believers feel about the Bible. It's an honest comment, but one that leaves us squarely in the land of fideism.

Feiler once more:

> As with many places in the Sinai, the absence of evidence hardly matters, as modern visitors have decided these sites are the ones mentioned in the text. As we were sitting, a tour bus rolled up and fifty South Koreans disembarked, said a quick prayer by the spring, and prepared to re-embark. "This is the site of Marah," the minister explained, when I asked why he had come. Moments later a car full of American college students appeared and repeated the ritual. Their professor was less confident, "I don't worry about assigning places," he said. "In the end it doesn't matter whether they took the northern

---

7   Ibid., 322.

route, the central route or the southern route. What matters is that they were here." Minutes later, a carload of Frenchwomen arrived. "Who cares if the Israelites were actually here?" one woman said. "We're here because it's biblical!"[8]

Yes, with orthodoxy trumping text, you see things as you are, not as they are.

THE TALMUD LENS EXPANDED

A quotation sets the scene here:

> The stories in the New Testament as well as the Old are also fictionalized works of art, written imaginatively by authors for certain purposes. These authors drew from historically based traditions that had been handed down to them, but they created "history" by drawing on symbols, metaphors, myths, fables, and legends that were part of their culture at the time. They filled in the historical gap, supplying dialogue and narrative interpretation out of their own rich imaginations to convey some revelatory truth as they saw it.[9]

A fair summary, but the trouble is that "as *they* saw it" is not the way *we* see it today. The result is considerable tension between the Word *of* God and the Word *about* God. The fact is, as more and more information has been revealed about the ancient past—a deeper sense of sociology, language, and comparative religion, and the way the sacred writers embellished and "filled in the gaps"—the Church, being committed to an inspired and inerrant scripture, has poured out endless ongoing commentaries in an effort to rearrange, re-explain, or neutralize its former teaching. As a result, it has invented various senses of scripture, resorted to allegory and metaphor, and, as we have seen, in some cases made outright reversals clothed in face-saving language.

---

8   Ibid., 202.
9   Sandra Levy, *Imagination and the Journey of Faith* (Grand Rapids: Eerdmans, 2008), 96.

To make our case, we won't pause with, say, the Book of Leviticus, which is definitely uncomfortable with homosexuality, menstruating women, shellfish, pigskin, lending money at interest, sabbath observance, circumcision—all commands and prohibitions that even biblical literalists seem to find it perfectly permissible to disregard. Rather, let's take a look at three broader foundational beliefs that have been or are being revised or recast—though surreptitiously.

THE ONE WHO IS TO COME

The first thing to remember is that the first Christians were Jews. They could only explain Jesus in the God-talk they knew, the language of the Old Testament. Israel's story was their story and Jesus had to fit into it—or, rather, it had to fit into Jesus. So, the New Testament writers adapted the old sacred story to explain Jesus. They couldn't do so literally, so they transformed the Old Testament by using it as more of a jumping-off point. They were, as we are now used to saying, "creative." To be blunt, they read into the text.

A case in point: Since it is foundational Christian belief that everything in the Old Testament should be interpreted through the revelation of God in Jesus Christ, the claim that Jesus is the long-awaited, long-predicted Messiah is a given. It's a concept found in almost every page of the Old Testament if you know what to look for. On the contrary: Any talk of an Anointed One or Messiah came very late in Israel's history—at best, the second century BCE—and so there is no long tradition of a Messiah being "foretold."

Let me bring in some heavy Catholic hitters to back this up. Jesuit Joseph Fitzmyer says that any attempt to speak of Isaiah's Messianic prophecies is "still born." More forcefully, he adds, "The idea of a suffering Messiah . . . is found nowhere in the Old Testament or in any Jewish literature prior to or contemporaneous with the New Testament. It is a Christian conception that goes beyond the Jewish Messianic tradition."[10] In this, he echoes another prominent

---

10   Joseph A. Fitzmyer, *The One Who Is to Come* (Grand Rapids: Eerdmans, 2007), 142.

Catholic scripture scholar, Raymond Brown, who said, "There are no predictions of Jesus, as we know him, anywhere in the Hebrew Scriptures."[11] Dominican theologian Yves Congar states firmly that a suffering Messiah is without foundation. So, it's a Christian concept with no roots in the Old Testament tradition, even though Luke (24:27) writes about "Moses" and "all the prophets" and "all the scriptures" testifying to it.

Another commentator, Franciscan Leslie Hoppe, adds this sad note:

> Early Christian writers sometimes projected the centrality of the Messianic idea in the New Testament into the theology of the Hebrew Scriptures and early Jewish religious texts imagining that every Jew of the first century was eagerly awaiting the coming of "the Messiah." That the vast majority of Jesus' Jewish contemporaries did not accept him as the expected Messiah was therefore explained as sinful obstinacy (for example, Acts 7:51). Certainly one of the roots of Christian anti-Semitism was the apologetic problem caused by the Church's confession of Jesus as the fulfillment of Jewish Messianic expectations, while those whose faith was supposedly shaped by those expectations did not make such a confession.[12]

So, in the light of these quotations, take this scene from the Acts of the Apostles (2:14, 22–28). Peter (really Luke), fresh from the Pentecostal Upper Room, is speaking to the crowd. He quotes Psalm 16, where David says:

> I saw the Lord always before me,
> for he is at my right hand so that I will not be shaken;
> therefore my heart was glad, and my tongue rejoiced;
> moreover, my flesh will live in hope.

---

11 As quoted by Roger Karban, "An Unexpected Messiah," *National Catholic Reporter*, December 15, 2012, https://www.ncronline.org/blogs/spiritual-reflections/unexpected-messiah.

12 Leslie J. Hoppe, "The Significance of Messianism," *The Bible Today* 41.3 (2003): 152.

> For you will not abandon my soul to Hades,
> or let your Holy One experience corruption.
> You have made known to me the ways of life;
> you will make me full of gladness with your presence.

The psalm, in itself, is a standard plea by the psalmist that God will not permit a devoted worshiper to perish. That's all it says—period. Peter, however, goes on to argue that David was really speaking of Jesus, not himself, arguing that David was in fact a prophet who foresaw and "spoke of the resurrection of the Messiah."

Or, there's the famous road to Emmaus story, also from Luke, where Jesus, having heard from the two disciples about the "things that had happened" the past few days in Jerusalem, exclaims, "How slow of heart [you are] to believe all that the prophets have declared!" Luke goes on to say, "Then beginning with Moses and all the prophets, he interpreted to them the things about himself in all the scriptures" (Luke 24:25–27).

In the light of the scholars cited above, strictly speaking, none of this is literally true, but it's a form of appropriation that was legitimate at the time. But you had to buy into the faith, the orthodoxy of the speaker (Peter/Luke) to embrace it.

I know all this is a surprise for many, but these examples are another striking instance where Christian orthodoxy has been relentlessly read into the Old Testament texts. This means that all those stately scripture readings and splendid oratorios we have in our Holy Week liturgies from Isaiah and the psalms are magnificent poetry but misplaced prose if we take them as literal. Instead, we need to take them as allegories, metaphors, or suggestive allusions, which has been pretty much the mindset (at least among the intellectuals) ever since historical criticism took hold. As Kugel wrote, it's an interpreted Bible that we are reading. Once more, seeing all this through the lens of the Bible being the Word *about* God rests much more easily and comfortably than the forced apologies and interpretations of it being the Word *of* God.

SILENT NIGHT

Second, keeping in mind that the canons or rules of ancient biography were not like our own just-the-facts-ma'am style, but rather through the lens of creative interpretations, when we move to the accounts of Jesus' birth, we find two incompatible accounts that have been popularly conflated into one seamless tableau, the one of our crèches and Christmas carols. The Infancy Narratives are a good example of *theologically interpreted history* in antiquity. *If* they are taken literally, historical implausibility abounds. Both Luke's and Matthew's narratives, as we saw, place Jesus' birth in Bethlehem even though everywhere in the texts, Jesus is always referred to as a Nazarene. The astronomical records from the ancient world tell of no unusual star appearances for this time period. One also has to ask whether it is plausible that Herod, with his vast network of spies and soldiers, would ask total strangers (the Magi) where Jesus was born (the first recorded interfaith gathering). After all, it's only five miles from Jerusalem to Bethlehem. His spies could find out in a hurry.

Jesus is given royal heritage by having him go back to David in one case and Abraham himself in another. That's because Matthew is repeating an old tradition that Abraham himself was a king. He is relying on a translation of the word "king" found in the Septuagint version, but which is "prince" in the Hebrew version. Abraham is a king, David is a king, and so, therefore, Jesus is a king—and this is precisely the tension in Matthew: The Jewish leaders keep on rejecting his genuine kingship over the false kingship of Rome.

According to Catholic doctrine, Mary conceived Jesus by divine intervention and she remained a virgin before, during, and after his birth—although such a virgin birth was unknown to Paul and Mark, the earliest New Testament writers. Mary, moreover, is "ever" Virgin. Protestant doctrine, in contrast, states that yes, Mary conceived Jesus by the power of the Holy Spirit, but she had other children in the normal way, as several passages referring to Jesus' siblings testify. It seems that some early Church Fathers read the pertinent New Testament passages erroneously, ignoring the fact is that there is no Old Testament evidence of a virginal conception of the Messiah.

The angelic phrase "full of grace" did not refer to the later medieval notion of supernatural grace, but rather to today's translation of "highly favored one."

Moreover, as we have seen, the sentence, "A virgin shall conceive a child" was an incorrect translation of the word for a young (married or unmarried) woman. Add to this the apocryphal Gospel of Peter, which absorbed all these strains and used them in turn to interpret scripture, and you come up with Mary's perpetual virginity. It doesn't quite add up, but now, thanks to the back-and-forth osmosis between scripture and tradition, we have a "divinely revealed" doctrine, the very Word of God. All this has not prevented a prominent Catholic scripture scholar, another priest, John Meier, from publicly saying that Mary's virginity is a "theological" concept, not a physical one. By the way, speaking of Fr. Meier, he also points out that, out of the thirty-two miracles attributed to Jesus, only twelve have any real history behind them.

Matthew goes on to quote an Old Testament saying, "He shall be called a Nazorean," but there is no such quotation in the Bible. In short, the Matthew/Luke infancy narratives are revelatory parables featuring stars, angels, dreams, mangers, Wise Men, shepherds, and a wicked king that metaphorically make the collective point of the significance of this particular birth. (See chapter 11 for more on this theme.)

THE INTENDED PURPOSE

As one author, writing an introduction to the New Testament, expresses it:

> Biblical texts bear all the marks of human composition: historical conditioning, prejudice, factual error, and moral limitation, as well as deep theological and religious insight into the mystery of God's relationship with humanity.... In sum, the Gospels are not literal records of the ministry of Jesus. Decades of developing and adapting the Jesus tradition had intervened. For some, this calls the truth of the Gospels into question. Truth, however, must be evaluated in terms of the intended purpose. The

Gospels might be judged untrue if their goal was strict reporting or exact biography; but if the goal was to bring readers/hearers to a faith in Jesus that opens them to God's activity, then adaptations that make the Gospels less than literal—adding dimensions of faith, adjusting to new audiences—were made precisely to facilitate this goal and thus to make the Gospels true.[13]

A worthy and accurate description, but still, one wonders whether, if truth is not to be deterred by cultural conditioning, prejudice, error, or moral limitation, but found rather (and most determiningly) in terms of the intended purpose of the author bent on "adding dimensions of faith" (where these extra dimensions come from is another matter), then, of course, one could say the same thing about any book in the world—say, for example, the Qur'an. Muslims believe that their sacred book was revealed in one language (Arabic) to the prophet Mohammed over a period of twenty years. Perhaps, too, some Muslims might not accept the Qur'an, with its "historical conditioning, prejudice, factual error, and moral limitation," as a literally true work, but rather will evaluate its truth from its "intended purpose," which is to open them up to Allah's activity. In other words, if the Muslims bypass the awkward literalisms and limitations of the human author(s) and re-read the Qur'an as a metaphor and embrace the author's purpose to open his readers to Allah, then that book, no matter how erroneous, is true and evaluated as the "Word of God."

The Bible. The Qur'an. The Book of Mormon. Following the same strained logic and using the same criteria for all three, you can have three different "true" books from God.

DAVID, AUTHOR OF THE PSALMS?

While we're at it, mention David and most people automatically think of the psalms. Turns out, it's not an easy association. True, in his career, David not only took on the role of priest, led religious rituals,

---

13   Arthur E. Zannoni, *A Beginner's Guide to the New Testament* (Chicago: Thomas More Press, 2002), 22.

and controlled Israel's priesthood, but he was also a musician so notable that his reputation as a psalmist, as author of the 150 psalms, was launched. That reputation may have arisen from the episode where David is called in to soothe troubled King Saul by strumming his harp. David as harpist may have inspired the idea of David as musician; that, in turn, inspired the concept of David as the composer of the psalms. A nice theory, but not necessarily true. We now know that he did not write the psalms, or at least most of them.

Today, for internal reasons of structure, style, and chronology, most scholars have ruled him out as the author. As an example, Psalm 137 speaks those famous words, "By the rivers of Babylon—there we sat down and there we wept when we remembered Zion... there our captors asked us for songs [of Zion].... How could we sing the Lord's song in a foreign land?" The psalm is from the Exile, four hundred years after David.

Moreover, the psalms turn out to be not much different from the contemporary hymns and songs of other nations. The pre-Mosaic Canaanite library at Ugarit, it turns out, contains a great deal of material quite consistent with the psalms. The characteristics used to describe their gods are strikingly similar to those describing Yahweh. Even that gracious quality of mercy, so extolled as Yahweh's special prerogative, turns out to be a standard characteristic of El, the Canaanite god. The very same sacrifices and temples cited in the psalms can be found in the Ugarit tablets. Even the Canaanite and Hebrew literary styles, such as their parallelisms, are very close. It's sometimes hard to tell the Ugaritic psalms from the Hebrew psalms, and some of the later Hebrew psalms simply borrow "whole cloth" from the Ugaritic. Indeed, reading the Ugarit text has provided corrections for the long-held misinterpretations of some words in the Hebrew psalms. That's a synopsis of what we have been saying all along about the Bible and its contemporary culture.

Together, these various examples illustrate how commentators finessed biblical passages once held as the literal word of God into palatable interpretations that tempt one to read them all as flexible words *about* God rather than the inflexible words *of* God.

A SUMMARY

Perhaps this is the right place to end with a related quotation from the scripture scholar James Kugel. It is worth reading carefully and slowly to appreciate its full meaning.

> Gradually... the historical circumstances in which a particular biblical passage might have originally been uttered were eventually forgotten or, in any case, considered irrelevant. What was important by, say, the third or second century B.C.E. (and quite possibly, even somewhat earlier) was what was thought to be the text's deeper significance, that is, how it was explained by the traditional interpretations that now accompanied it. And this traditionally interpreted Bible—the Bible itself plus the traditions about what it really meant—was what was taught to successive generations of students, expounded in public assemblies and, ultimately, canonized by Judaism and Christianity as their sacred book.
>
> The way in which these traditions of interpretation came to cling to the biblical text may be difficult for people today to comprehend. We like to think that the Bible, or any other text, means "just what it says." And we act on that assumption: we simply open up a book—including the Bible—and try to make sense of it on our own. In ancient Israel and for centuries afterward, on the contrary, people looked to special interpreters to explain the meaning of a biblical text. For that reason, the explanations passed along by such interpreters quickly acquired an authority of their own. In studying this or that biblical law or prophecy or story, students would do more than simply learn the words; they would be told what the text meant—not only the peculiar way in which this or that term was to be interpreted, but how one biblical text related to another far removed from it, or the particular moral lesson that a text embodied, or how a certain passage was to be applied in everyday life. And the people who learned these things about the Bible from their teachers in turn passed on the same information to the next generation of students.
>
> And so, it was this *interpreted Bible*—not just the stories, prophecies, and laws themselves, but these texts as they had, by now,

been interpreted and explained for centuries—that came to stand at the very center of Judaism and Christianity. This was what people in both religions meant by "the Bible." Of course, Judaism and Christianity themselves differed on a great many questions, including the interpretation of some crucial scriptural passages, as well as on just what books were to be included in the Bible. Nevertheless, both religions had begun with basically the same interpreted Bible. For both inherited an earlier, common set of traditions, general principles regarding how one ought to go about reading and interpreting the Bible as well as specific traditions concerning the meaning of individual passages, verses, and words. As a result, even when later Jews or Christians added on new interpretations—sometimes directed against each other or against other groups or ideologies within the world in which they lived—the new interpretations frequently built on, and only modified, what had been the accepted wisdom until then.[14]

The Bible is a complex collection with many, many fingerprints on it besides God's—maybe *instead* of God's?

---

14 Kugel, *How to Read the Bible*, xix, xv; his emphasis.

Chapter 7

GODS, GOD, AND HOLY ABSENCE

> The God whom ancient Israel worshipped arose as the fusion of a number of gods whom a nomadic nation had met in its wanderings.
>
> —*Jack Miles*

Israel told stories, as we have seen—marvelous, compelling ones stitched from scraps of the past and the needs of the present—and literally rewrote history. The rewrite even included their God, and we'll start with him.

YAHWEH

Yahweh as the one and only God, the monotheistic deity, became the orthodoxy. It wasn't always this way. Monotheism didn't catch on until the time of Second Isaiah. The idea of Yahweh, it turns out, seems more the product of a gradual evolution of society rather than a singular, original revelation to a particular people. The biblical authors inadvertently left clues of Yahweh's past. For instance, the Bible gives him several names—Yahweh, El, Elohim, and Shaddai—and stated that he is one of many gods. Exodus 15:11 inquires, "Who is like you, O Lord, among the gods?" Psalm 89:6 asks, "For who in the skies can be compared to the Lord? Who among the heavenly beings is like the Lord?" It is obvious that there existed a hierarchy in the heavens. Yahweh was even worshipped in the form of a calf (see I Kings 12:28 and Hosea 8:6).

Yahweh, in fact, as Tom Holland observes, was the end of a process by which, to a degree unparalleled by any other deity, Yahweh "had come to contain multitudes within himself. When, in the very first sentence of Genesis, he was described as creating the heavens and the earth, the Hebrew word for God—*Elohim*—was tellingly ambiguous. Used throughout Jewish scripture as a singular, the noun's ending was plural. 'God' had once been 'gods.'"[1]

Psalm 82:1 declared, "God has taken his place in the divine council; in the midst of the gods he holds judgment." Those gods are soon demoted (Psalm 82:6–7):

> I say, "You are gods,
> children of the Most High, all of you;
> nevertheless, you shall die like mortals,
> and fall like any prince."

To interject Bruce Feiler again:

> Even the *shema*, the holiest words in Judaism and what one commentator calls "the great text of monotheism," *seems to imply that other gods exist*. The traditional translation is "Hear, O Israel! The LORD is our God. The LORD is One." But the words, which come from Deuteronomy 6, are considered vague by Bible scholars and are often translated today as, "Hear, O Israel! The LORD is our God, the LORD alone." God, the words suggest, should stand apart and above other gods, meaning that he is the superior god but not the only god.[2]

The fact is that, until Moses' time, God was "El Shaddai" or other "El" combinations, "El" being the name of the Canaanite god,

---

1 Holland, *Dominion*, 63.
2 Feiler, *Walking the Bible*, 281.

to whom Yahweh bears a striking resemblance. This god was seen as a bull (a raging warrior), yet he was also called "El, the Compassionate" just like Yahweh, who is pictured as a fierce warrior giving no quarter, but who shows compassion to his people. Both El and Yahweh spoke through prophets, both are paternal creator gods, and, often, the Hebrew word El appears in the Bible as the word for God. This is not to say necessarily that Yahweh started life as El, but to suggest there is a close link: "I am Yahweh. I appeared to Abraham, to Isaac, and to Jacob as El Shaddai."

Finally, during the monarchial period, Yahweh has a female consort known as Asherah. Later, Proverbs will speak of "Lady Wisdom," who was with Yahweh at the creation, hinting that perhaps she was a disguised consort.

Summarizing the composite nature of Yahweh, Jack Miles offers this litany:

> The God whom ancient Israel worshipped arose as the fusion of a number of gods whom a nomadic nation had met in its wanderings.... Here the sky blue of El, there the earth tones of "the god of your father," over there the blood red of Ba'al. Psalm 29, most scholars believe, was originally a Ugaritic hymn to Ba'al or Tiamat, not to Yahweh or the evergreen memory of Asherah.... Historians have generally recognized the powerful originality of Israel's religious synthesis even when they did not also believe on religious grounds that this originality was revelation from God himself.... The most coherent way to imagine the Lord God of Israel is as the inclusion of the content of several ancient divine personalities in a single character.... Moreover, this Lord God of Israel was not the sole deity and this God was quite tolerant of other gods at the time of Adam, Noah, Abraham, Jacob, and Joseph. Suddenly, with Moses and Joshua he becomes "jealous" and even though, once you have the book of Deuteronomy with its prohibitions of further fusions of various gods into Yahweh, the syncretism continues.[3]

---

3   Miles, *God*, 20, 21, 72, 162.

The bottom line belongs to Karen Armstrong: it is almost impossible to find "a single monotheistic statement in the whole of the Pentateuch."[4]

POLYTHEISM AND MONOTHEISM

Polytheism, we must admit, had advantages. For one thing, it was a lot more tolerant. The monotheistic religions tended to have an "all or nothing at all" approach and so more easily clashed with other religions and did not hesitate to use torture or death against dissidents. For another thing, polytheism handled the problem of evil better than monotheism. Evil could come from angry, careless, arbitrary, or drunken gods, or simply "stuff happens," and would have to be defeated by the gods. But once you have monotheism, you have the conundrum of why that one God, reputed to be loving and forbearing, kind and merciful, who made all things and saw that they were good—how could he decide to do harm to the human race? (The monotheists eventually came up with an answer: because we sinned.)

So, where did monotheism come from? Historically, it seems to have arisen at the same time among disparate peoples of the Middle East, such as those of Babylon, Egypt, and Israel. We know that around 1340 BCE, the pharaoh Akhenaten (a.k.a. Amenhotep) came up with the concept of one god, Aten. Ultimately, it didn't catch on. The Greek philosopher Xenophanes, around the fifth century BCE, posited a single, all-powerful deity. Evidently, the growing notion of one god was beginning to have certain emotional and intellectual attractions. For example, if there is a single being that created and sustains the universe, then that means there is a coherence to life and everything must be part of a divine plan. It gave life a sense of unity and purpose. Rowan Williams, former Archbishop of Canterbury, argues:

> It guarantees a coherence and stability in the world we inhabit, and in how we understand human well-being. You don't have

---

4   Karen Armstrong, *A History of God: The 4,000-Year Quest of Judaism, Christianity and Islam* (New York: Ballantine, 1993), 23.

a god of this group and that group, who may or may not get on with each other. You don't have a god who looks after this bit of the universe, which may or may not hang together. You have a single purpose.... It is that sense of deep ultimate coherence that is one of the most significant things about monotheism.[5]

THE PROBLEM OF EVIL

As noted above, after the establishment of a single, monotheistic God, who made all things and saw they were good, the problem of evil was exacerbated. Where did evil come from? Even Eden's cunning snake was created "good." The non-canonical book of Enoch steps in to recount a revolt in heaven that spilled over to earth. There, the rebel angels mixed with humans to create a race of giants who were killed off in the flood. There are hints of this story in the "sons of God" references in Genesis 6:1–4 or in Leviticus 16, where Israel's sins are placed on a goat who is then sent off to "Azazel" (scapegoat), the name of one of the rebellious angels.

Whatever the case and no matter how much we proclaim the One God, in practice, dualism prevails and the God versus the Snake motif (polar opposites of good and evil) gets constantly replayed. Prominent in Zoroastrianism, it slipped into Judaism and Christianity. In spite of St. Augustine's insistence that there was only One Reality and that Evil was not an independent force, but rather the corruption of goodness, the myth of Satan, the tempter, gradually became standard. Zechariah cites Satan. The Dead Sea Scrolls relate the fall of rebellious angels. One text even describes a final war of Light versus Darkness.

Jesus himself believed in him, recounting how he saw Satan falling from heaven (Luke 10:18). In John's gospel (8:44) he calls the Jews the offspring of Satan. The book of Jude cites Enoch and relates, "The angels who did not keep their own position, but left

---

5   As quoted in Neil MacGregor, *Living with the Gods: On Beliefs and People* (New York: Alfred A. Knopf, 2018), 341.

their proper dwelling, he has kept in eternal chains in deepest darkness for the judgment of the great day" (Jude 6). Jude also mentions the archangel contending with the devil over the body of Moses. 2 Thessalonians makes reference to Satan: "The coming of the lawless one is apparent in the working of Satan" (2:7–11). The dystopian Book of Revelation, reluctantly accepted into the New Testament canon, also references Satan (12:9).

The third century Church Father Origen put all the pieces together and came up with Satan as a former morning star, "Lucifer," who wanted to displace God on the throne and was cast down from heaven like lightning. With a gloss on the Adam-Snake encounter and in defiance of the monolithic, monotheistic God who made all things good, the dualism (thanks to Plato and Descartes) has ever persisted: James Bond and Spector, Batman and the Joker, Holmes and Moriarty, Simba and Scar, Luke Skywalker and Darth Vader, Superman and Lex Luther, Captain Kirk and the Klingons. In fact, dualism, like the concept of the afterlife, is a variation of that hardwired human instinct for justice and its distinction between good and bad—and they should never be treated in the same way.

GOD IS A HE

I suppose this is the place to mention that the monotheistic God that emerged, though genderless and, in some biblical passages, imagined as female—for example, Deuteronomy 32:18: "the God who gave you birth"—there is no doubt that the biblical God is overwhelmingly male, a slant that irretrievably skews the Bible. The prophets speak of Yahweh as the husband of Israel and the psalms praise him as king and father. Jesus directs us to pray, "Our Father." The Church's universal creed proclaims forthrightly, "I believe in God, the Father Almighty." The doctrine of the Trinity gives us Father, Son, and Holy Spirit and, with delicious irony, while the *Catechism of the Catholic Church* proclaims that "God's parental tenderness can also be expressed by the image of motherhood... [and] God transcends the human distinction between the sexes," it continues with, "*He is* neither man nor woman: *he* is God. *He* also transcends human fatherhood and motherhood."[6] Even subconsciously, we can't get around God's maleness.

THE TRINITY FACTOR

Concerning the Trinity, the conservative Englishman Hilaire Belloc once jingled, "I wish there were four of Them so I could believe in more of Them." But this chapter isn't saucy. It's a reflection of everydayness, of where-we-are questions.

The Faithful Father

A good mantra to remember, the scholars tell us, is not that the Bible tells us who God is but who *we* are. Much of the Bible does, in fact, focus on the nature of human beings. It's a collection of reflections on sinful and lost humanity and the God who consistently saves it from itself. We see this "people focus" particularly in the so-called wisdom books, even though these books disagree with one another and are lifted sometimes verbatim from other cultures. Nevertheless, the fact remains that much of the Bible is all about resistible humanity and an irresistible God; about a wayward people and a God who nevertheless remains faithful to them; a God who, in spite of threats, keeps covenant with them. They are forever his people and he is forever their God. They are a Chosen Race, a Holy Nation, a People Set Apart. God is faithful.

Well, yes and no. To show what I mean, let me transition with a hoary old joke.

> Abe was dying. His wife, Sarah, was at his bedside. Abe said to her,
>
> "You know, Sarah, when I fell and broke my leg, you were with me.

---

6   Libreria Editrice Vaticana, *Catechism of the Catholic Church*, 239. My italics.

"When I lost my job, you were there.

"When I failed in my business, there you were.

"When I lost my lottery ticket, you were at my side.

"When I nearly drowned, there you were on the shore.

"When my car was stolen, you never left me.

"When the roof collapsed and I nearly lost my life, you were present.

"You know what, Sarah? You're bad luck!"

And that's my critique. To put it bluntly—and no disrespect intended—Yahweh may be faithful, but he is bad luck. Yahweh always "being there" is small comfort when you're in dire straits, in unspeakable mental, emotional, or physical pain day after day, week after week, month after month, year after year, century after century, without relief. The history of the Jews, the endless persecutions against them—the Christian crusades that slaughtered them, the pogroms that sought to eliminate them, the Holocaust that killed some six million of them, the relentless discrimination—no wonder some Jews prayed to God that he pick another people if this is the way he treats his chosen ones. "Choose somebody else." The bloody pages of history belie any observable and effective sense of covenant, of closeness, of God's fidelity. This makes one wonder: Would the Jews' history have been any worse *without* Yahweh? That question, as befits my state of mind, kicks in with this long aside.

Christianity claims that we are living in the messianic age. No one ever consciously attends to that fact. The Messiah, the Prince of Peace who came to make all things new again, has come. Yet, outside of the incredible impact for good that Christianity has made on the world, it's hard to detect a difference. David Klinghoffer, in his book *Why the Jews Rejected Jesus*, points out that it is hard to tell any difference as he asks, concerning Jesus, "Where is the Messiah's signature kingdom of peace?" Although Jesus said the kingdom of God is within you, it is clear to many scholars that the "Kingdom of

God" was something meant to happen here on earth. There would need to be a transformation here since the Jews did not believe in an afterlife.

Yet, two thousand years after the arrival of Jesus' Messianic Kingdom, after several genocides and holocausts, forty million killed in World War I and seventy-five million killed in World War II, religious wars, inquisitions, plagues, pandemics, earthquakes, Hiroshima, Dresden, Rwanda, Zimbabwe, Bosnia, Cambodia, Iraq, Afghanistan, Libya, Syria, Chernobyl, Treblinka, Newtown, and 9/11; after terrorism, Agent Orange, drones, mass graves, disappearing forests and water, global warming, and pollution; after slavery (even among the ancient Hebrews), colonialism, Manifest Destiny, ethnic cleansings, Wall Street meltdowns, disproportionate wealth, the growing chasm between the super-rich and the poor—the litany is never-ending—after all these and more, it challenges the mind to think that, if we are living in the time of Jesus' Messianic Kingdom, how could things possibly be worse without it?

Besides, if Yahweh promises Elijah he will no longer withhold the rain (1 Kings 18:1), should not God be accountable for nature's horrors as well, even in Messianic times? Think then of the massive classic extinctions—the Cretaceous-Paleogene, the Triassic-Jurassic (the one that got the dinosaurs), and so on, where most life forms were destroyed. Think of tsunamis, and the 20,000 people who died in 2005. What's the old saying: "God forgives always, man sometimes, and nature never"? But God is the author of nature.

I am, ironically, writing this at the apex (perhaps!) of the global coronavirus pandemic of 2020. The pope and the entire Catholic world have prayed to God for relief, in unison via telecast, but nothing is happening except that the pandemic grows worse daily, infecting millions and killing thousands of people. Is God dead, impotent, "with us" but not listening, or listening but, for his own reasons, not responding? Two prominent Protestant preachers weighed in on the conundrum. Lewis Smedes wrote, "Sometimes I hang on to faith by my fingernails; when the dream of a new world of Jesus' peace and love is more than two thousand years old and still shows no clear sign of coming true, anybody's faith is bound to turn to doubt."[7] Another noted, "Fred Craddock used to point out that there is always enough suffering in the world to make the idea of a messiah a powerful one. On the other hand, he says there is always enough pain in the world to render ridiculous the statement, 'The Messiah has come.'"[8]

Again, although the biblical Yahweh could be quite erratic, petulant, bloodthirsty, and revengeful, there are passages extolling his mercy and forgiveness and his declaration that he has loved his people "with an everlasting love." In testimony to this, the psalmist cries out: "Even though I walk through the darkest valley, I fear no evil; for you are with me; your rod and your staff—they comfort me" (Psalm 23:4).

Being There

Question: Has "with me" made a difference? On the contrary, it is a consistent human lament that, even though one prayed to God for release, or at least some sign of his presence, some sign that he cares, he is absent. "My spouse died anyway." "I was forced to watch soldiers rape my three-year old daughter." Elie Wiesel's famous question, "Where is God?" as a child swung back and forth on the end of a noose, and his answer, "This is where: hanging here from this gallows,"[9] is a statement that ultimately means nothing. The point is the nature of God: compassionate, kind, forgiving—and powerful.

It's not just that one has to "have faith" that God "will make all things new again," but a question of when. It's the intolerable delay. It's his absolutely consistent absence, his non-use of his power that perplexes. Still, we claim God is faithful, or there's the last-ditch response that God really *is* there—and, you know what? He is suffering with you. *He feels your pain.* So, the immutable God feels your

---

7 Lewis Smedes, *My God and I: A Spiritual Memoir* (Grand Rapids: Eerdmans, 2003), 175.

8 Unnamed preacher, "Draw a Bigger Circle," *Latham United Methodist Church*, February 3, 2013, https://lathamumc.org/?sermon=draw-a-bigger-circle.

9 Elie Wiesel, *Night*, trans. Marion Wiesel (New York: Hill and Wang, 2006), 65.

pain. What good is that if nothing changes? He has power, *is* power. He could relieve the situation. Yes, yes, suffering brings nobility and growth. Suffering tests. But you can't have it on such a daily, massive, consistent scale, millennium after millennium, and not wonder, "So what? God is present. God feels my pain. That's it? Is God the 'Sarah' of our joke—you know, 'bad luck'? Do those words mean anything when nothing changes?"

During the coronavirus of 2020, clergy of various faiths echoed the same theme. Rabbi Noam Marans of New York noted the overlap between Catholics and Jews on this perennial question of suffering. Reciting Psalm 23, Marans resorted to the old formula, "We believe that God is there with the sufferer."[10] Rabbi Irving Greenberg tells us that the biblical days of miraculous deliverance are over and that the Talmud says that God is "self-limited" so as to give human beings greater freedom and responsibility. God shares our pain (that phrase again), but asks *us* to take action to end suffering.[11] (Makes you wonder: Why pray for miracles?) The noted Catholic bishop Robert Barron's reply is similar: God doesn't take away suffering. He enters into it. So, God enters into it. We're still suffering. Nothing changes. The words are meaningless. The whole thing is like a man standing on the bank, watching a struggling woman and her two children sinking in quicksand. He shouts to her that he shares her pain. All the while, he has a branch in his hand.

Or there's the favorite last-ditch ploy that says that yes, of course, God is, *was*, present and active. He was present and active in the solidarity of people in distress, in all of the first responders, in the huge, unsung army of caregivers. That is a much-cherished thought, but, at bottom, it's an empty one. The picture of the thousands of people who ministered to the millions of victims is not quite commensurate

---

[10] Nick Mayrand, "New York's Religious Leaders Finding God at Virus's American Epicenter," *Crux*, April 10, 2020, https://cruxnow.com/church-in-the-usa/2020/04/new-yorks-religious-leaders-finding-god-at-viruss-american-epicenter/.

[11] Irving Greenberg, "The Coronavirus Isn't God's Will," *The Wall Street Journal*, May 28, 2020, https://www.wsj.com/articles/the-coronavirus-isnt-gods-will-11590706772.

with the claim of bountiful mercy. The presence of the emergency crew that pulled the dead bodies out of the quicksand doesn't quite compensate for the senseless deaths of three people. The collateral damage of the many far overrides any notion of God's presence in the few. Insisting that God was there still doesn't capture the magnitude of the ongoing suffering, not only of God's "chosen ones," but of all of humanity and all of sentient nature. The bottom line is that if you want to hold onto faith, these things are the best anyone can say and we just have to live with the inscrutableness of the mystery.

This is not just a rehash (though it is that) of the theodicy question. It's trying to come to terms with the injunction to read the Bible and expect that God will reveal himself in its pages—but precisely what is that revelation? It is, we are told, that in Israel's worst moments, in its most sinful and idolatrous moments, God remains faithful to the covenant he made with them, his chosen ones, in perpetuity. Empirically, historically, as we have seen, such a claim hasn't made much practical difference. True enough, one can read the biblical stories about how often God *has* come through and delivered his people and be inspired, but by this time, as the preceding pages have shown, we know that the stories, quite inflated, are suspect as nationalistic. They are partisan, reworked, interpreted stories that don't always hold up under scrutiny. Those biblical underdog stories are the wishful thinking of a perpetually minor, second-rate nation.

Not for a moment do I think the stories are not necessary. On the contrary, take away our stories, our myths, and we perish. I am just trying to say that the concept of Yahweh as Emmanuel—"God with us"—is a comfort, and many have felt it, but it is not an experienced reality in the massive maw of human history.

Anyway, back to the Bible: In spite of the predominance of Jews garnering Nobel Prizes, along with their fierce intelligence, huge influence on civilization (Moses, Jesus, Freud, Marx, Einstein, etc.), and the incredible wealth of some, they have suffered throughout history—and, in some places, still do. Like all of us, they have advanced noble causes and backslid into ignoble ones, but the biblical God is still with them—although it can be hard to tell. No matter what the Bible says, no matter what palatable communications God always seems to make in the Bible's ancient pages, in life's everyday chronicle, he's not perceptably there for a world struggling in a tsunami of evil, physical and moral.

On this subject, let me quote Richard Holloway. We can sense the anguish and struggle in his words:

> As the creator of all things, ultimate responsibility for everything had to rest with [God], especially for the pains and sorrows of the admittedly weak but not entirely wicked children of the earth whose unanswered cries had been beating against his gate for centuries. My wrestling with my own compulsions, as well as my experience of the tragedies of others, did not demonstrate any discernable improvement in the human condition as a result of the death of Jesus—allegedly decreed by God for our salvation.... In spite of the claims of the Revivalists, the world did not seem any more redeemed after than before Christ....
>
> I knew we could help to *ameliorate* the human condition. Christianity, in spite of its flaws, had been good at that, was still good at it. That's why those people came to our door and were insistent on being helped. This, they seem to be saying, is what you are for. We know it, you know it, so open up and get on with it. And we did. We fed the hungry and visited those in prison and clothed the naked and tried to share our goods with the poor. But the dead did not rise, the lame did not walk, the blind did not see. We could help the poor of the world but we could not heal the woe of the world that made them poor and would go on making them poor forever.... God needed to be accused not excused, challenged not crawled to on bended knee.[12]

The searing photo that went viral, if you remember it, of the lifeless body of the four-year-old immigrant child washed up on a Turkish beach in 2005, sums up the theodicy problem for many. This is religion's biggest challenge: keeping people believing in a God who saves the world in spite of consistent evidence to the contrary.

---

12 Richard Holloway, *Leaving Alexandria: A Memoir of Faith and Doubt* (Edinburgh: Canongate, 2012), 221–224.

The Faithful Son

Harking back to the theme of the Father being with us in the valley of death, we find the same resonance with Jesus in the New Testament. The Incarnate God tells us that the hairs of our heads are numbered; that we are no longer slaves but friends; that we are worth more than the birds of the air, and, if we strive for his Kingdom of God and his righteousness, God will give us food and clothing; that if we ask, what we ask for will be given us. For, after all, if we know how to give good things to *our* children, "how much more will your Father in heaven give good things to those who ask him!" (Matthew 7:11)? Moreover, Jesus did say that he came, not only to give us life, but to give it abundantly. Not only that, but wherever his followers are gathered in his name, he is there (Matthew 18:20). He is the one moved with compassion for the crowds and the one who wept over his friend Lazarus' death (John 11:35). He is in their midst.

Jesus affirms his presence with us: "Remember, I am with you always, to the end of the age" (Matthew 28:20). He is there. Once again, however, presence and abundant life have not precluded massive, irrational suffering. Jesus' cry on the cross, "My God, my God, why have you forsaken me?" (Matthew 27:46) has been humankind's harrowing question throughout the millennia.

Still, to move off our theme for the moment, allow me to editorialize a bit. Jesus' teaching—think of the Beatitudes—and Jesus' conduct, his own suffering and death, offer empathy. One of the common statements going around today is that we must return to the centrality of Jesus. There is a commonsense and growing recognition that Jesus was clearly concerned about the specific healing and transformation of real persons and human society. The Church, on the other hand, historically focused on doctrinal belief and moral stances, and also asks almost nothing of us in terms of real change. Quaker pastor Philip Gulley summarizes how we must rebuild spirituality from the bottom up in his book, *If the Church Were Christian*. Here, in ten statements, Richard Rohr uses his own words to restate Gulley's message:

1. Jesus is a model for living more than an object of worship.

2. Affirming people's potential is more important than reminding them of their brokenness.

3. The work of reconciliation should be valued over making judgments.

4. Gracious behavior is more important than right belief.

5. Inviting questions is more valuable than supplying answers.

6. Encouraging the personal search is more important than group uniformity.

7. Meeting actual needs is more important than maintaining institutions.

8. Peacemaking is more important than power.

9. We should care more about love and less about sex.

10. Life in this world is more important than the afterlife.[13]

These liberal-oriented "ten commandments" are not meant to be in opposition to the Church, but rather a philosophy that defines the Church. Shifting away from the concept of a totally institutionalized entity, yet preserving its dogmas and its laws, the Church must seek a new identity, a new focus, a new way of being "in Christ," as St. Paul would put it.

There must be a new awareness of Jesus as clearly teaching nonviolence, simplicity of lifestyle, peacemaking, love of creation, and letting go of ego, both for individuals and groups. His radical social critique of the systems of domination, money, and power is more or less ignored by Catholic, Orthodox, and Protestant Christians, concentrating as they did on private sinfulness, personal salvation, and the next world. There is a growing recognition that Jesus was clearly

---

13   Richard Rohr, "If We Were Christian," *Center for Action and Contemplation*, November 1, 2019, https://cac.org/if-we-were-christian-2019-11-01/.

concerned about the specific healing and transformation of real persons and human society here on earth. All this is meant to be an indictment of the status quo and a suggestion that the future thrust of the Church must be on spirituality and mysticism if it is to survive.

The Faithful Holy Spirit

This section will be brief, for I am hesitant to show any disrespect to the topic at hand. My view is strictly utilitarian and my point is succinct: The Holy Spirit has been misused. The Holy Spirit figures, of course, in the New Testament, some seventy-three times in Luke's two books alone. In Acts 13:2, for example, Luke speaks of a gathering in Antioch. "While they were worshipping the Lord and fasting, the Holy Spirit said, 'Set apart for me Barnabas and Saul for the work to which I have called them.'" The Holy Spirit *said*. Was it an audible voice, like the one Jesus heard at his baptism—"This is my Son, the Beloved" (Matthew 3:17)—or some other kind of communication? We don't know, except that apparently back then, the Holy Spirit was palpably more active and unmistakably direct than our freely used and vague "inspired by the Holy Spirit," which never delineates any such specifics.

In John's Gospel, Jesus speaks of the Spirit of Truth, the Advocate who will be with the disciples forever (14:16). That Holy Spirit, "whom the Father will send in my name, will teach you everything, and remind you of all that I have said to you" (14:26). "When the Spirit of truth comes, he will guide you into all the truth" (16:13). Such sayings are the basis of the claims that the Spirit is with the Church, especially the hierarchical magisterium.

But it has gone beyond that. The reference to the Holy Spirit has become an imprimatur to justify all sorts of things. I recall that when Cardinal Montini was elected Pope Paul VI, someone remarked that the Holy Spirit was at work in the choice. Where was the Holy Spirit at the election, say, of Alexander VI or, to add some spice to this heavy chapter, how about Adrian II, who was married and whose wife and daughter lived within the Lateran Palace? Stephen VI was imprisoned and strangled in 896. John VIII was hammered to death,

John X murdered. Sergius III had a son by the notorious Marozia Theophylact and that son later became John XI, who later witnessed the marriage of his mother to her brother-in-law. John XII was not yet twenty when he became pope; he died while visiting his mistress. John XIX was a layman who in one day received all of the ecclesiastical orders in order to ascend the papal throne. He was assassinated in 984. Sylvester III sold his papal title to Gregory VI. Imagine what a great TV series this would make!

Anyway, to get off the scandal page, be careful of "Holy Spiriting" your candidate or your cause. For example, some authors today speak of the Holy Spirit leading us to a new, revised future. Vatican II and the *Catechism of the Catholic Church* frequently cite the Holy Spirit as validating this or that. So many partisan ventures claim to be the work of the Holy Spirit. "This is clearly the work of the Holy Spirit" is the joyous conviction of devotees of various causes. It's an overused claim that, in some cases, does not stand up to scrutiny and sometimes becomes an embarrassment.

One such author opines:

> Prompted by the Spirit, Paul VI and the participants at the Second Vatican Council acknowledged that all Christians "are joined with us in the Holy Spirit for to them also the Spirit gives gifts and graces and is operative among them with sanctifying power...." (*Lumen Gentium*, #12)
>
> Further prompted by the Spirit, the council also acknowledged that the two-thirds of the world's population who are not Christian "are most dear to God," and therefore "we ought to believe that the Holy Spirit, in a manner known only to God, offers to every human being the grace of being blessed by the paschal mystery.... For it is God ... as Savior, [who] calls that all be saved" (*Lumen Gentium* #16; *Gaudium et Spes* #22).[14]

Notice the multiple references to the Holy Spirit. Indeed, God's ways are mysterious. We cannot help but point out, for example,

---

14 Patricia Sánchez, "Preaching Resources: Freedom of the Spirit, September 27, 2009," *Celebration* 38:9 (September 2009).

that the Holy Spirit, the Busy Prompter, delayed his advocacy of non-Catholics, the world's vast majority, for some eight hundred years until, at last, in the 1960s, in an act of progressive revelation, he inspired a latter-day pope and the bishops to reverse course by discovering in scripture and tradition reasons for doing so.

Surely the Spirit does abide and does guide, but that Spirit seems uneven in the timing of the doctrines and pronouncements it putatively inspired, doctrines and pronouncements that were reversed in a later day under its guidance. But that's not my point here. My point is that we should make a more cautious and judicious claim than our project is "clearly" the work of the Holy Spirit and leave that judgment for a later date, when time and distance provide a better perspective. The Church, I suggest, should stop invoking the validations of the Holy Spirit for a while—limiting it, say, to every two or three centuries, to give time for reality to take hold.

Chapter 8

UNFINISHED BUSINESS

> Adam ate the apple and we got the stomachache.
>
> —*traditional saying*

In this brief chapter—an excursus really—we probe a bit deeper to examine three contested areas about which people who read the same Bible radically disagree (challenging, once more, the literal "word of God" trope). Here, I confess, I enter into deep waters because I'm not sure I fully understand the material, but it does seem to bear on our theme.

FAITH IN JESUS?

The first consideration is the current "faith *in* Jesus versus the faith *of* Jesus" controversy. Scholar Richard Hays asserts that when St. Paul writes about the salvific effects of faith, he is primarily referencing the faith *of* Jesus, not faith *in* Jesus, maintaining that faith is not in Jesus being a part of our story, but we being a part of his.[1] The New Perspective on Paul agrees with him in declaring that *"Pistis Christou,"* a Greek genitive usually translated as "faith in Christ" ought to be "faithfulness *of* Christ." Finally, it is worth noting that Jerome's

---

1 Richard B. Hays, *The Faith of Jesus Christ: The Narrative Substructure of Galatians 3:1–4:11* (Grand Rapids: Eerdmans, 2002).

Vulgate and Tyndale's translation also say that we are saved by the "faith of" and not "faith *in*" Christ.

Be it noted that these simple statements turn Protestantism on its head, undermine it at its root. I continue to build up the case by giving a more complicated explanation, citing some comments from David Bentley Hart:

> The authenticity of Colossians has often been denied by some scholars on the grounds that it seems to contain doctrines (a strong "moralism" of good works, for instance) incompatible with those found in the authentic letters. That, however, is where a trap may have been laid. What those scholars generally mean is that Colossians seems somewhat hard to reconcile with Paul's authentic letters *as interpreted by magisterial Protestant tradition*. But the problem with this is that (pardon my bluntness) those traditional Protestant readings of Paul are demonstrably wrong [that is, declaring that justification through works is wrong; justification through faith is right].... But Paul taught nothing of the sort. Instead he taught that human beings cannot be "justified" (that is, "proved" or "made righteous") by "works of the Law" (such as circumcision or kosher dietary practices), but by a "faithfulness" that necessarily entails "works" of love.[2]

John Barton agrees. He notes that "central ideas... such as St. Paul's theory of 'salvation by grace through faith,' that at least until the Reformation were never part of official orthodoxy at all, and even now are not in the creeds."[3] Hart's judgment seems sound: "In the end it may not be entirely possible to write a translation of scripture not shaped by later theological and doctrinal history."[4] If that is so, can we categorically hold up today's Bible and declare, "This is the Word of God," buried as it is under human manipulation and partisanship?

---

2   David Bentley Hart, *The New Testament: A Translation* (New Haven, CT: Yale University Press, 2017), 571.

3   John Barton, *A History of the Bible: The Book and Its Faiths* (New York: Viking, 2019), 3.

4   Hart, *The New Testament*, xvi.

ORIGINAL SIN

Concerning Original Sin, the first truism about it is that it is strictly a doctrine of Western Christianity. Few people realize this. Judaism, which gave us the Adam and Eve story, has no such doctrine, no sense of being lost without grace. It has no emphasis on a fall-and-rescue scenario. Its focus is on election, guidance, and promise. Abraham, not Adam, is the man of the hour. Neither does the most ancient form of Christianity, the Orthodox Church, have such a doctrine as Original Sin. The doctrine comes solely from the brilliant fifth-century Roman Church of St. Augustine, an inveterate Platonist (matter is evil, the noble soul is weighted down by the ignoble body). He was the one who was so influential in shaping Christianity.

His theory was that Adam and Eve disobeyed God and ruptured the relationship. Adam passed on a fallen nature through the act of sexual intercourse, which Augustine only barely tolerated as a necessary evil to continue the human race. Humanity was inherently evil. Only baptism could take away the stain of Original Sin. The Fourth Gospel had made that clear: "No one can enter the kingdom of God without being born of water and Spirit" (John 3:5). This teaching became enshrined in Western theology, leading devout nurses over the centuries to clandestinely baptize non-Catholic infants and doubling the grief and guilt of mothers whose children died before they were baptized. Limbo, now lately disenfranchised, was a poor substitute. Yes, common sense finally provoked the sleight-of-hand "baptism of desire" and "baptism of blood," but the message was clear: Unbaptized infidels stand no chance of salvation and humanity remains permanently wounded. Orthodox Christianity couldn't disagree more.

Remember David Bentley Hart's take on St. Paul (or his translators), who made matters worse. Writing in his new translation of the New Testament, he underscores Paul's famous words in Romans 5:12 that challenge Western theology's notion of original sin (my italics): "Therefore as sin entered the world through one man [Adam] and death through sin, so also death spread to all *because all have sinned.*" This, Hart maintains, is a mistranslation. "A fairly easy verse to follow until one reaches the final four words [*because all have sinned*], whose precise meaning is *already obscure,* and whose notoriously *defective rendering* in the Latin Vulgate ... constitutes one of the most consequential mistranslations in Christian history."[5]

Hart means that the standard Latin version of the verse, that all have sinned *in Adam,* meaning we have an inherited culpability (Original Sin) from which we must be "redeemed"—which is the basis of Western theology—is shaky, to say the least. Hart feels that the correct reading of Paul goes something like this: "just as sin entered into the cosmos and introduced death into all its members, so the contagion of death spread into the whole of humanity and introduced sin into all its members."[6] No exact "Adam" connection, needing a "new Adam." Rather, "by [Christ's] triumphant righteousness he introduced eternal life into the cosmos, and so as that life spreads into the whole of humanity it makes all righteous."[7]

Once more, as for "faith alone," Hart points out that the Protestants' traditional interpretation of St. Paul about justification by faith alone, not good works (a slap at Catholicism's sacramental and indulgence systems), is totally wrong. It's another case of orthodoxy (Protestant) shaping the interpretation of the biblical text. For the sixteenth-century Protestant Reformers, Paul supposedly inveighed against belief in "justification" through human effort but accepted instead justification through intellectual and emotional assent to Jesus as sole Lord and savior as the criterion for salvation. Faith, *si*! Works, *non*! But, as Hart writes (italics mine), "Paul taught nothing of the sort. Instead he taught that human beings cannot be 'justified' (that is, 'proved' or 'made righteous') by 'works of the Law' (such as circumcision or kosher dietary practices) but only by a *'faithfulness'* that *necessarily* entails 'works' of love—good deeds—in respect of which one will be justified and either rewarded or 'punished.'"[8] In this, Paul is faithfully reflecting Matthew's Jesus (25:31–46), who makes salvation precisely contingent on "good works": feeding the hungry, giving

---

5   Ibid., 296.

6   Ibid., 297.

7   Ibid.

8   Ibid., 571.

drink to the thirsty, clothing the naked, and so on, for "just as you did it to one of the least of these who are members of my family, you did it to me." The ones who did not do these works "will go away into eternal punishment, but the righteous into eternal life."

Then there was Paul's letter to the Colossians, which clearly opted for good works. Colossians is one of those epistles attributed to Paul, but which is written by another hand. Nevertheless, Hart concedes, "I had come to believe that many doubts regarding its authenticity are based on poorer stylistic evidence than is generally claimed, as well as on theological arguments that may say more about certain scholars' theological presuppositions than about the rather unsystematic, late antique 'system' of thought to which Paul actually held."[9] Translation: Protestant orthodoxy was read into the text.

Hart makes an observation we noted earlier in the chapter.

> The relation between Christian theology and scriptural translation has a long and complicated history; theology has not only influenced translation, but particular translations have had enormous consequences for the development of theology (it would be almost impossible, for instance, to exaggerate how consequential the Latin Vulgate's inept rendering of a single verse, Romans 5:12, proved for the development of the Western Christian understanding of original sin).[10]

This is mind-blowing stuff. Hart's words undermine some of the very foundations of Catholicism and Protestantism. But, more to our theme, they show, once more, that the Bible as the word *of* God, so fervently held but so grievously misunderstood, is a dubious attribute. The Bible as the word *about* God leaves room for believers throughout the ages to try to correct what was wrong without guilt or contorted apologetics.

Finally, I make mention of the practical impact of these speculations. True to its nature, the Roman Catholic Church does not dismiss or deny Original Sin. Doctrinally, it's stuck with it. Currently

---

9   Ibid., 572.
10 Ibid., xv.

it just downplays it or lets it fade away as pastoral teaching and practical catechisms now (rightly) emphasize baptism as entrance into the Christian community, as initiation into the life of Christ. Baptism, in fact, is the source of ministry, not the priesthood.

MORE AMMUNITION

Here's another challenging quotation on the same subject, also by Hart:

> The long history of defective scriptural exegesis occasioned by problematic translations is a luxuriant one, and its riches are too numerous and exquisitely various adequately to classify. But I think one can arrange most of them along a single continuum in four broad divisions: some misreadings are caused by a translator's error, others by merely questionable renderings of certain words, others by the unfamiliarity of the original author's (historically specific) idiom, and still others by the "untranslatable" remoteness of the author's own (culturally specific) theological concerns. And each kind comes with its own special perils and consequences.
>
> But let me illustrate. Take, for example, Augustine's magisterial reading of the Letter to the Romans, as unfolded in reams of his writings, and ever thereafter by his theological heirs: perhaps the most sublime "strong misreading" in the history of Christian thought, and one that compromises specimens of all four classes of misprision. Of the first, for instance: the notoriously misleading Latin rendering of Romans 5:12 that deceived Augustine into imagining Paul believed all human beings to have, in some mysterious manner, sinned "in" Adam, which obliged Augustine to think of original sin—bondage to death, mental and moral debility, estrangement from God—even more insistently in terms of an inherited guilt (a concept as logically coherent as that of a square circle), and which prompted him to assert with such sinewy vigor the justly eternal torment of babes who died unbaptized. And of the second: the way, for instance, Augustine's misunderstanding of Paul's theology of election was abetted by

the simple contingency of a verb as weak as the Greek *proorizein* ("sketching out beforehand," "planning," etc. [cf. Romans 8:29, 1 Corinthians 2:7, and Ephesians 1:5]) being rendered as *praedestinare*—etymologically defensible, but connotatively impossible. And of the third: Augustine's frequent failure to appreciate the degree to which, for Paul, the "works" (*erga, opera*) he contradistinguishes from faith are works of the Mosaic law, "observances" (circumcision, kosher regulations, and so on). And of the fourth—well, the evidence abounds:... his entire [mis]reading of Romans 9–11....

Regarding that part of [Augustine's] intellectual patrimony that has had the widest effect—his understanding of sin, grace, and election [predestination teaching]—not only do I share the Eastern distaste for (or, frankly, horror at) his conclusions; I am even something of an extremist in that respect. In the whole long, rich history of Christian misreadings of Scripture, none I think has ever been more consequential, more invincibly perennial, or more disastrous.[11]

Quite an indictment. This timely quotation encapsulates the issues: a massive misreading of an inherently unstable Bible by a foundational theologian, Augustine, that got firmly fixed into Christian theology, doctrine, and practice, thereby to burden Christians for almost two millennia. Today, as the quiet dismantling of Augustine's legacy in this regard goes on, one has to question the authority of the Bible and the official, far-reaching teaching of a fallible Church that claims the infallibility of the Holy Spirit.

ATONEMENT

"Jesus died for our sins" or as "a ransom for many" is bedrock Christian doctrine. The problem is that no one knows precisely what the words mean. The Church has wisely never officially defined it. The New Testament writers gave various explanations to help their

---

11 David Bentley Hart, "Traditio Deformis," *First Things,* May 2015, https://www.firstthings.com/article/2015/05/traditio-deformis.

communities understand what Jesus' criminal death meant. Was Jesus' individual death a sacrifice for us, a "sacrifice of atonement" as Paul wrote (Romans 3:25)? Was Jesus the biblical scapegoat onto whom the sins of the people were transferred? Was he "a ransom for many" as St. Mark has Jesus say (10:45)? But a ransom paid to whom—the devil? (Gregory of Nyssa, among others, thought so.) God? Is God really a cosmic pawnbroker, demanding his blood money, a Shylock demanding blood? (Some call this "divine child abuse.") Certainly, everything we have seen about the character of Yahweh would support this view. Was our guilt really transferred to Jesus? If so, what about moral responsibility? Is violence redemptive? St. Paul does teach that we are all under the wrath of God (Romans 3), and that Jesus' shed blood turns it away: "Much more surely then, now that we have been justified by his blood, will we be saved through him from the wrath of God" (Romans 5:9; cf. 1 Thessalonians 1:10). Is the "substitutionary atonement" theory right—namely, that our sins leave us owing God a debt we cannot pay, but Christ came along and suffered and died for our sins, doing on our behalf what we cannot do?

Was St. Anselm right when he wrote that the dignity of the Offended must be matched by the dignity of the Apologist, and so the Son was the only sufficient candidate to appease the Father? Was Jesus' death the result of his steadfast fidelity to the principles of his Father, or was his love so cosmic and deep that it canceled all the world's cumulative hate? Are we talking about retributive justice or restorative justice? Did Jesus, going meekly and silently to his Passion and death, become an inadvertent model of passivity before injustice? Did the Father really send him to die like the son in one of Jesus' parables, whom the Master sent into his vineyard hoping that the vineyard workers, who had manhandled his servants, would respect his son? Is Jesus Luke's forgiving victim (23:34)?

Whatever the questions, there is no doubt that there is a strong Christian sense that God is deeply involved here, that he is the ultimate reason why Jesus had to die on the cross. ("Not my will, but yours be done.") His death was according to God's plan. Yes, Jesus was sent into the world to die for our sins, to die in our place, taking on the penalty for our wrongdoing. He was the one who loved me "and gave himself for me" (Galatians 2:20). This is the doctrine of substitutionary atonement, but modern folk are uneasy with the notion that Jesus' painful death was something demanded by God.

Theologians as well as ordinary people have always had trouble with any kind of "payment" or God-appeasement scenarios and have refocused on God's love. The thirteenth-century Franciscan Duns Scotus held that the incarnation had nothing to do with the sin of Adam and Eve. Theologian Elizabeth Johnson, for example, reminds us that in the Prodigal Son story, the father wouldn't even let his son apologize, saying instead, "Look, it doesn't matter now. You're home. Let's have a party."[12]

Some make an end run around all this and say that God, out of love, entered into the human condition to save humanity from ourselves: our follies, our self-absorption, our stepping over others to get ahead, our vindictiveness, our cruelty. This meant Jesus had to take on human darkness and suffering and transform them. In the crucifixion, humanity could throw its worst at him and he would respond with forgiveness. His crucifixion was an act of love, not payment. As spiritual writer Ron Rolheiser puts it:

> Jesus...takes in hatred, holds it, transforms it, and gives back love; he takes in bitterness, holds it, transforms it, and gives back graciousness; he takes in curses, holds them, transforms them, and gives back blessing; he takes in chaos, holds it, transforms it, and gives back order; he takes in fear, holds it, transforms it, and gives back freedom; he takes in jealousy, holds it, transforms it, and gives back affirmation; and he takes in Satan and murder, holds them, transforms them, and gives back only God and forgiveness.[13]

---

12   Elizabeth A. Johnson, *Creation and Cross: The Mercy of God for a Planet in Peril* (Maryknoll, NY: Orbis, 2018).

13   Ron Rolheiser, "The Agony in the Garden—The Place of Transformation," *Ron Rolheiser, OMI*, April 4, 2004, https://ronrolheiser.com/the-agony-in-the-garden-the-place-of-transformation/#.X20FFT-Sl9A.

Yes, Jesus takes away the sins of the world in the same way a water filter takes impurities out of water, by absorbing and holding all that isn't clean and giving back only what is.

Still, all this is a modern conceit, not traditional Christian understanding. There's too much "ransom" and the "Father's wrath" overtones in Paul's letters to dismiss them. In the last analysis, William O'Malley, SJ, who puzzles over it all, speaks for all of us:

> Note well: I do not deny the centuries-old teaching on atonement. I just no longer pretend I understand it. Not even a fool could deny the effects of original sin. But I balk at the economic metaphor—an almost irreparable debt to explain what caused human inconstancy.
>
> If the degradation God endured for us has not been deadened by repetition, I wonder if we could find a depth beyond atonement. In his forthright confrontation with evil and suffering, Christ did indeed free us—from fear: fear that our sins might defy forgiveness, fear that our sufferings have no meaning, fear that only a few loved ones really care.[14]

---

14 William J. O'Malley, "Forgiving God: Can We Make Sense of Suffering?" *America*, September 22, 2008, https://www.americamagazine.org/issue/668/faith-focus/forgiving-god.

Chapter 9

RELIGIOUS VISIONARIES AND VIOLENCE

> But as for the towns of these people that the Lord your God is giving you as an inheritance, you must not let anything that breathes remain alive. You shall annihilate them—the Hittites and the Amorites, the Canaanites and the Perizzites, the Hivites and the Jebusites—just as the Lord your God has commanded.
>
> —*Deuteronomy 20:16–17*

In this chapter, we move away from the Bible itself to an ancillary issue about the Bible's Creator—God, the One, remember, who made all things and saw that "it was good." The issue at hand is how violence fits into the divine persona of goodness and the religious visionaries who promoted it in his name.

We begin with a quote.

> Fix in your mind the idea of an invisible reality outside time and space that can communicate directly with human beings. Get hold of that thought and you will have grasped the central idea of religion. There is a power in the universe beyond what is available to our physical senses *and it has made itself known to special people who proclaim its message to others.*[1]

---

1   Richard Holloway, *A Little History of Religion* (New Haven, CT: Yale University Press, 2016), 8.

So Richard Holloway reminds us in his insightful book *A Little History of Religion*. History is full of seers and visionaries (special people) and the verdict is split on their worth or legitimacy. The modern secular mindset is skeptical and suspects that these prophets' revelations are actually projections from their own subconscious or are signals of an emotional disorder. Because it's more accessible to our times, the Book of Mormon and its founder Joseph Smith often fall under this suspicion.

VISIONARIES WHO CHANGED THE WORLD

Here are some of the major visionaries who changed the world. Siddhartha passed into a state of ecstasy to become the Buddha, the Enlightened One. Moses heard a voice from a bush. Ezekiel and other Hebrew prophets heard voices and saw visions. Paul had a vision and heard a voice on the way to Damascus. Jesus, dazzled by light at his baptism and hearing God's voice calling him his beloved son, began his mission then and there. Mohammed had a vision in a cave outside Mecca and heard his first voice; visions and voices continued for the rest of his life. Sun Myung Moon had a vision in the 1930s in which Jesus told him to marry and produce sinless children since Adam and Eve blew it.

Quaker George Fox claimed to have a revelation from God telling him that he didn't need ministers and rubrics and vestments and creeds. No, he was told, just be still; sit and be quiet and let the Holy Spirit speak to his heart. He and his followers pitted their consciences against the Bible and established churches. They knew the difference between what was right and what the Bible said was right. For example, the Quakers were a key factor in the abolition of slavery, no matter what the Bible said.

Joseph Smith, mentioned above, had delusions of being "president pro tem of the world," pronouncing himself "King, Priest, and Ruler over Israel on the Earth." He taught that Earth was created near some planet called Kolab and the Garden of Eden was near Kansas City. He said that Jesus had actually visited America in the year 34 and that the American Indians were the descendants of the Israelites who had been there hundreds of years before Christ (a point disproved by modern DNA tests). He had dozens of wives, some of whom were already married to other men, and founded Mormonism. He had a vision where an angel told him of the existence of a collection of writings from the prophet of ancient America, writings inscribed on gold plates by a man called Mormon. It became the genesis of the Book of Mormon.

Whatever the origins of the authors of these religious revolutions, almost all of them—or their later interpreters—have enforced their vision by violence. Even the normally peaceful Buddhists have persecuted the Burmese Christians in Myanmar in recent times.

RELIGIOUS VIOLENCE

All the major religions, at one time or another, have espoused violence and, as the pages of history show, are no strangers to it. This theme is so prevalent that some critics have cited religion as the cause of violence and declared that the sooner it and its God are deleted from society, the better. Restricting ourselves to the three main Abrahamic religions, there's no denying there is a lot of violence in the early and subsequent history of Judaism, Christianity, and Islam.

The Hebrews, under God's direct command, killed the Canaanites mercilessly. There's the Bible's legendary God-directed violence (wiping out the guilty with the innocent), putting other nations to the ban, and David's butchering of so many people. Yes, the Bible teaches, every person will answer for their own acts, but their children will pay for their parents' sins. Universal brotherhood is extolled, but kill the Amorites. The books of Joshua and Judges are "bibles" to every gun-toting colonialist and supremacist. In Judges 11 we have the horrific story of Jephthah, who made a vow to God that if God gave his enemies into his hands, then whoever would first come out the door to meet him when he returned home victorious would be offered up to Yahweh "as a burnt offering." (Human sacrifice was not unknown to the Hebrews.) After his victory, the first one to come through the door was his lovely daughter, his only child. Still, he had to sacrifice her. Note that, unlike God's interference with Abraham's sacrifice of Isaac, there was no intervention, so Jephthah sacrificed her. In Numbers 25, a man named Phinehas, when he saw an Israelite bring home a Midianite woman, went into his tent and speared the two of them through the belly as they were having sex. That pleased Yahweh so much that he called off a plague. Even more, he praised and rewarded Phinehas because "he was zealous" for his cause.

CHRISTIAN VIOLENCE

Christian violence started early, in spite of Jesus' teachings to turn the other cheek when struck, give your cloak to anyone who would sue you for your coat, and, if forced to go one mile, go two (Matthew 5:38–41). Jesus also taught, "When you are offering your gift at the altar, if you remember that your brother or sister has something against you, leave your gift there before the altar and go; first be reconciled to your brother or sister" (Matthew 5:23–24); "Love your enemies and pray for those who persecute you" (Matthew 5:44); and forgive seventy times seven times. Plus, there is Jesus' forgiveness to those who killed him and his making of breakfast on the shoreline for those who had abandoned him—all these never seem to have caught on with his later followers. It was scarcely fifty years later when the author of the eccentric Book of Revelation presented Jesus, the Prince of Peace, as one wearing a golden crown and having a sharp sickle in his hand to reap the earth (14:14–16), the Word of God who rode a white horse with his clothes dripping in blood while from his mouth came a sharp sword with which to strike down the nations (19:11–16).

After the Romans made Christianity the state religion in 313 CE, the persecuted became the persecutors. In spite of Jesus' teaching, with power came intolerance, secular control, and organized killing. That lasted nearly nonstop for a thousand years. Most of the bloodletting was blessed. The biblical Jesus, who never lifted a hand in violence (outside of overturning the moneychangers' tables in the Temple), was unrecognizable among the armies who murdered thousands in his name.

So, it wasn't long before monks rioted during the Arian controversy. Near the year 400, a group of what we would call right-wing Christians of the Donatist party attacked a Catholic bishop of the left-wing party, stripping him naked and flinging him from a tower. They pulled out the tongue of another and cut off his right hand. Thus did Jesus' followers treat one another. Around the same time, St. Augustine, tapping Jesus' parable of the great dinner, justified the persecution of the Cathars by citing Luke 14:23: "The Master said to the slave, 'Go out into the roads and lanes, and *compel* people to come in.'" Now that's a twist Jesus never envisaged.

Christian Charlemagne, newly crowned by the pope, gave Saxon rebels a choice between conversion or death. Almost 5,000 were beheaded at his orders. In 1190, Pope Innocent III decreed that Jews must be publicly distinguished from other people by their dress (think of the Nazis demanding the Star of David badges be pinned to Jews' clothes or worn as armbands). In the year 1208, nearly 500,000 of the Cathars perished miserably under a Crusade called by Pope Innocent III. The Abbot of Citeaux led the Crusade with Dominic Guzman among his soldiers—later known as St. Dominic, founder of the Dominicans. Pope Julius II led his troops into battle. The great St. Bernard of Clairvaux did not hesitate to proclaim, "Cursed be he who does not stain his sword with blood!"[2] He later issued an apology, but "he wasn't sorry about the many innocent lives taken, the orphans created, the villages torched, the property stolen. He was sorry that his side lost the Second Crusade, prompting many people to give up their faith."[3]

INTOLERANCE

Think of all the centuries when the message was, "Convert or be killed." Think of the people who were put to death because they believed in science over dogma. Think of all the murders committed

---

2   Timothy Egan, *A Pilgrimage to Eternity: From Canterbury to Rome in Search of a Faith* (New York: Penguin, 2019), 38.

3   Ibid., 123.

in the name of Christian orthodoxy. Think of the irony that heretics were persecuted and burned by the very same people who, for the greater honor and glory of God, were building magnificent cathedrals. In 1215, at the great Lateran Council presided over by Innocent III, "sanctions explicitly targeting heresy had provided the Church with an entire machinery of persecution"[4] and thousands and thousands of Waldensians and Albigensians were slaughtered under Church auspices to achieve this end.

Think of the edict of Pope Boniface VIII in the year 1300: "We declare, we proclaim, we define that it is absolutely necessary for salvation that every human creature be subject to the Roman pontiff."[5] Consider the acts of Pope Alexander VI, father of ten through multiple mistresses: He divided the New World between Portugal and Spain in 1494, natives be damned, and those natives were persecuted near to extinction. Think of the Inquisition, initiated by a later pope who said he would gather the wood to burn his own father.

Pope Urban II cried *Deus Vult* ("God wills it") in kicking off the Crusades. The Crusaders massacred thousands of Jews in places like Cologne and Mainz. In thirteenth-century Europe, there was almost no actual knowledge of Islamic culture or religion, but rather only stereotypes of "the enemy." The vast majority of voices in the Western Church—popes at their lead—had been swept up in the fervor of the anti-Islamist Crusades that began in 1095. Popes repeatedly used promises of eternal life and offered indulgences and total forgiveness of sin for those who would fight these "holy wars," which were then backed up by kings and official Crusade preachers. Hardly anyone objected or recognized that this was a major abuse of power and of the Gospel. Some 1.7 million people were killed overall.

In the war on the Huguenots, the Catholic Duke of Guise murdered some sixty-three people praying inside a barn. In 1572, some 50,000 Huguenots were slaughtered during the Bartholomew's Day Massacre in Paris, the pope issuing a medallion to mark the occasion. The Thirty Years War—Christians versus Christians—which began in

---

4   Holland, *Dominion*, 254.

5   Pope Boniface VIII, *Unam Sanctam*, November 18, 1302.

1618, led to the death of 20 percent of the German population. Think of the nineteenth-century invention of papal infallibility, of papal condemnation of freedom of speech and freedom of worship.

What is noticeable in all this is that everyone could appeal to the Bible for justification. Even those who had misgivings over the persecution of heretics, like some Puritans, were reassured by the words of God's licensing of slaughter in defense of Israel. "Sometimes the Scripture declareth women and children must perish with their parents," they were told. "We had sufficient light from the Word of God for our proceedings."[6]

Speaking of the Huguenots, here's a nasty piece of American history. In 1564, fleeing Catholic persecution in France, some Huguenots fled to America to establish a settlement called Fort Caroline in Florida. When the Catholic Spaniards came and claimed Florida under the conquistador Pedro Menendez, they fought the Huguenots in a naval battle and eventually captured Fort Caroline. They butchered the inhabitants and when the remainder of the Huguenot fleet surrendered, the captives, despite promises of clemency, were executed. The brutal massacre at Fort Caroline shocked even Europe, as accustomed as it was to wars of religion.

During the French Revolution, its leaders destroyed churches, temples, and all elements of religion, and in their places established the Cult of Reason. It launched a program of suppression of anything religious, all in the name of freedom and tolerance. Science and culture would liberate humanity—but just the opposite happened: bloody repression and mass killings. It reminds me of Chesterton's quip: "The madman is not the man who has lost his reason. The madman is the man who has lost everything except his reason."[7] When Mussolini gassed thousands of people in Ethiopia, the Church did not protest. It backed Mussolini and Franco.

Then there are the horrors and genocides that Christian settlers inflicted on the Native Americans in both South and North America.

---

6   Holland, *Dominion*, 344.
7   G. K. Chesterton, *Orthodoxy* (London: William Clowes and Sons, 1927), Chapter II.

The irony was that not only did the Spanish conquistadors visit unpardonable cruelty on the native peoples, not only did they call themselves Christians, but they also maintained that all the atrocities they committed against the heathens were done for the sake of Christendom. As the Christian Europeans colonized the globe, they brought with them a sense of superiority and often a program of exploitation. Rudyard Kipling's poem "The White Man's Burden" touted the supposed or presumed responsibility of white people to govern and impart their culture to nonwhite people and was often advanced as a justification for European colonialism. Europeans seized lands; plundered copper, diamonds, ivory, and rubber; and formed a colonial hierarchy in which native peoples were deemed inferior.

No wonder Mohandas Gandhi used to say that every world religion knows that Jesus taught nonviolence, lived nonviolently—except one: Christianity! Yes, in 1995, Pope John Paul II said he was sorry for the massacre of French Protestants. He issued a formal Vatican apology aimed specifically at France. Five years later, he made an even more sweeping apology for two thousand years of violence and persecution, against Protestants throughout Europe, Jews, women, heretics, and so-called Gypsies. He had already apologized for the Crusades, centuries of anti-Semitism, and the Inquisition. The apologies were welcomed, but they still do not erase the violence associated with religion.

A caveat: It is important that we do not press "religion equals violence" too far, for research has shown that wars and conflicts were often manufactured and manipulated by emperors, kings, and other outside political forces that had vested interests and supplied pressure in promoting warfare. In other words, social and political components were never far away from alleged "religious violence."

Sidebar

In modern times—when we are in practical denial about death; when we euphemize, cosmeticize, and perfume corpses; when even the Roman Catholic Church has jettisoned black vestments at funerals and dropped the hauntingly moving *Dies Irae*; when the liturgical color is white and resurrection is the theme—we can't imagine death's dominance in previous eras of history. In premodern times—before miracle drugs and antibiotics—with high infant mortality, diseases, famines, plagues, epidemics, and constant warfare, life was "solitary, poor, nasty, brutish, and short."[8] Death was a dreadful companion. It was everywhere, a constant presence. Natural death was exacerbated by the legal punishments of church and state of those criminals, from rapists to doctrinal deviants, who were perceived to be so by whoever defined orthodoxy, whether pope or elder or prophet or leader of the ever-proliferating religious sects. Religion had to be "pure" at all costs and those who polluted it must be eliminated and made examples of. The means of enforcing this was death, preceded by torture beyond belief.

The *Catechism of the Catholic Church* states that "torture ... is contrary to respect for the person and for human dignity"[9] and then it coyly adds,

> In times past, cruel practices were commonly used by legitimate governments to maintain law and order, often without protest from the Pastors of the Church, who themselves adopted in their own tribunals the prescriptions of Roman law concerning torture. Regrettable as these facts are, the Church always taught the duty of clemency and mercy.[10]

Significantly, what is notably missing is a phrase that is constantly and continually used almost everywhere in the *Catechism* when explaining doctrine or practice: "under the breath of the Holy Spirit" or "enlightened by the Holy Spirit" and similar phrases. It does not say here (or elsewhere where embarrassments may lurk), "Regrettably, the Pastors of the Church, influenced by the Holy Spirit, adopted torture." This isn't meant to be sarcastic or snarky, but torture *was* a legitimate and approved practice of the Spirit-guided Church, as much as any tradition, and we can't have it both ways.

---

8   Thomas Hobbes, *The Leviathan* (New York: Penguin, 1982), Chapter XIII.
9   *Catechism of the Catholic Church*, 2297.
10 Ibid., 2298.

Anyway, flaying, waterboarding, pulling out tongues, plucking out eyes, tearing off skin, cutting off genitals, burning at the stake, hanging heads on posts for all to see, and any other way excruciating pain could be extended—perpetrators were masters at this and for centuries it was commonplace. As noted, many people at the time were appalled, but such gruesome acts, vigilante or legal, were often justified, as we have seen, by an appeal to Scripture, "for thus jealous Yahweh clearly treated his opponents."

But there were other scriptural passages conveniently overlooked. As Christians tortured, slashed, maimed, and broke human bodies, there was never the slightest official nod to the belief that all were made in the image of God (Genesis 1:27), or to Jesus' dictum that "Truly I tell you, just as you did it to one of these who are members of my family, you did it to me" (Matthew 25:40), or to St. Paul's words, "Do you not know that your bodies are members of Christ? . . . that your body is a temple of the Holy Spirit within you, which you have from God, and that you are not your own?" (1 Corinthians 6:15–19), or his "For as the body is one and has many members, and all the members of the body, though many, are one body, so it is with Christ. For in the one Spirit we were all baptized into one body—Jews or Greeks, slaves or free—and we were all made to drink of one Spirit" (1 Corinthians 12:12–13). Not to mention the example of the stunning charity of the early Christians, who, during the many plagues, cared for believer and unbeliever alike, causing total awe among the pagans at such unprecedented and indiscriminate charity. For the first time in history, a people believed itself called to provide compassion and care to everyone. How was all this juxtaposed with commonplace torture? Again, there were many protesting voices raising these questions, but nevertheless, *officially*, the Church tortured.

ALL GOD'S CHILDREN

In any case, all this consistent religiously based carnage is appalling and as far away as it can be from Jesus' teaching. It is positively stunning when we realize how deeply challenging it is. Richard Holloway frames the problem this way:

> Most religions are based on the claim that God is the supreme reality. And that he is the author of their moral code. They may have different ways of putting it, but they all see God as the universal parent. Humans are God's children. As the New Testament says, in God "we live and move and have our being."
>
> But if we are all God's children, why does God spend so much time in history ordering one branch of his universal family to wipe out another branch? Why did his love for his Jewish children have to be expressed by the extermination of his Palestinian children? Why did he later abandon his Jewish children in favor of his Christian children and encourage his new favorites to torment their older siblings? Why did he order his Muslim children who worship him as One to persecute his pagan children who worship him as Many [the Trinity]? Why is there so much violence in religious history, all done by groups who claim God is on their side?[11]

But claim it they did, citing the clear words of their sacred writings for justification. That makes many people wonder about the authority and credibility of the synagogues and churches that claim to interpret God's book correctly, know God's mind, and pass the laws he enjoined. Others question the very existence of God or, in our therapeutic world, insist that humankind, in its sacred books, has projected onto him its own cruelty. As for the Bible, it is obvious that humankind has consistently misused, misread, and misinterpreted it over the centuries, justifying if not glorifying the violence in its own heart. That again raises the question: Where was the Church's claimed Spirit of Truth, the Abiding Presence, the Guiding Paraclete, during all this time when religious people were killing one another in the name of God?

Timothy Egan sums it up: "You can see why people shun a supposedly beneficent creator who presided over the slaughter of the

---

11   Holloway, *Little History of Religion*, 230.

Wars of Religion, the African slave trade, the butchery of the Great War, Stalin's mass executions, genocide in Germany and Uganda and Cambodia."[12]

ET TU?

These days, it is worth noting that, in spite of common misunderstanding, the Qur'an's jihad is mainly associated, not with warring on others, but with nonviolent resistance. From the beginning, jihad was not meant to forcefully convert others, but to share the gifts of the Qur'an with the rest of the world. Reconciliation and nonviolent resistance were forever its goals. At its heart and soul are peace and toleration. It even accepted other scriptures as inspired: the psalms of David, the Torah of Moses, the Gospel of Jesus, and even the Indian and Chinese sacred writings.

The Qur'an is not a book of information or even inspiration. It exists as a means of exciting worship and right living. What some remember, however, is the famous "sword" verse in the Qur'an (9:5) that reads, "When the [four] forbidden months are over, wherever you find the polytheists, kill them, seize them, besiege them, ambush them." This sounds strange, since, in Islam, killing a human being is considered a grave sin, and the only situations in which Muslims are allowed fight is in self-defense or to defend the oppressed who ask them for help. So Islamic apologists soften the verse by reminding us that the verse was revealed at a time when Muslims were under a treaty with non-Muslims and some non-Muslims kept breaking it. Finally, in desperation, they gave the enemy notice that, after the four sacred months mentioned in the sword verse, the Muslims would wage war on them. The verse, in short, was a limited permission made for Muslims in order to defend themselves under a specific circumstance.

Unfortunately, as time went on, new leaders, bent on empire building, gave entirely new aggressive, imperialist interpretations to

---

12   Egan, *Pilgrimage to Eternity*, 235.

the Qur'an that justified warfare. Verses were reinterpreted to justify warring on one's enemies indiscriminately in the name of Allah. Our own time bears witness to how far that has come. For instance, a front-page *New York Times* article on May 26, 2020 quoted Mawlawi Mohammed Qais, the head of Taliban's military commission, as saying these words: "We see this fight as worship. So if a brother is killed, the second brother won't disappoint God's wish—he'll step into the brother's shoes."[13] Yes, once more, the God of a sacred book is invoked to justify violence.

THE ECOLOGY OF KILLING

That bothersome question raises another, broader question—one that, to this day, has exercised people of all stripes, believers and non-believers alike: the question of suffering, the age-old, insoluble theodicy question: How do we reconcile a good God with human pain? Why does God not intervene to stop the torture of little children? The usual, but inadequate, responses run from "a lot of human suffering comes from the free actions of human beings themselves and God respects our free will as a greater good" to "suffering is vital to human growth—no pain, no gain—and often provokes loving compassion and heroic charity." "Love is the law of sacrifice" is the mantra here.

Still, the excessiveness, magnitude, and randomness of human suffering are deeply perplexing and any sense of God's presence in the world is mightily challenged, especially when tragedy hits home. Charles Darwin may have had some misgivings about God as he developed his *Origin of Species*, but it was the death of his beloved daughter that led him to abandon religion. So, skeptics continue to sneer and believers continue to step beyond the rational, bow before the mystery, and trust in the Lord.

But I do not want to talk about this aspect of suffering because I too don't know what more to say. Rather, I want to deal with the more

---

13 Mujib Mashal, "How the Taliban Outlasted a Superpower: Tenacity and Carnage," *The New York Times*, May 26, 2020, https://www.nytimes.com/2020/05/26/world/asia/taliban-afghanistan-war.html.

basic issue that predates human suffering or even human existence. I want to deal with the suffering that is cosmic: the idea that suffering, so to speak, is intrinsic to our cosmological existence. Bypassing the innate violence of nature, as seen in our planetary origins—the Big Bang theory, for instance, the collision of the asteroids, the cacophony of the life and death of stars, the eruption of suns—let me move to the nearer term, when life began and moved from microbe to monkey.

I begin by mentioning one of those magnificent Public Broadcasting (PBS) series, titled *Nature*, with its fascinating science and stunning photography, a series that explored the ravages of nature when the balance of power is ruptured. Examples were given as follows. The starfish eats the sea urchins that eat the kelp forest. As long as the starfish are there, the ecology stays stable. When the starfish are absent, the sea urchins proliferate, take over, overeat the kelp, and destroy it all. The dependent fish and ocean life suffer and, before you know it, stagnant water and dead vegetation replace a living, vibrant ecosystem. The same with otters. When they are present and eat the clams, the balance is maintained. When they disappear, the clams proliferate and kill other forms of life that rupture the chain of life. It's the same with the largemouth bass. When they are present and feed on the minnows, all flourish. When they are not there, the minnows proliferate and scrape off all the green vegetation, which eventually dies. Trees dependent on the vegetation disappear and soon you have a desert where once a forest thrived. When hunters killed off all the wolves in Yellowstone Park, the elk and deer populations exploded, ate all the vegetation that had no time to recover, and soon whole forests disappeared.

Not all disappearing species have this effect, but certain ones do. The scientists have dubbed those that do, like the starfish, otters, largemouth bass, and wolves Keystone Species. They, above all others, for some reason, are essential factors in keeping nature in balance. Knowing this, the scientists now reintroduce starfish, otters, wolves, wild dogs, and the like to areas where they had disappeared so they can prey on the overpopulating culprits. Scientists see that enough gazelles are supplied for a lion population that may be declining for lack of (living) food. Again, when all is in balance, the ecosystems flourish and are restored. Now, we should not ignore that this is the way restored nature works: *Balanced killing is the absolutely essential factor for life to continue, and that balance has to be readjusted if total annihilation is to be avoided.* Not only does the macabre dance between predator and prey never end—and likewise the suffering—but it cannot *not* go on.

I am an addict of the *Nature* series on PBS. The photography, as I said, is stunning. Two segments I recently saw were on the eagle and the tiger. The eagle is truly a regal bird, with a fearsome look. It is gorgeously designed, the product of an evolutionary spiral that produced a master of the sky and a fierce predator. To see it soar effortlessly, to sense its magnificence, to watch in awe its maneuverability, speed, and keen eyesight, to be drawn into its acrobatic pursuit of prey as it sinks its deadly talons into a rabbit, is utterly fascinating, a choreography of the death dance. It's a work of art. It has its own compelling admiration. That terrible beauty, the finesse of its attack, stirs something in us, something in our own evolution, that makes us identify with it, admire it. Yet, at the end of the day, the gorgeousness of the eagle has one goal: to kill that rabbit, whose screams of terror and pain are unsettlingly like a human's.

As for the tiger, one recalls Blake's lines:

Tiger, tiger burning bright
In the forest of the night

Tiger is grace in motion, compelling in loveliness, awesome in purpose, fierce in pursuit. It too speaks somehow to us, our commonality, our aspirations to be top predator, and it too is designed to kill. Eagle, tiger, you and I—by design, we all must kill to live.

All this simply confirms the verifiable and obvious fact that all life is contingent on death. Living things in the vast chain of life must kill, and often kill violently, to survive. From the orcas who ravage the sea lions, to the snakes that constrict the raccoons, to the wolves that rip apart the sheep, to the tiniest microbe that feeds on living tissue, to the larvae that eat their host alive, to humans themselves slaughtering the food we eat: fish, chicken, cows, lambs, and so on—such necessary violence is the indispensable condition, the *sine qua non*, to stay alive. The daily, nonstop, excruciating suffering is beyond calculation. The lion pride biting into the buffalo, the crocodile snapping its huge jaws into the wildebeest, the raptor birds digging their talons into prairie dogs or fish, the cheetah bringing down the rabbit, the boa constrictor squeezing the life out of the hedgehog, and all the rest are inflicting unbearable, searing pain every second of every day. But that's the way it is. Existence is designed that way. In order to live, living things must take life from creatures that, with every fiber of their being, want to stay alive and evolve every subtle device to do so—but, in the long run, it is futile. It goes against nature to resist.

Death remains the indispensable condition for life. Suffering is the indispensable flip side of death. "The wolf shall live with the lamb, the leopard shall lie down with the kid, the calf and the lion and the fatling together" (Isaiah 11:6) may sound attractive, but it cannot endure if we, the wolf, the leopard, and the lion are to live. As Woody Allen said, the lion and the lamb may lie down together, but the lamb won't get much sleep. Yes, those nature documentaries showing the brutal killing of squealing prey are hard to take, but what choice do we all have? Searing pain and terrible violence are inseparable from the eating of living things that, more than anything else, want to live.

BOTTOM LINE?

It's a lousy system.

One would think that a loving, tender, compassionate, almighty, and intelligent Creator Deity could have come up with a better scenario than suffering and death as the condition for life. Were there not alternatives? Maybe we could have been nourished by rays of the sun or by a certain photosynthesis or osmosis of the atmosphere or a thousand other ways to survive. Is this what the Creator had in mind when he said, "Let us make humankind" and let them "fill the earth and subdue it; and have dominion over the fish of the sea and over the birds of the air and over every living thing" (Genesis 1:26, 28)—

meaning that "subduing" would *necessarily* involve terrible, neverending suffering as intrinsic to life on earth? And even though the Lord proclaimed that he preferred "mercy not sacrifice," he never once proscribed the ritual slaughter of animals at Noah's landing, at Covenant time, or at the Temple dedication. There were no "animal rights" signals from Yahweh. Life dependent on death; like the theodicy question, it perplexes the mind.

Sidebar

To repeat a theme we have touched on before: It is interesting to note that apologists of the atonement-substitutionary school of salvation respond that animal sacrifice was a deeply symbolic ritual, reminding worshippers of death. Rebellion and sin required death—though a simple act of forgiveness, as Jung remarked, would have done the trick. Anyway, the theory goes that, in order for the Israelites to gain forgiveness, something had to die. Sin led to death (but death, as we have seen, was here a long time before human beings were on the planet). In order to avoid their own destruction because of their sin, the Israelites had to offer something innocent to die in their place—in this case, an animal without blemish. That's where we get animal sacrifice.

The story deepens when the Israelites realized that animal sacrifice was not enough. As an obdurate people sinned again and again, no amount of animal blood could completely wash them clean or pay the death price they owed. Hence the necessity of Jesus and his blood sacrifice of atonement. Whatever the value of the theory—and increasingly it's being called into question—the painful slaughter of innocent animals as an offering to God begs the question of an alternate solution besides suffering and death for those who did not desire, earn, or deserve either. The bottom line seems to be that somehow, blind evolution seems more palatable than the belief in one who said we were worth more than many sparrows—most of whom, with winged predators above and slithering snakes below, would not survive.

Let me allow Annie Dillard the last word to this chapter: "Evolution loves death more than it loves you or me.... We are moral creatures, then, in an amoral world. The universe that suckled us is a monster that does not care if we live or die—does not care if it itself grinds to a halt."[14]

---

[14] *The Annie Dillard Reader* (New York: HarperCollins, 1994), 381–382.

Chapter 10

BE AWARE OF THE SCRIBES AND PHARISEES

> Beware of the scribes.
>
> —Luke 20:46

> Woe to you, scribes and Pharisees, hypocrites!
>
> —Matthew 23:13

As we play off the words of this chapter's title and the epigraphs from Jesus, as we contrast the words "Beware" and "Be Aware," this refresher chapter, a gathering and repetition of previous thoughts, becomes an important bridge to the next one, a restatement of our theme of "of" versus "about," so we must attend carefully.

Matthew's Jesus teaches us to speak kindly, to love our enemies and pray for those who persecute us (5:44). Later, in chapter 23, he levels the most vicious—or, shall we say, "unchristian"—woes against the scribes and Pharisees, calling them hypocrites, blind guides, lawless, snakes, brood of vipers, murderers, and whitewashed tombs. That's a lot of invective from the Prince of Peace, the one who calls us to be meek and gentle of heart. In fact, it's quite uncharacteristic of Jesus, which is why most scholars say that this is not the Jesus of the year 32 or 33 talking, but the persecuted Christians of some fifty years later, who were in a fierce ideological war with their fellow Jews: the Pharisees, the "bad guys" of the gospels.

There's more. Mark tells us that the Pharisees tried to cause trouble by accusing Jesus of doing what is unlawful on the sabbath (Mark 2:24). Luke adds that the Pharisees were a suspicious lot, pretentious, arrogant (18:11), and self-righteous (18:9). John joins the chorus and tells the story of the woman caught in adultery, whom the Pharisees demanded should be stoned (John 8:1–11),[1] then recounts their jealousy after Jesus' triumphal entry into Jerusalem (12:19) and their final alignment with Judas (18:3).

The tension arose from the fact that the Christian Jews claimed that Jesus, not Moses, was now the God-approved and certified interpreter of the sacred writings. Jesus replaced the recently destroyed Temple as the center of holiness. The debate has left a terrible legacy of dissing the scribes and Pharisees, as we would say today, and marking them forever as synonyms for deceit and cunning. Actually, the Pharisees, often lumped together with the scribes, were one of many sects of Judaism and a decent lot, even though they did tend to an oppressive legalism. Several noble Pharisees are mentioned in the New Testament, including Nicodemus and Paul's teacher, Gamaliel (Acts 22:3). In the turmoil of the times and the destruction of the Temple by the Romans, they were the only ones left standing. As we have seen, they saved the day by moving Torah from the Temple to the book.

In any case, this is a pivotal chapter that centers on a word play, moving from Jesus' "Beware of the scribes and Pharisees" to "Be Aware of the scribes and Pharisees." This simple distinction is critical to the whole biblical enterprise and, in particular, to the chapter that follows.

SCRIBAL INNOVATION

Let's revisit some ground we've covered here and there and repeat a bit of history. The first time the Temple was destroyed by

---

[1]   A floating story that doesn't belong in John.

the Babylonians, the people were dispersed. Without the Temple, the exiles sought comfort in their oral traditions and remembrances (actual or inflated) of past deliverance. The exiles gathered together the multiple ancient stories, hymns, laws, and genealogies that they had memorized in a way that gave them new significance. Northern and southern traditions had begun to merge after the fall of the kingdom of Israel in 722 BCE, but during the exile the editors reassembled them in a way that reflected their own tragic circumstances. In the process they—the scribes—created the Hebrew Bible.

"Reassemble" meant that the scribes had no qualms about abandoning any "original" version. They simply ransacked the past to find meaning in the present. From their exile experience and perspective, the scribes offered a very different view of Abraham's story. They had no hesitation about giving the old tales a new twist. As Karen Armstrong observes,

> The stories of Moses were already well developed by the sixth century BCE, but during the exile, the editors seem to have introduced new elements. Hitherto, the oral traditions had focused on the crossing of the Sea of Reeds, the Sinai revelation and the years in the wilderness. But the exiled Judahites seem to have added new details about the Israelites' enslavement in Egypt, which closely mirrored their own experience in Babylon.[2]

Let that sink in. The scribal editors freely rewrote the Exodus story to fit their times, even adding totally new elements such as when Ezra, who was inventing and giving commentary on the old traditions (*midrash*), said that Yahweh had instructed Moses that during the seventh month Israelites should live in leafy shelters (*sukkoth*) in memory of their ancestors' years in the wilderness. This was a complete innovation; Israel had never done such a thing, from the days of Joshua to Ezra's time. So, it is clear that during the post-exilic period several of the old texts were rewritten so that they could address the contemporary situation. Jeremiah's letters, for example,

---

2   Armstrong, *Lost Art of Scripture*, 104.

were altered to reflect Jerusalem's destruction and the ensuing exile. The two books of Chronicles, composed by priestly authors, glossed passages of Genesis, Samuel, and Kings, giving them new meaning. The authors were reading between the lines of the old texts and adding new reflections. Ezra, who sparked the project, would be remembered as a creator of scripture as well as an exegete.

Later on, during the rule of the Hasmoneans, the scribes created a renewed scriptural canon including the blatantly propagandist books of Maccabees, which are retained in the Catholic and Orthodox canon, but not the Protestant canon, which excluded later works written in Greek. When the Romans supplanted the Hasmoneans, they installed Herod, who began extensive building programs and supported Judahite communities outside Palestine. During this time new scriptures appeared, written in Greek, including Tobit and the Wisdom of Solomon. Finally, when the Romans destroyed the Temple, a group of Pharisees repeated the process. They and the scribes brought about a textual revolution that replaced the Temple with a new scripture. The Pharisees and the Sanhedrin had fled to Yavne, east of Jerusalem, and assembled an academy where creative and brilliant rabbis led the work of a massive project to revise the Torah. Gradually, the rabbinical scribes put together the final text of the Bible, again making adjustments to reflect their changing times. Eventually, with the Temple gone, the "divine presence" would now be found in the communal study of the Bible, and so we get today's rabbinic Judaism.

BE AWARE OF THE SCRIBES

Again, this is important in the context of this chapter. Notice that the emphasis in each case was not on the scriptural text but on the one who wrote, read, performed, and commented on the text: the scribes. In other words, the written Torah, which few could read, gave way to the oral Torah, which all could hear. The scribes or rabbis, after much heated discussion, would creatively improvise and come up with new insights. These many, very practical interpretations and commentaries became the *Mishnah*. Soon, scribes and the people in general did not quote written scripture (they couldn't read it anyway) as much as quote a gifted rabbinical commentator as the source of revelation. (Recall Kugel's words in chapter 6.)

Further, opposing opinions among the great rabbis and their schools were not trashed, but tolerated and saved, just in case changed circumstances might demand their adoption, for it was axiomatic among the rabbis that there was no last word, and never could be. You never knew what would be around the corner. Likewise, it was understood that the Torah had multiple meanings and the interpreter applied them as current concerns demanded. In fact, the rabbis felt quite free to challenge and even change the wording of scripture itself! Rabbi Meir, for example, is on record as completely reversing a ruling in Deuteronomy. Rabbi Yohanan reversed a saying found in Hosea. So, at times, the interpretation varied from and superseded the written text—the scripture—and the interpretation prevailed. The eighth-century CE thirty-volume Babylonian Talmud is a tribute to the subtle thoughts of the rabbis and sages and their debates over God's law and the meaning of the Bible.[3]

In this sense, we can readily define the gospels as *midrash*, weaving, as they do, scriptural verses together to create a story, using the Hebrew scriptures to interpret Jesus' life, even citing the Hebrew text as prophecy where there was in fact no explicit prophecy. We've seen already that St. Paul felt free to tell his followers that Christ died for our sins, was buried, and raised *in accordance with the scripture*, when in fact, no such scripture citations exist beyond those concerning a suffering Messiah. Both Jewish and Christian scholars agree on this, but Paul was acting according to *midrash* norms. Matthew's gospel, notice, is almost completely *midrash*. As we can plainly see, from the beginning, he never misses a chance to quote a scriptural precedent from the Hebrew Bible for the events of Jesus' life. His argument, in fact, is that the entire Hebrew corpus points to Jesus, who becomes the new Moses. It's all creative *midrash*. None of his citations are literally referring to the Messiah in the Hebrew Bible. It's a matter of

---

[3] See Barry Scott Wimpfheimer, *The Talmud: A Biography* (Princeton: Princeton University Press, 2018).

interpretation. That's why we find Jesus, in Matthew's gospel, in the spirit of the debates among the rabbis, sharply and nastily arguing with the Pharisees, telling them they got it all wrong: "Moses said, but *I* say...."

THE FALLOUT

History has amply shown that, over the centuries, various influential interpreters, under pressure from social, political, and scientific upheavals, have wound up changing what we call scripture. They actually changed, or even reversed, what was solemnly taught in previous eras, claiming that now *this* is the truth. Yet, we pick up the Bible and seek certainty, a clear, unambiguous message—something, as we have seen, that the ancients never attempted, for God was too large, life was too mysterious, and Yahweh was too unsteady, puzzling, and inconsistent. The ancients insisted that the scriptures could never tell us completely about a God who was so ineffable, and certainty was an illusion, which is why we have not one, but four gospels that each give a very different view of Jesus. Dogmatic statements of what scripture really means were not in their consciousness. They would find the Roman Catholic Church's claim of eternal, unchanging doctrines incomprehensible.

A delightful story about how oral tradition works: A young rabbi was completely dismayed to find serious division and quarreling among members of his new congregation. You see, during the Friday evening services, half of the participants would stand during one part of the worship while the other half would be seated, and all semblance of decency and decorum was lost as they shouted at each other to conform to their way. Members of each group insisted that theirs was the correct tradition. Seeking guidance, the young rabbi took a representative from each side to visit the synagogue's founder, a ninety-year-old rabbi, living in a nursing home.

"Rabbi, isn't it true that tradition was always with the people who stand at this point of the service?" inquired a man from the standing-up side.

"No, that was not the tradition," the old man replied.

"Then it is correct for people to stay seated," said the sitting-down representative.

"No," the rabbi said, "that was not the tradition."

"But, Rabbi," cried the young rabbi, "what we have now is complete chaos. Half the people stand and shout, while the others sit and scream."

"Aha," said the old man, "*that* was the tradition!"

I repeat: In the past, scriptures were freely altered, revised, and reinterpreted to meet changing conditions. This is true of all religions. We know that the Hindus freely added texts to their sacred writing, the *Rig Veda*. The Chinese freely added their own ideas to the teachings of Confucius and the Hindus reinterpreted the *Upanishads*. The Jews, during the Babylonian exile, completely recast the ancient traditions; after the Roman destruction of the Temple, they created the *midrash* that distanced itself from the written Torah. Nothing was written in stone—until the Church arose, and now the Church is stuck with trying to explain the changes that did, in fact, occur. One thinks of Pope Paul VI's hesitation in not confirming the evils of contraception. He felt bound to let it stand, for his biggest fear was that, in changing the doctrine of his predecessors, the whole house of cards would collapse. My point: If only the Church had been "aware" instead of "beware" of the Scribes and the Pharisees—their flexibility, their creativity—it would have saved itself a lot of embarrassment when it was forced to reverse itself, as the following two chapters will show.

Chapter 11

THE CHURCH TO THE RESCUE (PART I)

> The bishops and theologians at the [Second Vatican] council accepted the reality of change as a matter of course. Their only questions were about how to explain it.
> —*Father John O'Malley, SJ*

We'll unpack that quotation in a moment. For the time being, we might observe that Catholic believers at least are relieved of the impact of the issues we mentioned in the previous chapters because they have a backup: the magisterium of the Church. The *Catechism of the Catholic Church*, expressing itself in the terms of the documents of Vatican II, says quite clearly:

> To the Church belongs the right always and everywhere to announce moral principles.... The Roman Pontiff and the bishops are "authentic teachers, that is, teachers endowed with the authority of Christ."... The law of God entrusted to the Church is taught to the faithful as the way of life and truth.[1]

In short, the Church has extracted certain eternal dogmas and truths from the biblical accounts and stories and codified them,

---
1   *Catechism of the Catholic Church*, 2032, 3034, 2037.

guaranteeing their truthfulness in its magisterial teachings. Building on this confidence, the noted Catholic biblical scholar Raymond Brown can readily admit:

> Let me be precise about the limits of this discussion of the Bible as the word of God, lest I arouse misunderstanding or false expectation. First, I fully accept the Roman Catholic doctrine of the Bible as the word of God, and the whole discussion assumes that fact. This may disappoint those who think proof is needed that the Bible is the word of God—*no such proof is possible beyond biblical self-claim and Church doctrine; it is a matter of faith.*[2]

That's an accurate statement and backs up what I have been saying all along: Orthodoxy trumps text. So, true to my theme, let me teasingly suggest replacing terms for the following hypothetical followers:

Mary Mormon: "I fully accept the Mormon doctrine of the Book of Mormon as the word of God.... This may disappoint those who think proof is needed that the Book of Mormon is the word of God—no such proof is possible beyond the Mormon self-claim and Mormon doctrine; it is a matter of faith."

Mohammed Muslim: "I fully accept the Muslim doctrine of the Qur'an as the word of Allah.... This may disappoint those who think proof is needed that the Qur'an is the word of Allah—no such proof is possible beyond Muslim self-claim and mosque doctrine. It is a matter of faith."

Josiah Jew: "I fully accept the Hebrew doctrine of the Torah as the word of God.... This may disappoint those who think proof is needed that the Torah is the word of God. No such proof is possible, beyond biblical self-claim and synagogue doctrine. It is a matter of faith."

Albert Atheist: "I can't accept the Hebrew-Christian doctrines of the Bible as the word of God. The proof is in the errors and contradictions, in the heavy borrowings from contemporary cultures. It's a matter of science."

---

2   Raymond E. Brown, *The Critical Meaning of the Bible* (New York: Paulist, 1981), 3. Italics mine.

This is what gives postmodernism a good name! No matter. We still cling to the testimony of the unchanging Church, with its venerable, unchanging doctrine—yes, unchanging—or do we?

This brings us back to our epigraph: explaining the reality of change. How indeed to explain what seems to many, not a development of doctrine, but an actual change of doctrine, a reversal of what was previously believed and taught, with the full authority of the Teaching Church, buoyed by scripture, tradition, and the abiding presence of the Spirit of truth? The apologists and theologians have tried to provide answers, to explain what seems "apparent" change, but they are far from convincing. This leaves the average Catholic, conditioned for centuries by the extravagant claims of the Church, to wonder how that which was once forbidden is now allowed and what was "eternal truth," enshrined in official teaching, ecumenical councils, papal pronouncements, and everyday catechisms, is not only no longer held, but often condemned.

Let us take a look at some turnarounds that have provoked some fancy wordplay.

THE CHURCH EVOLVES

We'll skip over the fact that the first church, comprised of circumcised Jews—the apostles—for whom circumcision, divinely declared to be a sign of the "everlasting covenant" (Genesis 17:13), quickly declared circumcision obsolete and dropped it. Also relatively quickly, Sunday replaced the ancient, inviolable Sabbath observance. More notable is that Jesus' divorce policy, "What God has joined together, let no one separate.... Whoever divorces his wife, except for unchastity, and marries another commits adultery" (Matthew 19:6–9), was quickly modified by St. Paul. He wrote in 1 Corinthians 7:10–16 that, in the case of two unbelievers, if one converts and the other does not and deserts his or her partner, the convert "is not bound." The Church Fathers, based on this reading, allowed the convert to divorce and remarry, thus reversing Jesus' teaching.

Moving ahead some sixteen centuries, we find that Pope Gregory XIII allowed the dissolution of the marriages of African slaves who were torn from their spouses and shipped to the Americas. In 1924, Pius XI dissolved a marriage of an unbaptized man from an Anglican woman "in favor of the faith" when the man wanted to marry a Catholic. Prior to 1924, according to official Church teaching and tradition, found in both papal encyclicals and episcopal universal ordinary teaching, this arrangement would have been morally (not civilly) considered bigamy and adultery. No wonder scholar John Noonan commented, "That the moral teachings of the Catholic Church have changed over time will, I suppose, be denied by almost no one today."[3] He was echoing Charles Curran's observation, "others claim that the discontinuity [in the Church] is so great that one cannot properly speak of development."[4]

ABORTION

I know I'm putting myself in the firing line, but let's tackle the highly sensitive subject of abortion. At Mass, in the prepackaged Prayers of the Faithful, there is usually included some sort of petition such as, "That all may respect human life from the moment of conception to natural death, let us pray to the Lord." That human life begins at the moment of conception is Catholic doctrine, going back to Pope Pius XI in the nineteenth century. Therefore, abortion at any stage is gravely sinful. The only problem is that tradition contradicts this.

In the beginning, there was no doubt that the Christian consensus, in contrast to the Greek and Roman state religions and the various mystery religions, was fairly unanimous: Abortion was morally wrong. But note this: There was some debate as to whether there was a real human being in the womb for the first forty (males) or ninety (females)

---

3   John T. Noonan, Jr., "Development in Moral Doctrine," *Theological Studies* 54 (1993): 662.

4   Charles E. Curran, *Change in Official Catholic Moral Teachings* (Mahwah, NJ: Paulist, 2003), ix.

days. The argument went that, as yet, no "ensoulment" had taken place. However, after the first trimester, it definitely was murder to kill the unborn child. The Church's greatest theologians, St. Augustine and St. Thomas Aquinas, taught this. So did Pope Gregory XIV.

Only relatively recently did the Roman Catholic Church contradict this tradition and teach that ensoulment was present from the moment of conception. Still, there remains the question, "When *does* a person become a person?" Some modern theologians, buoyed by science, wonder if a soul can reside in just a primitive, single sperm-egg combination and not in some kind of a body, without a womb to animate it. Can the simple sperm-egg combination, without a formative or forming body, be considered a person? After all, it is not a fully animated fetus. It is still in the process of becoming a person. Some further note that modern science has shown that many eggs are fertilized but never get implanted in the womb and therefore die. Are these really "persons"? Science also shows us that sometimes a fertilized egg can divide and eventually become more than one person, just as two fertilized eggs can merge and eventually become one person. Do the "souls" of these people similarly multiply or contract? Given these considerations and citing tradition, it would seem that, early on, before the fertilized egg attaches to the womb, there is some leeway for a termination.

After the first trimester, it is unconscionably horrible to terminate a pregnancy and the current "abortion on demand" at any stage is monstrous, as is the rare case of leaving a baby who survived the abortion to die. The Church is right to condemn such barbarism. Still, according to Christian-Catholic tradition, those first thirty to forty days provide some leeway for the sincere woman who, for serious mental or physical reasons, must agonize over a decision she wishes she did not have to make. She doesn't need the added oppression of moral condemnation, especially when there is a tradition that supports her. This is the kind of speculation that brings hate mail, but the Church, looking at its history, may have to modify its position.

SLAVERY: ROOT AND BRANCH

We will spend a little more time on this subject, for it is still a healing in progress. In Minneapolis, in June 2020, while America was in the midst of the coronavirus pandemic, a white policeman killed a Black man using a knee-on-neck hold. It was caught on video and went viral, provoking massive peaceful protest marches for months, all over the country's major cities. Unfortunately, like unwanted collateral damage, the dark side of looting, fires, destruction of property, general mayhem, and killing accompanied the protests. The prevailing slogan, "Black Lives Matter" got a new lease on life as officials from the top down struggled to contain the riots and promise reform of police forces.

The marches were the culmination of centuries of the systemic exploitation and suppression of people of color, especially Black Americans saddled with the legacy of slavery. Blacks have been the living contradiction of the United States being founded on the premise that "all men are created equal," words ironically written by Thomas Jefferson, who physically and sexually exploited slaves. The first dozen American presidents, except for the Adamses, all owned slaves.

Slavery in this traditionally Judeo-Christian country goes way back, but with an interesting sidebar. When, in 1619, a ship arrived at the Jamestown settlement in Virginia, it carried some "20 and odd Negroes" who were kidnapped from their village in Africa. Let's pause on that word "kidnapped," for it reveals the unpleasant fact that African slavery could not have survived at the time without the connivance of some African leaders and chieftains. Their descendants acknowledge this and, in 1995, many gathered to take part in a cleansing ceremony that asked forgiveness on behalf of their ancestors, whose chiefs accepted guns and promises in exchange for people from their villages. Fred Swaniker, the founder of the African Leadership Academy, regretfully said that, "It would be worth looking at and acknowledging the role Africa did play in the slave trade. Someone had to find the slaves and bring them before the Europeans."[5] Back in 1998, Yoweri Museveni, the president of Uganda, told an audience: "African chiefs were the ones waging war on each other and capturing their own people and selling them. If anyone should apologize it should be the African chiefs."[6]

As far as America goes, slavery started early. Christopher Columbus sailed home from his second voyage with over a thousand Native American captives bound for the slave auctions in Cádiz. Many died en route and their bodies were simply tossed overboard. Columbus envisioned a future market for New World gold, spices, cotton, and, as he wrote, "as many slaves as Their Majesties order to make, from among those who are idolaters,"[7] whose sales might underwrite subsequent expeditions. The discoverer of the New World became its first transatlantic human trafficker. To round out the picture, we really should note that, in all this sad story of African slavery, there is the often-forgotten chronicle of the enslavement of the American Indians.

The recipients of the slave trade were Christian countries, which would seem like a spiritual oxymoron. That's why there were always those who felt unease about slavery, not only because it made a mockery of "All men are created equal," but also because it flew in the face of the gospel. On these grounds, slavery and unequal treatment should be abolished.

In England in 1833, when the ban on the slave trade had finally been followed by the emancipation of slaves throughout the British Empire, a small, eccentric religious group, neither Catholic nor Protestant—the Quakers, long and insistent advocates of the abolition of slavery—savored victory. They had stood up against strong arguments for slavery. After all, from time immemorial, slavery had been an accepted practice. Even the Bible embraced it. But the Quakers finally won.

---

5   David Smith, "African Chiefs Urged to Apologise for Slave Trade," *The Guardian*, November 18, 2009, https://www.theguardian.com/world/2009/nov/18/africans-apologise-slave-trade.

6   Ibid.

7   Andrés Reséndez, *The Other Slavery: The Uncovered Story of Indian Enslavement in America* (Boston: Houghton Mifflin Harcourt, 2016), 23.

Then Britain, now fully abolitionist and prompted by financial and expansionist motives, approached the Mideast Muslims, and for the sake of public relations, they asked the Muslims to ban the African slave trade. After all, it wouldn't be consistent to deal with a people who held slaves. The Muslims looked at them with blank faces. Everyone knew that slavery had always been a part of the human endeavor, from the time of Adam. It was part and parcel of civilization. Thus, the Brits' request was incomprehensible. Besides, the abolition of slaves was against their religion. Indisputably, the owning of slaves was licensed by the Qur'an, the unbreakable Word of God. Mohammad himself, like the patriarchs of the Bible, owned slaves. The Sunna, the book of Islamic traditions and practices, allowed it. What were the British thinking?

The Muslims could not, would not, disobey the Holy Book. They could not go back on scripture and tradition, especially if pressured by Christians. But there were other compelling interests to be served. So finally, to save face, they reinterpreted the Qur'an, arguing that, if read in the proper light, it would certainly approve of the freeing of slaves, a noble deed. Thus they reversed more than twelve centuries of teaching and practice and eventually the Muslims, arguing from Islamic scripture, abolished slavery.

Then there is the Christians' Holy Book. The conundrum here is that both Testaments clearly condoned slavery. The Church, for close to twenty centuries, buoyed by the Bible, did likewise. As we have noted, in spite of frequent and sincere misgivings, hesitations, and calls for the gentler treatment of slaves, the Church officially tolerated, if not embraced, slavery. Even as late as the nineteenth century, Pius IX averred it was not against the law for slaves to be sold, bought, or exchanged. It's a matter of record that the Church, at one time or another—its institutions, its clergy, religious orders, both male and female—had slaves. In other words, the Bible, Jesus, St. Paul—who urged slaves to be obedient to their masters "as you obey Christ"—and popes throughout the ages, no matter how solicitous they were about treating people lovingly, never outright condemned the institution of slavery. That was the tradition.

And then, one late day, prodded by the Quaker success and the change of heart of some nations, in a complete reversal, the belief that slavery was lawful was condemned as a grave moral evil with the highest decibel of rhetoric. Our morally virtuous and biblically taught ancestors centuries ago did not sin when they bought and sold slaves, but today they would be civilly prosecuted and ecclesiastically condemned as immoral sinners in need of repentance and susceptible to excommunication. Only the most dedicated apologist would offer the word "development" for a moral tradition so thoroughly reversed.

People of the Book have to be nimble.

THE "FAITHLESS" JEWS

No one will deny the Church's two millennia of doctrinal, liturgical, and lived anti-Semitism. From the time of the Church Fathers onward, Jews were deemed Christ-Killers, a deed they boasted about: "His blood be on us and on our children" (Matthew 27:25). They were "clearly" ridiculed in the Bible itself, condemned as the inferiors of the Christians who had supplanted them as God's chosen ones, and their covenant had been nullified. Disbelievers in a Trinitarian God, rejecters of Jesus as the Messiah, mis-readers of their own scriptures, Jews were considered beyond the pale. Forced or freely chosen conversions were their only hope of salvation.

But no more. In the last century, the Church has officially declared that the Jewish expectation of a coming Messiah is valid and the Jewish covenant with Yahweh has *not* been abrogated, but continues, even after the coming of Jesus. Furthermore, it is now forbidden for Catholics to proselytize the Jews. Pope Benedict XVI has firmly and unequivocally stated that Christians should not seek the conversion of the Jews: "Israel is in the hands of God, who will save it 'as a whole' at the proper time, when the number of Gentiles is complete"[8]—whenever that "proper time" comes. No one knows the answer to that, but there is the sequence: Gentiles first,

---

8   Pope Benedict XVI, *Jesus of Nazareth: Holy Week: From the Entrance into Jerusalem to the Resurrection* (San Francisco: Ignatius, 2011), 46.

Jews second. While rightly rejoicing in the more kindly, tolerant, and accepting attitudes in Jewish-Catholic relationships—let's be clear on that—some do find the statements of Vatican II and of Pope Benedict puzzling and wonder about Jesus' injunction to baptize "*all* nations."

Then there's that Epistle to the Hebrews. Father Joseph Fitzmyer, SJ pointed out that the Vatican II document on the Jews conveniently omits passages in Hebrews that completely contradict the thesis of a viable Judaism. He cites Hebrews 8:6–13, which concludes: "In speaking of 'a new covenant,' he [Christ] has made the first one obsolete. And what is obsolete and growing old will soon disappear." That's quite clear. He also cites Hebrews 10:9, which reads, "Then he added, 'See, I have come to do your will.' He abolishes the first in order to establish the second." This seems to reflect Matthew 21:43, where Jesus says, "Therefore I tell you, the kingdom of God will be taken away from you and given to a people that produces the fruits of the kingdom." Therefore, starting with Peter's (Luke's) words in the Book of Acts, urging his fellow Jews to be baptized and accept the Lord Jesus, the conversion of the Jews was an imperative.

Add to this past council documents, like the Council of Constance (1414–1418), and other official teachings that call for conversion of the Jews, plus Pope Paul VI's encyclical *Evangelii Nuntiandi*, which forthrightly states, "There is no true evangelization if the name, the teaching, the life, the promises, the kingdom and the mystery of Jesus of Nazareth, the Son of God are not proclaimed."[9] Cardinal Dulles summed up the tension by observing, "Once we grant that there are some persons for whom it is not important to acknowledge Christ, to be baptized and to receive the sacraments, we raise questions about our own religious life."[10] The bottom line in all this reversal comes from the Jewish writer Lazare Landau, who rejoiced that,

---

9   Pope Paul VI, *Evangelii Nuntiandi*, 22.

10 Avery Dulles, "Covenant and Mission," *America*, October 21, 2002, https://www.americamagazine.org/issue/408/article/covenant-and-mission.

thanks to Vatican II, "the Church's doctrine has indeed undergone a total change."[11] Change. Total.

NO SALVATION OUTSIDE THE CHURCH

It is a centuries-old teaching of the Roman Catholic Church that there is no salvation beyond its borders. So-called religious liberty is heresy. The scriptures, along with several councils and popes have insisted as much: Innocent III in 1206, Boniface VIII in 1302, the Council of Florence in 1442, Pius IV in 1564, Pius IX in 1854, and so on. These popes insisted that, in matters of religion, error had no rights because it threatens people's souls. People who held such errors represented a danger to church and society. Such attitudes were at the heart of the crusades and inquisitions. Only in the twentieth century, at Vatican II, was this stance modified, but not without obvious problems and strained rhetoric. As John O'Malley put it:

> Since the French Revolution, the popes had repeatedly condemned religious liberty and separation of church and state. But proponents of them at the council argued that they were legitimate developments of church teaching, an argument that to the opponents seemed like legerdemain. Development was supposedly movement to a further point along a given path, but *Dignitatis humanae* ["On Religious Liberty"] seemed to jump off the given path to forge a new one.[12]

The council wound up saying, "we ought to believe that the Holy Spirit in a manner known only to God offers to every man the possibility of being associated with this paschal mystery."[13] But it was a stretch.

---

11   As quoted in John Vennari, "Judaism and the Church: Before and after Vatican II," *Society of Saint Pius X*, January 24, 2013, https://sspx.org/en/news-events/news/judaism-church-after-vatican-ii-1342.

12   John O'Malley, "Does Church Teaching Change?" *Commonweal*, August 9, 2019, 20.

13   Paul VI, *Gaudium et Spes*, 22.

This also goes for the sacred writings of others. A professor from Notre Dame University, Gabriel S. Reynolds, has produced an excellent audio series on the Qur'an and the Bible. In introducing the series, he recounts sitting with a devout Muslim friend who was reading the Qur'an, lifted his head, and said to him with great fervor, "This is the Word of God! This is the Word of God!"[14] Do we have two Words of God? They agree in some places, but seriously disagree in other, critical places, but still, both traditions claim their book is *the* voice of God. At one time, the Church consigned such writings to the category of heresy. Today, in more ecumenical times, it admits there is some merit, some truth, some partial revelation in other scriptures, but is quick to add that we have the "fullness" of truth. I suggest that these adherents have different paths, different reflections and experiences *about* God, and have recorded them as such.

SAME-SEX MARRIAGE REVISITED

Finally, to revisit a delicate hot-button topic, many Christian and non-Christian institutions today have accepted same-sex marriage, thereby not only reversing their own perennial teachings and traditions, but also, as an unintended consequence, completely reversing sexual morals. That is to say, the assumption is that two gay men, for example, who marry, may and will express their love genitally, any form of which was once severely condemned, the most dramatic example being sodomy. "You shall not lie with a male as with a woman; it is an abomination" (Leviticus 18:22); "sodomites ... will not inherit the kingdom of God" (1 Corinthians 6:9–10). In no uncertain terms, St. Paul condemned homosexual acts in Romans 1:18–32. The Church Fathers weighed in similarly.

Dante put sodomites at the very bottom of the seventh ring of hell, well below those who commit suicide or homicide. The *Catechism of the Catholic Church*, while urging that gays "must be accepted with

---

14   Gabriel S. Reynolds, *The Bible and the Qur'an: A Comparative Study* (Learn25).

respect, compassion, and sensitivity,"[15] steadfastly declares, "Basing itself on Sacred Scripture, which presents homosexual acts as acts of grave depravity, tradition has always declared that 'homosexual acts are intrinsically disordered.' ... Under no circumstances can they be approved."[16] Such condemnations, in fact, went beyond Christianity and were quite universal, the ancients' horror being that men were being treated like women! Today, for some biblical religions that remain heavy with tradition, in the context of a loving marriage, these expressions are now permissible.

The late scripture scholar Marcus Borg gives one reason why: "Passages in the New Testament that affirm slavery and patriarchy and condemn same-sex marriages tell us how some of our spiritual ancestors saw things, not necessarily how we should see things. Of course, what they thought in their then matters—but it may not be normative for our now."[17]

Recall the quote regarding Episcopal Bishop Gene Robinson from Chapter 2: "Ten years ago I would not have been happy about this because I would have felt it's clearly contrary to the Bible, contrary to the traditions of the church. It's all because I've experienced the ministry of this man and a couple of others that I think I was mistaken."

Catholic scripture scholar Luke Timothy Johnson [disclosure: He has a lesbian daughter.] also references experience. He admits that the scriptural texts are clear and straightforward. They *do* condemn homosexuality, although, in fact, the original Greek terms referring to homosexuality and/or specific homosexual acts are not as clear as formerly thought. Whatever the case, Johnson adds that there are grounds for standing in tension (scholarly jargon for disagreement) with the commands of the "word of God." He writes:

> I think it important to state clearly that we do, in fact, reject the straightforward commands of Scripture, and appeal instead to

---

15 *Catechism of the Catholic Church*, 2358.
16 Ibid., 2357.
17 Marcus J. Borg, *Evolution of the Word: The New Testament in the Order the Books Were Written* (New York: HarperOne, 2012), 6.

another authority when we declare that same-sex unions can be holy and good. And what exactly is that authority? We appeal explicitly to the weight of our own experience and the experience thousands of others have witnessed to, which tells us that to claim our own sexual orientation is in fact to accept the way in which God has created us. By so doing, we explicitly reject as well the premises of the scriptural statements condemning homosexuality—namely, that it is a vice freely chosen, a symptom of human corruption, and disobedience to God's created order....

Implicit in an appeal to experience is also an appeal to the living God whose creative work never ceases, who continues to shape humans in his image every day, in ways that can surprise and even shock us....

Our situation vis-à-vis the authority of Scripture is not unlike that of abolitionists in nineteenth-century America. During the 1850s, arguments raged over the morality of slaveholding, and the exegesis of Scripture played a key role in those debates. The exegetical battles were one-sided: all abolitionists could point to was Galatians 3:28 and the Letter of Philemon, while slave owners had the rest of the Old and New Testaments, which gave every indication that slaveholding was a legitimate, indeed God-ordained social arrangement, one to which neither Moses nor Jesus nor Paul raised a fundamental objection. So how is it that now, in the early twenty-first century, the authority of the scriptural texts on slavery and the arguments made on their basis appear to all of us, without exception, as completely beside the point and deeply wrong? The answer is that over time the *human experience* of slavery and its horrors came home to the popular conscience....

Many of us who stand for the full recognition of gay and lesbian persons within the Christian communion find ourselves in a position similar to that of the early abolitionists.... We are fully aware of the weight of scriptural evidence pointing away from our position, yet we place our trust in the power of the living God to reveal as powerfully through personal experience and testimony as through written texts.[18]

---

18   Johnson, "Homosexuality & the Church."

IMPLICATIONS

That's a lot to think about. I suspect that the average Catholic is not tuned into the subtleties of his distinctions and wonder if they have just been handed a key to make scripture say what the modern mindset wants it to say today—and who knows what tomorrow's "experience" may bring? Scholars like N.T. Wright also have second thoughts. He writes, "If 'experience' is itself a source of authority, we can no longer be addressed by the word which comes from beyond ourselves. At this point, theology and Christian living cease to be rooted in God himself, and are rooted instead in our own selves."[19]

You can't get more direct than that: We need a new interpretative theory in reading the Bible, a critique that turns the Bible on itself. There's no mention of the centuries-old and ecclesiastically guaranteed "truth" of the old interpretations that we'll explore later, but for now, the statement does say, in effect, we've been wrong—often tragically wrong—all these centuries.

Anyway, my interest is not in whether same-sex marriage is right or not, but rather in the question of the radical change it implies, the reversal of an unambiguous, persistent teaching and tradition. If the Roman Catholic Church ever does change its stance, it will have to come to terms with a lot of practical and theoretical history. However, for what it's worth, my very guarded and conflicted opinion is that, sooner or later, the Church will accept same-sex marriages.

In 2013 Pope Francis, when he was asked about his attitude to a man who was gay, famously replied, "if a person is gay and seeks God and has good will, who am I to judge?"[20] In October 2020, Pope Francis, while still opposing gay marriage within the Church, went further by publicly approving same-sex civil unions. He instantly upended not only the Church's traditional teaching of marriage as between one man and one woman but also its long-standing opposition

---

19 N. T. Wright, *Scripture and the Authority of God: How to Read the Bible Today* (New York: HarperCollins, 2013), 103.

20 Pope Francis: Who am I to Judge Gay People?" *BBC News*, July 29, 2013, https://www.bbc.com/news/world-europe-23489702.

to such civil unions as being a threat to it. The pope went on to say that "Homosexuals have a right to be part of the family.... Nobody should be thrown out, or be made miserable because of it."[21] His remarks gave a boost to liberal Catholics and angst to conservative ones, including the hierarchy. Earlier in 2020, the German bishops had expressed their desire to see the *Catechism of the Catholic Church* revise its wording on homosexual acts as "intrinsically disordered." They have asked for a change of thinking in evaluating same-sex partnerships and indeed have suggested the blessing of such unions. The Archdiocese of Salzburg has published a book entitled *The Benediction of Same-Sex Partnerships*. Something's in the air and pressure will continue to mount, especially when, in June 2020, the United States Supreme Court ruled that gay and transgender people cannot be fired for their sexuality, putting tremendous pressure on evangelical and Roman Catholic institutions.

In actual pastoral practice, consider this: two civilly married gay men, respected members of the parish—"part of the family"—approach for Communion. There is no way they can be denied and so their status becomes a distinction without a difference, a doctrinal shadow without substance.

On top of all this, let me add this startling thought: that one day in the foreseeable future, the whole issue of same-sex marriage versus traditional marriage will become moot. That's because technology has changed the whole pattern of childbearing. We are already aware that people can have children via a surrogate mother. Two women can purchase a sperm donor. An older woman can use an egg from a younger one. IVG (in vitro gametogenesis) has advanced so far that it can now take different cells outside the body and theoretically manufacture in laboratories an egg or sperm cell from a tiny sliver of a person's own skin. This means that, in the foreseeable future, a single woman could mix her egg with sperm fashioned from the genetic material from

---

21   Henry Austin, "Pope Calls for Civil Unions for Same-sex Couples, in Major Departure from Vatican Doctrine," *NBCNews.com*, October 21, 2020, https://www.nbcnews.com/feature/nbc-out/pope-calls-civil-unions-same-sex-couples-major-departure-vatican-n1244137.

one or two or more of her male friends—material from which potentially inherited diseases can be extracted. The result could be a family threesome or foursome, all genetically connected. The resulting child would have three or more genetic parents.

In short, technologies such as IVG have completely severed reproduction from sex. Procreative unions no longer just come from pairs. The necessity of the traditional family is obviated, reduced to a personal choice. Yes, people will still use the usual means of sexual reproduction to have children, but the new technologies that enable people to have children without it will give us a whole new concept of what it means to be family. Just as we are becoming used to that nice family next door being two men or two women or a single person with children, so someday we may take for granted the three or four people who are all genetically related to their children and consider them family. We can be sure that the law which in 2015 extended the right of marriage to same-sex couples will in due time sanction the poly-parents of tomorrow. Society and the Church will have to come to terms with this new reality. Our current arguments over same-sex marriage will seem, if not irrelevant, at least less cogent in the face of a new reality.

A PASTORAL ASIDE

Can you imagine preaching from the altar Borg's statement that scriptural words may not be normative for us today, or Johnson's declaration that "I think it important to state clearly that we do in fact reject the straightforward commands of Scripture.... We appeal [rather] to the weight of our own experience"—given, as we shall see in the next chapter, the deep, unassailable conviction drummed into us by centuries of catechesis and teaching of the immutable word of God and the authority of the immutable Church to which it has been entrusted? If those words are anywhere near true, we have massive re-education to do, not to mention the delicate task of face-saving.

Chapter 12

THE CHURCH TO THE RESCUE (PART II)

Every day I have less belief and more faith.

—*Graham Greene*

More reversals, more changes are quietly going on right now. In the light of modern scientific discovery, there is, for example, the slow but discernable leaching of belief in Adam and Eve as the first parents of humankind, whose sin brought death into the world. Belief in the guilt of Original Sin that, according to St. Augustine, is passed on by sex and removed by baptism, is slowly losing ground; not many theologians speak of it that way. Nor do they accept Augustine's insistence that all will be damned to hell unless they *are* baptized, even infants—unless, of course, God, in his mercy, decides to save them. Limbo as an option was downgraded by Pope Benedict XVI in 2005; he did not deny limbo exists, just that most unbaptized infants would not go to heaven. His declaration provoked attacks from rightwing Catholics for changing doctrine just as, later on, Pope Francis would come under the same charge for permitting divorced Catholics to receive Communion.

Again, many spiritual writers and teachers today treat the Genesis account of Adam and Eve symbolically or metaphorically, while "original sin" is seen as an expression of our estrangement from God. Baptism is seen as not primarily for removing the stain of Original Sin but an entrance rite into Church membership:

> Baptism is a naming.... In baptism we are identified as beloved children of God, and our adoption into the sprawling, beautiful, dysfunctional family of the church... is why the baptism font is typically located near the entrance of a church. The central aisle represents the Christian's journey through life toward God, a journey that begins with baptism.[1]

In today's climate, Confirmation is less likely to entail a promise to be a strong Catholic and profess the faith openly and courageously forever. Rather, as one father put it to his doubtful and hesitant daughter, "What you promise when you are confirmed is not that you will believe this forever. What you promise when you are confirmed is that this is the story you will wrestle with forever."[2] That could have been my dad!

Evolution has shown that other people, like death, were around long before Adam and Eve. Jesus, the new Adam who "died for our sins" and ransomed us from the wrath of the Father, is being recast. The concept of "natural law" is evaporating in a world of heart transplants, test tube babies, gender fluidity, and artificial intelligence. Just as the seven-day creation story—of a 6,000-year-old earth-centered universe, formed by a "Prime Mover"—must now be seen in terms of creative myth rather than history, so the dynamics of moral truth are seen from a new perspective and are forcing reinterpretations, if not reversals, of doctrine.

---

1 Rachel Held Evans, *Searching for Sunday: Loving, Leaving, and Finding the Church* (Nashville, TN: Nelson, 2015), 14–15.

2 Lauren F. Winner, *Still: Notes on a Mid-Faith Crisis* (New York: HarperOne, 2013), 172.

CATHOLIC CONFLICT

Still, any doctrinal change is a hard sell for Fundamentalists and, for different reasons, for Roman Catholics. First, for Catholics, the concept of new consciousness may indeed be valid, but they're stuck with the Church's perennially overblown claims. Two millennia of conditioning and teaching have left a deep and cherished (and comforting) conviction in the Catholic imagination that truth, as taught by the Church, is "always the same" and can never change. The *Catechism of the Catholic Church* is full of reminders:

- 892: Regarding the ordinary teaching of the Magisterium, the faithful "are to adhere to it with religious assent."

- 890: "The pastoral duty of the Magisterium is aimed at seeing to it that the People of God abides in the truth that liberates. To fulfill this service, Christ endowed the Church's shepherds with the charism of infallibility in matters of faith and morals."

- 2034: "The Roman Pontiff and the bishops are 'authentic teachers, that is, teachers endowed with the authority of Christ.'"

- 2037: "The law of God entrusted to the Church is taught to the faithful as the way of life and truth."

Vatican II adds:

The entire body of the faithful, anointed as they are by the Holy One, cannot err in matters of belief. They manifest this special property by means of the whole people's supernatural discernment in matters of faith when 'from the Bishops down to the last of the lay faithful' they show universal agreement in matters of faith and morals.[3]

---

3   Pope Paul VI, *Lumen Gentium*, 12.

Older Catholics, raised on the Baltimore Catechism, knew the drill:

Q. 444. Will the Holy Ghost [sic] abide with the Church forever?

A. The Holy Ghost will abide with the Church forever, and guide it in the way of holiness and truth.

Q. 567. How is the Church Apostolic?

A. The Church is Apostolic because it was founded by Christ on His Apostles, and is governed by their lawful successors, and because it has never ceased, and never will cease, to teach their doctrine.

We can see in all of this official teaching the hubris of the Church, its subversion of faith. Faith, by definition, implies doubt, but the Church will have none of that. The Church wants and sells certainty. Catholics are not invited to live with unanswerable questions. They are directed to embrace the certainties embodied in the Church's catechism and propositions. We're not on a pilgrimage. We have arrived.

So, the understanding is that the Church does not, has not, cannot change its doctrines. They are the very deposit of faith revealed by Jesus Christ, taught by the apostles, and handed down in their entirety by the apostles to their successors. Revealed truth cannot change. Yes, Jesus' words to the apostles in Matthew 18:18–19 do grant authority to the apostles to "bind" and to "loose," but that "loosing" does not mean the apostles or their successors can modify doctrine.

The result of all this is that the pithy old axiom, "*Roma locuta est. Causa finita est,*" was solid and unyielding: "Rome has spoken. The matter is closed," and that was that. Let other religions flounder all over the place, but the Roman Catholic Church teaches the same "yesterday, today, and forever." As a result of this enduring conviction, the ceaseless flow of history becomes a big problem for a Church that claims a timeless revelation that answered every question and solved every problem. And when the Church is forced to seemingly propose something new, its apologists resort to serpentine and convoluted logic to prove that the new challenge is not only consistent with the old convictions but is actually mandated by them! As one wily Jesuit put it, in Rome, everything is forbidden till it is made compulsory. Peter Steinfels weighs in on the same thought:

> Historically Catholicism solved the problem of change simply by denying it. Understandings of the Trinity, the priesthood, the papacy, the Mass and the sacraments that emerged over a long time were *projected back into New Testament texts*. Theologians joked that when a pope or other official circuitously introduced a modification of church teaching, he would begin, "As the church has always taught...." Such denial, still widespread, means that examining change in official teaching... poses two challenges: first, to establish that alterations—some more than minor—have unquestionably occurred; and second, to show how they can be reconciled with the church's claim to preach the same essential message Jesus and his disciples did 2,000 years ago.[4]

A ROLL OF THE MORAL DICE

Secondly, for Catholics as for other believers, there are the existential questions of doubt that a history of Church certainties provokes. We no longer torture homosexuals, publicly pray for the "faithless" Jews on Good Friday, consign non-Catholics to hell for their heresies, or buy and sell slaves. But, with good conscience, we *did* do all these things at one time—officially, with approval. They were all taught, encouraged, and rewarded, or at least permitted, by the Spirit-filled Church, the same promised Spirit of All Truth that was to guide and guarantee the Church at every moment. Then, suddenly, these acts are all wrong, wicked, immoral. One cannot help but think about how, at one time, scientists or doctors who, in their limited knowledge and ignorance, unwittingly brought untold misery

---

4   As quoted in Clifford Nichols, "Historical Amnesia," *Commonweal*, September 27, 2013, 8–9.

and even death to others. Their mistakes are in the graveyard. The Church's mistakes are in hell.

Thirdly, as the Church does encounter new experiences and, as a result, winds up reversing age-old "infallible" doctrines and practices, the issues (a variant of the old theodicy conundrum) of proportion, justice, and fairness correspondingly come into play. The fact that we finally got it right seems, in hindsight, a small comfort for the centuries of abusive horrors women have suffered as the "property" of men. Apologetically cutting their bodies down from tree limbs is small comfort to the slaves who hung there for 3,000 biblically approved years. Embracing them as separated "brethren" is small comfort for those "infidels" who had to be eliminated by torture and fire in the name of orthodoxy. Being accepted "with great respect, compassion and sensitivity" is small comfort for the endless shunning, condemning, and persecuting of "intrinsically disordered" gays.

However unarticulated, people are pondering why the Jesus-promised and Truth-Guided Spirit allowed errors so early and truth so late, with such suffering in the in-between time. Yes, moral consciousness grows, but we're talking about the Church, where people were condemned to hell for the simple accident of being born in the wrong century. That's a dissonance that not only questions the notion of a so-called loving, just, and compassionate Deity, but challenges the unforgiving authority of the "always the same" Church and, by implication, the circular biblical interpretations that support it.

FUTURE QUESTIONS

We asked before: Who knows what tomorrow's "experience" may bring? What other changes lie further down the doctrinal pike? The average Catholic can deal with moveable disciplines such as changing the Mass from Latin to awkward English, the possibility of married clergy, and even, someday, women deacons, but what about those foundational things that, as far as they can plainly see, reverse the Bible, Tradition, Church practice, and official Church teaching? How do ordinary people deal with a Church that claims immutable transcendental authority and then flip-flops with the new interpretations because of "experience"? They have already witnessed how today's secular system, backed by very punitive laws, legally permits everything that they were taught was morally wrong: divorce, contraception, abortion on demand, the right to die. How soon before polygamy (biblically approved), the killing of defective babies, and the lowering of the age of sexual consent follow suit and are morally permitted? Someday, citing experience, could Catholic dissenters also embrace these things, claiming they are being prophetic and the Church will catch up, sooner or later? If you change one traditional doctrine, is any teaching safe?

A LONG ASIDE

Before we end with a speculation about the next Church council (yes, there will be one), let's backtrack. The early Christians were familiar with development and reversal. St. Paul was an outlier who ran counter to the apostles who were convinced that their message was to Jews only. They reluctantly came over to his side as Gentiles became the majority of Christians. Most Christians, including St. Paul, thought the world was ending soon and Jesus would be returning, only to have the author of 2 Peter (3:8) clear his throat and reverse the timetable. Early Christian leaders with apparently open eyes put together a New Testament that ran the wide Christological gamut from Mark to John, the former not knowing what to make of the latter. More changed as Christians embraced more deeply a Greco-Roman worldview, where they adopted "the Platonic notion that true reality, the spiritual reality of the divine, is unchanging (strongly contrary to the Old Testament image of God as a deity always acting in history and even changing his mind—cf. Gen. 6:6). They also became wary of change, idealizing and idolizing the apostolic age and making that the fixed reference point."[5] That, again, is because they were children of their time.

---

5   Joseph F. Kelly, *History and Heresy: How Historical Forces Can Create Doctrinal Conflicts* (Collegeville, MN: Liturgical, 2012), 51.

In other words, the architects of our faith, like all of us, came from *somewhere*, that "somewhere" being laden with its innate presuppositions. For us Christians, Christianity came to maturity in Europe. It may have started out in the Mideast, but soon became a legal and dominant entity in the Hellenistic "Europe" of the Roman Empire. As such, it lived and breathed the famous Roman legal way of governing and coding, plus Platonic and Aristotelian ways of thinking, seeing, and understanding the world. As a result, the Roman Catholic Church's New Testament was written in Greek (not Aramaic), its liturgy was celebrated for centuries in Greek, and its councils, canons, decrees, proclamations, laws, and theologies are unconscious expressions of European Greco-Roman philosophies. We're not called the *Roman* Catholic Church for nothing. For many centuries, this European Church knew little or nothing of African, Asian, and Arctic worldviews and their ways of expressing faith and living life.

Furthermore, although two ecumenical councils—Chalcedon in 451 and Nicaea II in 787—were called by women, think of this: The only people making the canons, decrees, proclamations, and laws for twenty centuries have been men. Although it has its heroines, the Bible itself is a collection written by men for men (the Ten Commandments, for instance, are written in the second person masculine). God was male. Jesus was male. Since Jesus and his twelve disciples were men, the Church decided only men could make decisions. Only men could be priests. In spite of the roles women played in the canonical gospels and epistles, the last saying (#114) in the Gospel of Thomas sums up the prevailing attitude:

> Simon Peter said to them, "Let Mary go away from us, for women are not worthy of life." Jesus said, "Look, I will draw her in so as to make her male, so that she too may become a living male spirit, similar to you." [But I say to you]: "Every woman who makes herself male will enter the kingdom of heaven."

That these things are part of the mental furniture of the Church should not be surprising. Plato downgraded women, wondering why, if not for sex and children, men needed them at all. Aristotle claimed women were biologically inferior. Jewish tradition equated a good woman with one who married the man her parents chose and gave him sons so his name would continue. Medieval Christianity's greatest theologian, Thomas Aquinas, wrote,

> It was necessary for woman to be made, as the scripture says, as a "helper" to man; not indeed as a helpmate in other works, as some say, since man can more efficiently be helped by another man in other works; but as a helper in the work of generation.... As regards the individual nature, woman is defective and misbegotten, for the active force in the male seed tends to the production of a perfect likeness in the masculine sex; while the production of woman comes from defect in the active force or from some material indisposition.[6]

Once all this formation, all the subconscious cosmological and philosophical underpinnings are revealed and grasped, then it is obvious that an all-male clerical-establishment church needs to make room for modern realities, where science is acknowledged, other cultures are heard, women have equality, and lay theologians and scripture scholars are welcome. So, with that long aside in mind, we turn to the question of the next council.

VATICAN III?

Ilia Delio writes, "Theology must *begin with evolution* if it is to talk of a *living* God, and hence it must include physical, spiritual, and psychological change as fundamental to reality."[7] That may be true, but surely the pastoral challenge is how one can get this across to Catholics whose consciences have been formed by unambiguous, inviolable, static Church teaching. It has been

---

6   Thomas Aquinas, *Summa Theologiae*, First Part, Question 92, Article 1.
7   Ilia Delio, *Making All Things New: Catholicity, Cosmology, Consciousness* (Maryknoll, NY: Orbis, 2015), 147.

proudly stated that the Roman Catholic Church does not change, and when change does happen, conservative Catholics are outraged by a sense of betrayal and liberal Catholics are incensed by a lack of coherence, while faithful middle-of-the-roaders are left hanging. It won't be easy.

The Church, like all institutions, is a conservative institution. Like so many institutions, it has become self-enclosed. In fact, it has always felt itself to be immune to the historical process, assuming that Church teaching in any era was continuous with the gospel. It has tended to conflate faith with certainty. Its rules, while truly useful, became absolute. It is quite unsettling for sincere Catholics when changes are made and they realize people of good conscience from another era were penalized. To this day, even while proclaiming in its Vatican II document "On Divine Revelation" that the tradition of the Church stemming from the apostles "makes progress in the Church and grows," the Church and its leaders have failed to provide an adequate catechesis, a deeper and more honest concept of tradition that makes sense of that phrase. This is important because it is clear that what is at stake here is nothing less than the credibility and authority of the Church.

One thing is sure, no matter how this gets resolved: The official Church has to drop its out-of-touch, overblown, static claims of rigid certainty and assume its Vatican II identity as a Pilgrim Church whose deep spirituality, ancient wisdom, and powerful traditions aid in the search for truth—and not prepackage it in binding formulas, irreversible canons, and unforgiving laws. The faithful need a new narrative catechism that invites dialogue rather than dictates answers.

So, we end as we began, with a quotation from John O'Malley, SJ. Speculating on the possibility of another Church council (which he believes will occur), he writes that when that time comes, the Church will find that:

> Some issues... are not subject to final resolution. One of them is the relationship of tradition to innovation. It is the challenge of maintaining identity while adapting to new situations, the problem of remaining true to oneself without lapsing into

irrelevance. For the church, this challenge is the result of being a historical institution, subject to the forces of the historical process. Such an institution is not an entity that can plow through the sea of history without being changed by the journey.[8]

The Church sorely needs to "be aware" of the ancient scribes.

Sidebar

I mentioned that the architects of our faith came from somewhere and, for us, we recall, it was Plato by way of St. Augustine. There is no doubt that their disdain of the body was whole-heartedly embraced by Christianity. As one reads through the lives of the saints, one is struck with the ferocious hatred of the body, hatred that is held up as an ideal. This is not just the discipline necessary for human living and growth, but the extremes of self-torture, deprivation, and deformity becoming part and parcel of holiness. The prophet-like eccentricities were one thing, but the vicious assault on the "despicable" body was another: saints beating and flagellating their bodies, fasting to the point of starvation, holing themselves up in enclaves, wearing heavy chains. St. Francis of Assisi and thousands of others shortened and crippled their lives through such spiritual antics.

Still, the more they punished themselves, the more they "suffered for Christ," the greater esteem they garnered. In Robert Ellsberg's noted book *All Saints*, the prevalence of self-punishing heroes and the religious visions of pre-menopausal girls is astounding. Today, we would harshly judge such rage against the body and proclaim nine-year-old visionaries as victims of hysteria and psychological disorder—certainly not to be imitated. The Church today would not—does not—tolerate such extremes, nor self-inflicted bodily punishment, but the point is that the Church extolled them at one time.

---

8   John W. O'Malley, *When Bishops Meet: An Essay Comparing Trent, Vatican I, and Vatican II* (Cambridge, MA: The Belknap Press of Harvard University Press, 2019), 211–212.

PART II:

WITNESSES FOR THE DEFENSE

Chapter 13

THE LIE THAT TELLS THE TRUTH

I create fiction to tell the truth.

—*Eudora Welty*

When it comes to atoms, language can be used only as in poetry. The poet, too, is not so nearly concerned with describing facts as with creating images.

—*Niels Bohr*

We Catholics are very much given to the Instant Answer. Fiction doesn't have any. It leaves us, like Job, with a renewed sense of mystery.

—*Flannery O'Connor*

These three quotations sum up this whole chapter. Substitute the Bible for atoms and you have it. So, let's begin.

Scripture scholar Philip R. Davies sets the tone:

> The Bible's moral teaching is actually not very remarkable. For the most part, it is typical of the values of the age in which the writers lived. It does not advocate democracy, freedom of speech or equality, whether sexual, racial or religious. Women are

subordinate, unbelievers are evil, slavery is acceptable. Its god is gracious to believers and vengeful to unbelievers, demanding obedience and even love. Like all gods, he expects sacrifice. The Bible is, with a very occasional lapse, monotheistic, and accepts that God is the source of all virtue.... Christian behavior conforms very closely to conventional Jewish morality.[1]

Still, on the other hand, there *is* an area that gives me pause. There is a key that I think might unlock the Bible's schizophrenias and innate contradictions. There is a framework increasingly used by scholars wishing to save the day that I find appealing. It is the distinction between what Karen Armstrong calls *logos* and *mythos*, between poetry and prose, if you will, between the literal and the imaginative, with *both* offering truth, but in different ways.

THE STORYTELLING LENS

We begin with Lesson 101. The collection we call the Bible is from times, cultures, and a mentality very different from our own. Therefore, like Shakespeare, it does require some study, some background. You may consider the Bible to be the word of God, God's self-revelation, not in the sense that God dictated it to scribes, but in the sense that the scribes, and the people they were writing for, experienced God in and through the writings. Mostly and by far, it's the stories they told and preserved that were the material for these glimpses of what God must be like—those stories that were not always factual, but true.

Suppose we read the Bible by applying, not the rules of history, but the rules of storytelling? Those rules are, you know, vastly different. There is a saying among writers that goes, "Some stories are factual. All stories are true." We can apply this to the biblical stories. There is, of course, some factual history in its pages, but, more often, there is the fiction that tells the truth as much as Harper Lee's fictional *To Kill a Mockingbird*.

---

1   Philip R. Davies, *The Bible for the Curious: A Brief Encounter* (Indonesia: Equinox, 2018), 142.

In 2003, Fr. Andy Greeley, always ahead of the times, said the biggest appeal of the Roman Catholic Church was its stories: the biblical stories, church history stories, martyrs' and saints' stories, legend stories, apparition stories, liturgical cycle stories: Advent, Christmas, Lent, Easter, Pentecost stories, and so on. The Bible's appeal, likewise, has always been its stories. The human reality is that stories speak to us at a deep, numinous level. Stories have their own logic. Unlike closed dogmas, they are open-ended. At each stage of one's life, the same story may carry a different message. It may also do so depending on where we're coming from. Women may read the biblical text differently from men, the Third world from the First world.

Norton Juster's children's book *The Phantom Tollbooth* makes this point. In the tale, the boy, Milo, travels to the Kingdom of Knowledge. Everywhere he goes, Milo learns life lessons. There is the lesson from a character named Alec Bings at the "Point of View Station":

> "For instance, from here that looks like a bucket of water," he said, pointing to a bucket of water; "but from an ant's point of view it's a vast ocean, from an elephant's just a cool drink, and to a fish, of course, it's home. So, you see, the way you see things depends a great deal on where you look at them from."[2]

In any case, standing by our contention that most of the biblical stories are recycled myths, they nevertheless carry myth's truths and myth's struggle with the Big Questions at different stages of life. The Christian faith is built on a story, and stories require imagination. In an article in *The Wall Street Journal*, Karen Armstrong explains:

> Most cultures believed that there were two recognized ways of arriving at truth. The Greeks called them *mythos* and *logos*. Both were essential and neither was superior to the other; they were not in conflict but complementary, each with its own sphere of competence. *Logos* ("reason") was the pragmatic mode of thought that enabled us to function effectively in the world and had, therefore, to correspond accurately to external reality. But

---

2   Norton Juster, *The Phantom Tollbooth* (New York: Yearling, 1961), 108.

it could not assuage human grief or find ultimate meaning in life's struggle. For that people turned to *mythos*, stories that made no pretensions to historical accuracy but should rather be seen as an early form of psychology; if translated into ritual or ethical action, a good myth showed you how to cope with mortality, discover an inner source of strength, and endure pain and sorrow with serenity.[3]

In her book *The Lost Art of Scripture*, she expands on this idea:

Myths help us understand our experience, give shape to shapeless events, order to our fears and desires, narrative to chaos. The huge step that *Homo sapiens* took away from Neanderthals in the Cognitive Revolution of 70,000 years ago was made possible by the ability of our species to collectively imagine things, as Yuval Noah Harari argues in his book on human origins. "... all religion is informed by myth, as are most cultural bonds...." "Mythology is not lie," said Joseph Campbell. "Mythology is poetry, it's metaphysical. It has been well said that myth is the penultimate truth—penultimate because the ultimate cannot be put into words."[4]

In other words, myth is naked truth with clothes put on.

A WORTHY DISTINCTION

This is a good distinction to keep in mind as we observe here that atheists and critics are alert to *logos* but deaf to *mythos*. They unleash a one-sided criticism of a book they consider literal history, ignoring the fact that biblical authors, like all the ancients, wrote in stories. They little appreciate that they are Western Greek-heritage thinkers trying to understand Mideastern Semitic thinkers, that they analyze while Semites synthesize, that they seek history

---

[3] Karen Armstrong and Richard Dawkins, "Man vs. God," *The Wall Street Journal*, September 12, 2009.

[4] Armstrong, *Lost Art of Scripture*, 223.

while the Semites are writing theology, being more concerned with the meaning of what happened than in narrating the facts of what happened. So, the Bible becomes an easy target, a mere repository of "bronze-age myths."

They don't realize that today, more and more modern scholars do appreciate the Bible as a collected book of stories, with perhaps some pretense, but little claim, to historical accuracy. Historical fiction might be a more accurate description. Scholars are beginning once more to recognize the Bible as an ongoing imaginative narrative, led to stopping at one sentence or paragraph or episode as if it were the final word, but always open to another "final" word. (Think of Joshua's exclusivism and Jonah's inclusivism.) Its stories deliberately have lots of gaps and leave much unsaid in order to bypass judgment or make a point. Just as people have learned how to read Winnie the Pooh, the Brothers Karamazov, and Ron Chernow's biography of George Washington, they must learn also how to read the Bible.

This means that the Bible circles and circles the imponderables of God and human life in exotic, poetic language. Its stories (thanks to the scribes) are ever evolving, ever expanding to fit new circumstances, and not in the sense of adding more technical or historical information or literary flair, but in the sense of taking another dive into the mystery. The Bible and its symbols (*mythos*) are not meant to compete with reason (*logos*); to judge the former by the latter is not fitting. In the Bible, we are dealing with a different dimension of search and meaning. If, as someone said, the best theology is akin to art and poetry, the best reading of the Bible is akin to story. As such, it follows the rules of oral storytelling and not the rules of written grammar, logic, and composition. If we don't apply oral rules to the Bible, but rather apply the literary canons of the later written text, then we're not far from the literalism and fundamentalism that furiously hugs facts, not meaning, and makes bestsellers of atheistic shortsightedness.

Thus, when the orthodox Christian view of the Genesis story began to insist that it was factual and built a theology around it, it became, as we saw, vulnerable to new discoveries. The first parents—Adam and Eve, the temptation, and the fall-and-rescue scenarios—got imbedded in Christian lore and art. Milton's *Paradise Lost* turned the story into a tragedy promoted by Satan. Somehow, Christianity forgot that for many centuries the story was not read literally. St. Augustine, who spent fifteen years composing "The Literal Meaning of Genesis," said it need not be taken literally if it goes against what we know to be true from other sources. First-century Jewish philosopher Philo presented Genesis as an allegory. The literalists missed, as Stephen Greenblatt tells us,[5] the story as mythology. In John Gray's excellent summation, "The story expresses universal conflicts within human beings, rendered into a vernacular language of monotheism."[6]

VIEWPOINT

The bottom line is that people of the pre-scientific age thought, told, and (those who could write) wrote stories rich in allegory, metaphor, and symbolism. This was not only because they were superstitious and ignorant of our scientific knowledge and our great ability to manipulate nature (which would have stunned their minds), but because, free of our resulting hubris, they innately sensed that reality could not be fully grasped by the human mind or categorized by human systems, however "scientific." They felt and respected the power of mystery and could only resort to mumbling about it in indirect ways, the ways of story and metaphor (what we call myth). Above all, they had a highly developed sense of God (under any title) as awesome, as ungraspable, and anything they had to say about him had to be unsaid almost immediately, or quickly cast in opposing and contradictory ways. (Yahweh is forgiving. Yahweh is cruel.) There

---

5   Stephen Greenblatt, *The Rise and Fall of Adam and Eve: The Story that Created Us* (New York: W. W. Norton, 2017).

6   John Gray, "The Rise and Fall of Adam and Eve: Exploring the Myth of the Original Sinners," *New Statesman*, September 9, 2017, https://www.newstatesman.com/culture/books/2017/09/rise-and-fall-adam-and-eve-exploring-myth-original-sinners.

was a transcendence whose existence could not be proved, but only intuited. When it came to God and life's mysteries, the Greek philosophical terms we've inherited, like "omnipotent," "omnipresent," and "omniscient" made no sense. Story and poetry, tale and folklore were the only adequate terms.

In summary, where we today are resigned to a meaningless universe and have embraced the palliative technical marvels and entertainments of the digital here-and-now, the ancients wrestled to find human meaning through the poetries and contradictions of allegory and metaphor. The Semitic ancients preferred *mythos* over reason—although, in a twist of history, reason via the Greeks eventually triumphed. Alas, as we have seen, the church also came down too often on the side of reason. Much to our loss, catechisms replaced narrative.

WHAT WE REMEMBER

It's the stories and their evolving interpretations, which we tell and pass on, that stir our moral imagination, not the scientific discoveries that speak to human life and how it is to be lived. That's why we covet our moral heroes and morality tales. Such stories mirror our own struggles and come closest to plumbing the hard-to-name nuances of life, the "something more" perfume that hangs in the air, even in laboratories. Stories, as befit the complexities of life, are ambivalent, multi-leveled, and, in one sense, never finished. Stories exist because we have learned that there are simply moments too precious, deep, mysterious, and unspeakable to be explained fully by science.

How often we say or hear said, "Words fail me," or "There are no words to express this bounty" or "this horror" or whatever. Normal, rational categories *do* fail us, so we turn to poetry and story. We struggle to make sense of human experience, and stories are really the only venue to express the messiness and ambiguities of life. They move beyond any simple, reductive, scientific answer. Their range is wide. They supply the language, metaphors, poetry, allegories, and paradoxes that come nearest to expressing our fears, joys, and desires for fulfillment. Human beings cannot understand themselves or the world without resorting to stories and myths. To this day, the great movies, novels, and even TV shows captivate us. We are a storytelling people, because science has its limits.

My labored point is that the Bible, like other great sagas, fits in here. It is a story anthology, one not meant to be taken literally, one not meant to be consistent or logical or historical or the last word. It is a *mythos* that challenges us and helps us, through its stories, to define ourselves and our place in this universe. The fact is, we can't understand Pliny or Shakespeare, what and how they wrote, without understanding their times and assumed allusions and metaphors. So, too, concerning the biblical stories, scholars expose the ways the ancients regularly took and recycled old myths to capture new truths.

For example, a biblical writer comfortably took the centuries-old Elijah story of bringing back the widow's son to life (1 Kings 17:17–24), and moved it forward to interpret Jesus' raising of the widow's son at Nain (Luke 7:11–17). This was his way of explaining who Jesus is, the tradition he stood in, what he was about. So, we don't necessarily have to literally parse the Jesus version with modern, one-dimensional scientific minds to "prove" Jesus raised someone from the dead. We have to parse the story, in its contextual, recycled metaphors, to discover what the story is trying to tell us about Jesus. Remember, in spite of some hot disputes, there are certain basics, certain elements of the Christian message that were quite clear very early in the middle of the first century. First, believers never doubted that Christ died to take away sin, the necessity of a moral and upright life based on Christ, the truth of Jesus' resurrection, and the centrality of the Eucharist. These fundamentals from St. Paul, a near contemporary of Jesus, were bedrock. What followed were the creative stories to convey them.

The biblical stories, then, are, in the words of scholar Raymond Brown, "imaginative retellings," inventive fiction, narrative parables. As such, the Bible is best presented as a compendium of wonderfully creative stories sacred to a particular people struggling to make sense of the world. If read literally, of course, the atheists and skeptics *will* have a field day, but why should we concede the day to them? If read metaphorically, believers will have something to ponder. And it's a shame that scholars themselves have also tended to compartmentalize their disciplines into unnecessary hostilities. It's a shame that our ecclesiastical leaders have disdained the "gods," if you will: folk religion and its icons, rituals, and stories. They should suspend their skepticism and take seriously the note of transcendence present in these expressions and integrate them more fully into church life.

The same with the Bible. If read with recognition, the biblical stories challenge us. The crises between parents and children are there in the sagas of Abraham and Isaac, David and Absalom. Sibling rivalry is found in the story of Jacob and Esau, jealousy in the story of Joseph and his brothers, fidelity in the friendship of Ruth and Naomi, hatred in the Cain and Abel saga, the reluctant and hesitant heroes with Jonah or Moses, pride and fall in the David and Solomon stories, betrayal in Judas, weakness in the face of human pressure in Peter, Thomas who doubted, Pilate who compromised, Barnabas who encouraged, Simeon who tried to buy his way into heaven, and so on. Many find a revelation of God in these stories.

Sidebar

The pastor in me kicks in here as what I just wrote leads me to ponder the problems of the young: living in uncertain times, saddled with a pandemic, staggering student debt, shrunken opportunities as businesses close or contract, some 70 percent now living with their parents, marriages delayed, raised in a polarized secular society hostile to religion and educated by an entrenched scientism that refuses to recognize the transcendent and has jettisoned the tales that would have given them the metaphors and images to live by. No wonder suicide, drugs, depression, and loneliness define so many of them today.

David Brooks, in a September 25, 2020 *New York Times* column, spelled out the consequences. After noting that in an ever-increasingly secular society we have more to fear from political dogmatism than religious dogmatism, and that people look to politics as a substitute for faith, he writes, "And we have most to fear from the possibility that the biblical metaphysic, which has been a coherent value system for believers and nonbelievers for centuries, will fade from our culture, the stories will go untold, and young people will grow up in a society without any coherent moral ecology at all."[7] Some have criticized Brooks' reference to society's loss through the fading of the biblical metaphysic, noting that the biblical metaphysic, as we have seen in previous chapters, has historically often blessed intolerance, prejudice, and suppression, but I think his concern stands. Whatever their failures, the biblical stories of fidelity, forgiveness, and the unity of humankind provide a vision of what can be.

STORYTHINK

Back to our text. The fact is, we moderns have trouble with the Bible because, in general, we have lost the taste for, perhaps even the ability to, think in stories. When it comes to the Bible, we seem to think we have only two choices: skepticism or fundamentalism, facts or truth. The figurative sense of story is foreign to us, and so we have relegated stories to the children's domain and have equated telling stories with telling lies. We have learned to distrust and disdain the imagination. It is not hard to figure why. Our whole educational system is in service to the practical needs of the corporations, the efficient, the predictable digital. This is why universities have shortsightedly dismantled the humanities and build science labs. Scientism is equated with truth, and the modern mindset is that only science is the path to it. Everything else is merely entertaining. "Real" knowledge is that which is observed, measured, and capable of being plugged into a database. Add to this the fact that today's students are raised on a diet of chatter, gossip, speed, demanding and competitive consumerism, constant action, and social media, all of which collectively absorb their attention, subvert their own imaginations, and undermine their ability to embrace silence and thoughtfulness.

---

7   David Brooks, "How Faith Shapes My Politics," *The New York Times*, September 25, 2020, https://www.nytimes.com/2020/09/24/opinion/religion-politics.html.

The one-dimensional "objective" conviction of today is close to the insight of Ursula Le Guin, the author of the wonderful fantasy series *EarthSea*, who writes words that should be on the frontispiece of every Bible:

> The language of the unconscious—symbol and archetype. Though they use words, they work the way music does: they short-circuit verbal reasoning, and go straight to the thoughts that lie too deep to utter. They cannot be translated fully into the language of reason, but only a Logical Positivist, who also finds Beethoven's Ninth Symphony meaningless, would claim that they are therefore meaningless. They are profoundly meaningful, and usable—practical—in terms of ethics; of insight; of growth.[8]

Perhaps no one put what I'm trying to say better than the Mormon speaker and apologist Clifton Jolley. When he was challenged by religious reporters about the DNA test that showed that American Indians are not descendants of the Hebrew tribes, as held by Mormon doctrine, Jolley replied, "After we have been defeated and all our stories proven untrue, we will perhaps come to know the more important reason and the only question that ever is—not whether the stories are true, but whether we are true to our stories."[9] It's like the curator of a famous museum overhearing two ladies sharing snide remarks about a masterpiece. He accosted them, saying, "Ladies, you are not here to critique the paintings. They are here to critique you!" *There's* the key to Bible reading. These attitudes characterize most religions (and politics) and are the challenge.

Rabbi Harold Kushner spoke for all religions when he wrote in his book *To Life!* "Judaism is less about believing and more about

---

8   Ursula K. Le Guin, *The Language of the Night: Essays on Fantasy and Science Fiction* (New York: G.P. Putnam's Sons, 1979), 62.

9   Valerie Weaver-Zercher, "After Faith," *The Christian Century*, September 7, 2009, https://www.christiancentury.org/reviews/2009-09/after-faith.

belonging."[10] He may be right, for he and all the others I have mentioned have chosen myth over reason, stories over doctrine. The biblical stories are enough to justify the Bible on its own terms, for they are stories about life and death, conquest and victory, humanity and God. It fits in nicely with my contention that the Bible is the Word *of* humans *about* God.

The stories are memorable and they give us a glimpse of what God is like. With that, let's take a look at just two characteristics of story.

STORY CHARACTERISTICS

First, antiquity is always revered. That's why, to digress a bit, the Roman Empire allowed the Jews to not worship the emperor—because they and their stories were very, very old. Indeed, some of the biblical stories are very old—dating back long, long before any of the writers lived. The song of Deborah in Exodus 15, for example, might go back to 1200 BCE. Some stories get patched together from different eras. The stories, of course, had purpose: encouragement, identity, inspiration, persecution, defection, healing.

Since the stories were about people whose relationship to God ebbs and flows, they are center stage, but did you ever notice this trivial point? There are precious few descriptions of those people, a factor so dear to our celebrity culture. Were they handsome and beautiful, or homely and ugly? How tall or short were they, where did they live, what did they eat, what did they wear? Outside of the description that Saul was tall or Absalom had long hair, Esther was beautiful or Zacchaeus was short—because these attributes were critical to their stories—there are no descriptions of anyone in the Bible, including Jesus. Again, the emphasis is on people: men, women, kings, servants, prophets, fools, magicians, warriors, slaves, farmers, fishermen, and how they each related to God. Fortunately, however, they talked a lot, and their talk is at the heart of the stories.

---

10   Harold S. Kushner, *To Life! A Celebration of Jewish Being and Thinking* (New York: Warner, 1993), 14.

THE ONE THAT GOT AWAY

Second, stories, by nature, expand. Check out this (pre-politically correct) comedy routine. The Braggart begins:

"There I was, surrounded by ten thousand hostile Indians!"

"How many?"

"Well, maybe five thousand."

"How many?"

"Well, there I was, surrounded by five hundred hostile Indians!"

"How many?"

"Well, maybe 75."

"How many?"

"Well, maybe 30."

"How many?'

"Well, I said to one old squaw . . . ."

Stories always expand for dramatic effect and the biblical ones are no exception. Here is a quotation from scripture scholar Margaret Ralph. She's explaining the incident of Moses and his rod that drove back the Rea Sea—or was it the wind?

> A modern reader might well ask, "Well, which was it? Was this a natural event, a wind, or a supernatural event, Moses and his rod?" The question ignores the intention of the authors. The distinction between natural and supernatural is irrelevant. In both accounts we are dealing with an event in which God's presence was experienced. The difference between the methods through which God acted—through wind or through the more dramatic and marvelous action in which Moses raised his rod—illustrates the exaggeration that is characteristic of legend. In

the later version the author has embellished the story by using exaggeration to make Moses' role more dramatic.

Remember that the legends were told and retold not merely to recall the past but to affect a present audience. To embellish a legend with marvelous details is to make it all the more interesting and inspiring to the next generation. In most legends exaggeration is used to build up a human hero. In these legends, however, the religious purpose of the author is always present. It is not really Moses, but God acting through Moses, who is being glorified. The author wished to inspire his audience with the marvelous nature of God's intervention in the history of God's people. Their God is a God who saves.[11]

(The skeptic is right to observe that this interpretation can apply to the Qur'an, the Book of Mormon, or any other claimant to divine revelation, but it makes its point here.)
Jack Miles expresses the same thought:

No responsible historian believes that at the time of the Exodus the Israelites actually outnumbered the Egyptians or that a company of 4 or 5 million people made its way through the desert and into Canaan. Despite the lack of any historical record outside the Bible, most historians do not believe that the story of the Exodus is a total fabrication. But were it an event of the size the Bible reports the likelihood of its leaving no record outside the Bible would be small. For the literary effect of the Book of Exodus to be what its authors intended, however, it is essential that readers imagine the numbers that the text reports rather than the ones the historians may, on other evidence, have good reason to believe. Historians of England have good reasons to believe that Richard III was not the monster Shakespeare made him out to be in the play that bears his name. Nonetheless, if the play is to work as Shakespeare intended, the villain must be allowed to be a villain. The same, analogously, goes for the Book of Exodus. Cecil B. DeMille's

---

11 Margaret Nutting Ralph, *And God Said What? An Introduction to Biblical Literary Forms* (Mahwah, NJ: Paulist, 2003).

"The Ten Commandments," with its mighty throng crossing the sea, may be more true to the intended literary effect of the Book of Exodus than scholarship's reconstruction of a band of minor tribes slipping through the marsh.[12]

That's story for you.

FINAL THOUGHTS

Stories say something to the faithful. They speak to them at a deep and numinous level. Stories, as Richard Holloway puts it, have

> the truth of art, not the truth of science. Science is interested in facts, the way things work. Art is interested in revealing to us the truth of our own lives. That's why a story can make you cry out in recognition: that's me! Religion is an art, not a science. So the question to ask of a creation story is not whether it is true or false, but what it means, what it's trying to tell us—a distinction many religious people never get hold of.[13]

As the old saying goes, stories are the fiction that tells the truth. So, whatever problems scholars have with the birth stories of Jesus or the Passion narratives, they are incidental to the message, to the genius of the constructed story that pursues meaning, not facts.

Take the perennial attraction of the expectation of Christ's Second Coming. I repeat that it is a matter of record that St. Paul and the early Christians fervently believed it would be soon, very soon— except that Jesus didn't come back, even though, throughout the ages, with great regularity, it has been predicted, with convinced certainty and to the disappointment of the Rapture folks—which never deters them from trying again. This delay has become one of the Bible's most awkward embarrassments: the fact that, after two thousand years of waiting and watching, Christ *still* hasn't arrived. Nevertheless, we

---

12   Miles, *God*, 104.
13   Holloway, *Little History of Religion*, 91.

go on rehearsing it each Advent, and each time we recite the Creed, because, in an ever-present world of terrible things—abuses of power, drug addictions, global implosions, terrorism, and the like—the story of a Second Coming speaks to the twin desires of the human heart for release from earthly horrors and for a justice that promises to level the field. As long as hope endures, so will stories in the face of disaster.

We must remember that the visionaries and the sacred books they wrote or inspired are ultimately wrestling with the age-old questions that bedevil us up to this day: Where did the universe come from? Why isn't there nothing? Is there somebody "out there" who made it? Why do we suffer? Why is life so unfair? Is there life after death? Is there more here than meets the eye? These questions are why we are drawn to special people who claim they have pulled back the curtain, so to speak, and glimpsed a new reality. They have been encountered, spoken to, and given the mandate to share the message. So, they tell the story which their followers eventually memorize and ultimately write down to produce a sacred book—the Bible, the Qur'an, the Book of Mormon—and religion is born. The stories attract and are told, parsed, and expanded, over and over again, until they become sacred and then canonized as the very word of God, never to be added to or subtracted from.

What soon gets forgotten is that the stories—creation stories, royalty stories, prophetic stories, apocalyptic stories—are just that: stories culled from the prevailing cultures and tweaked to fit into the plot of the original revelation. They are not science. They are not literal. They are powerful metaphors that wrestle with the eternal questions and great harm has come from a literal reading of these stories that are grounded in a different age, culture, and imagination.

Stories of God among us; dying and rising Saviors; a deity who favors the disadvantaged, poor, and rejected; who works miracles as a sign of another world, another power; the one who lifts up the lowly, sees beyond appearances, reclaims sinners, reverses expectations, and promises paradise—such stories are solace, fonts of hope, and patterns of inspiration and imitation. Once we unlock the mindsets of the authors who wrote and rewrote these stories, we can appreciate them as such. At their best, they are embraced to free. At their worst, they are manipulated to control. At their best, they are open-ended and liberating. At their worst, they are literalized and suffocating. At their best, they are in service to the people. At their worst, they are in service to the controllers of the stories, who claim to know what they mean.

Sidebar

Another fantasy: I know it's breaking tradition and will never happen, but, for what it's worth, I wish we could declare a moratorium for a while and replace the usual liturgical introduction, "A reading of the holy gospel according to Matthew" with "The *story* of Jesus Christ according to Matthew" or, better still, "The Story of Jesus Christ as told by Matthew." In the long run, it would help the people see, with sufficient catechesis, that the gospels follow the usual formulas of such ancients as Thucydides, Lucretius, and Suetonius, and so they need not try to harmonize the four gospels, but take them on their own merits and within the biographical canons of the times. It would save of a lot of verbal summersaults.

Chapter 14

A DIGRESSION

> All sorrows can be borne if you put them into a story or tell a story about them.
>
> —*Isak Dinesen*

> Catholicism is a religion not of hard mechanical rules but of stories and paradoxes and enigmatic parables. It is an invitation to mystery, not mastery, to communion, not control.
>
> —*Philip Klay*

As the title suggests, this digression, this excursus, is an idiosyncratic afterthought that may be skipped. It looks like a stray from another book, but if you want to indulge me, continue reading on as I fantasize a bit by stating that if I knew enough about the Bible (I don't), and in the extreme unlikelihood I were ever to teach a course on it, I would not start out with timelines and charts or anything that directly has to do with the Bible. I would spend the first semester on the arts—especially, as we shall see, the movies. With today's dangerous overemphasis on science and the STEM curriculums, with the elimination of the classics in our universities and the mass production of left-brain workers, few would be able to approach the mythologies of the Bible with understanding—not to mention life itself.

THE BIBLE: THE WORD *OF* GOD OR THE WORD *ABOUT* GOD?

I cringed when I learned that, when he was governor of Wisconsin, Scott Walker proposed removing the mottos "search for truth" and "improve the human condition" from the mission statement of the state university system and replacing them with "meet the state's workforce needs." Good grief! My students would need a pre-education. So, we would study poetry, fiction, art, and, again, mostly movies and movie directors: something my putative students could relate to. We would spend time on the art of making movies and all the intricacies of costume, casting, lighting, music, camera angles—all the manipulations, realistic or imagined, overt or subliminal, that help tell a whopping good story. We would speculate on how John Ford, David Lean, Alfred Hitchcock, Ridley Scott, Preston Sturges, Stanley Kubrick, or Sidney Lumet would handle the same story. (How did Matthew, Mark, Luke, and John do it?)

We will take note in the next chapter the powerful impact of the movie score and how it clues us in on how to emote and perceive. We know almost immediately, from the opening music, what kind of movie we're about to see: comedy, farce, tragedy, science fiction, fantasy, and so on. Now, let's read the words of the movie storyteller—namely, the director. Here, for example, is Sidney Lumet, who directed such well-regarded films as *12 Angry Men, Long Day's Journey into Night, The Pawnbroker, Serpico, Murder on the Orient Express, Network,* and others. He wrote a book called, not unsurprisingly, *Making Movies,* which ought to be required reading for any scripture course.

> What is this movie about?... What is the theme of the movie, the spine, the arch [the core tradition]? The theme will decide the specifics of every selection made... will determine how it will look, how it will be edited, how it will be musically scored.... First, comes an examination of each scene in sequence, of course. Does this scene contribute to the overall theme? How does it contribute to the storyline? To character?... Is the story being moved forward by the characters?[1]

---

1   Sidney Lumet, *Making Movies* (New York: Vintage, 1995), 10.

As an example, let me interject a scene from Alfred Hitchcock's *North by Northwest*. Recall the famous scene in which Cary Grant is alone in the Kansas plains. Suddenly, a double-wing duster plane comes out of nowhere to strafe him with bullets. Storyteller Hitchcock wanted to pursue his favorite theme: No matter where you are, no matter how safe you think you are, no matter if you're in the middle of nowhere, evil will get you! To convey this truth, Hitchcock turned off the soundtrack completely and simply panned the camera slowly in all four directions, showing nothing but miles and miles of empty land and sheer silence. All is utter, eerie stillness—until evil roars in.

EVANGELISTS IN THE DIRECTOR'S CHAIR

Movie making is a good analogy for what faced, say, the evangelists—the four sacred movie directors, if you will: Matthew, Mark, Luke, and John. What is the Jesus story about? What does it mean? How will that meaning determine the style? How will it be cast? It's all in the realm of storytelling: art, music, movies. That's the parallel.

By way of illustration, let's take a quick dip into the storytelling art (core tradition + creative details) in reference to Jesus' passion, the oldest core tradition written down. There is, for example, John's use of the "split screen." He does this all the time: The woman at the well is on one screen, telling her townsfolk about the man she met who told her life story, while, at the same time, on the other screen, Jesus speaks to his disciples. In another scene, Jesus is professing his faith before Pilate on one screen while, simultaneously, Peter is denying his on another. It is John who tells us, as Judas leaves to betray Jesus, "Now it was night." Did he mean night in the sense that the day is over or night in the sense that Judas' heart was black with a dastardly deed aborning?

Or consider the Garden of Gethsemane's carefully crafted "camera" choreography: the use of the mystical three. In this dramatic scene, Jesus moves in three stages. One, he is separated from the main body of his disciples. Two, he is separated from the three he took with him (Peter, James, and John). Three, he now goes alone to face death. This detailed, three-step movement dramatizes the core truth: Jesus' utter aloneness and abandonment. Then he goes back *three times* to his disciples, which illustrates how he can find no assistance from them. Notice the creative technique of three-ness: rejected three times! Moving in three stages toward a lonely death. What a scene sequence and how memorable!

The pattern of three is well-established, even in our own time. So many of our jokes and stories have threes. There is always a Franciscan, a Dominican, and a Jesuit. There is always an Italian, a Pole, and a Jew. Two is not enough to establish tension and four is too many and too complicated. Three is just right for dramatic purposes. Think of Glinda and Dorothy: click your heels—3 times!

So, in the passion narratives: three disciples, three times Jesus goes back. In Mark, the disciples fall asleep three times, Peter denies three times, Peter professes three times, Pilate declares Jesus innocent three times, Mark describes three hours—the third, sixth, and ninth hours—as a frame for his crucifixion narrative. These are powerful storytelling techniques. Even in our pious and devotional tradition, when we come to the stations of the cross, we have here things not in scripture. We have Jesus falling—how many times? Three!

How about this? Why did Jesus take Peter, James, and John with him into the Garden of Gethsemane? "He took with him Peter, James, and John and began to be distressed and agitated. And he said to them, 'I am deeply grieved even to death: remain here and keep awake'" (Mark 14:33–34). He chose Peter, James, and John because they are the only ones who said they would not fail! Peter promised, while James and John asked for places on Jesus' right and left and proclaimed that they could and would drink of his chalice. These unsettling details use the passion story to warn those whose words are stronger than their action.

To summarize: A story is verbal art. Like art, there is more than meets the eye (or ear). It's more than a simple tale. Story tells you more, on a deeper level than what the surface words imply. Stories should not be read (or heard) literally, but symbolically. (Even straightforward, literal, dry, official, "scientific," "objective" prose betrays an attitude, mindset, mentality, and philosophy of life.) And no matter how wild stories are, we must respect the fact that, somewhere behind the exorbitant language and fantastic imagery, there's some truth trying to be told, some people trying to be formed by what is being told.

This principle may also give us a handle on those terribly sadistic passages where Yahweh orders genocide and mass murder. Such words were not spoken by God, but were put there by the storyteller-writer to make a point he thought was important and which he expressed in the only cultural way he knew how. It will also help if you recall that scripture in those days was not something to be read (due to mass illiteracy), but performed.

The point behind such scriptural stories is that God is indeed sovereign, that God has a plan, that God has a will and desire to befriend Israel and, through it, the whole human race—and that nothing must get in the way of Yahweh's inexorable love. That thought is expressed by a primitive people through stories of violence which reflect the relentless drive to see that Yahweh's yearnings—"You are my people, I am your God"—will be, must be, fulfilled. So, putting women and children to the sword and dashing babies' heads against rocks is the culturally primitive storytellers' version of "Thy will be done." It's horribly gruesome and crude by our standards, but, still, within the bounds of story canons that include a melting wicked witch, a giant smashing to earth by the ax of an enterprising lad, and a wolf brutally beheaded who would have swallowed up the promise and fulfillment of a young girl.

Chapter 15

PRIVILEGED BUT NOT UNIQUE

> Stories are to society what dreams are to individuals. Without them, we go mad.
>
> —*Isabel Allende*

Whether you skipped the last chapter or not, and while I am uncharacteristically giving three cheers on behalf of the Bible as it is (it won't last), allow me to come at biblical storytelling another way, because I believe it to be so essential. To wit: A man walks into a restaurant with a full-grown ostrich behind him. As he sits, the waitress comes over and asks for their orders. The man says, "I'll have a hamburger, fries, and a coke," and turns to the ostrich, asking, "What's yours?" "I'll have the same," says the ostrich. A short time later, the waitress returns with the order. "That will be $6.40 please," she says, and the man reaches into his pocket and pulls out the exact change for payment.

The next day, the man and the ostrich come again and the man says, "I'll have a hamburger, fries, and a coke," and the ostrich says, "I'll have the same." Once again, the man reaches into his pocket and pays with exact change. This becomes a routine until, late one evening, the two enter again. "The usual?" asks the waitress. "No, this is Friday night, so I will have a steak, baked potato, and salad," says the man. "Same for me," says the ostrich. A short time later, the waitress comes with the order and says, "That will be $12.62." Once again, the man pulls exact change out of his pocket and places it on the table.

The waitress can't hold back her curiosity any longer. "Excuse me, sir. How do you manage to always come up with the exact change out of your pocket every time?" "Well," says the man, "several years ago I was cleaning the attic and I found an old lamp. When I rubbed it, a genie appeared and offered me two wishes. My first wish was that if I ever had to pay for anything, I would just put my hand in my pocket and the right amount of money would always be there." "That's brilliant!" says the waitress. "Most people would wish for a million dollars or something, but you'll always be as rich as you want for as long as you live!"

"That's right," replied the man. "Whether it's a gallon of milk or a Rolls Royce, the exact money is always there." The waitress then asks, "One other thing, sir. What's with the ostrich?" The man sighs, pauses, and answers, "My second wish was for a tall chick with long legs who agrees with everything I say."

EXEGESIS

That's a funny joke. We accept it on its own terms and let out a guffaw. But I'm going to do something that one should never, ever do with a joke: analyze it. To analyze a joke is to kill it but, in the interest of this chapter, allow me to commit some literary homicide. There are some things going on here, so subtle that we do not perceive them.

Notice, for example, how we suspended our judgment. You have an ostrich walking into a restaurant, for one thing. And the bird talks, for another. If you're telling the joke and, when you come to the part where the ostrich says, "I'll have the same," someone interrupts you and says, "Wait a minute! Hold it! Ostriches don't talk," and proceeds to make a big fuss over the point, you would probably strangle the clod and no jury would convict you. He's missed the point. (Snakes don't talk either, but one does in the Bible's very first book.)

Such a protestor is what we call a fundamentalist, and fundamentalists come in both Protestant and Catholic versions. Strictly speaking, the man's right, of course. Ostriches don't talk. We all know that, but the average person takes the joke-story on its own terms to learn what it has to say, even if it goes against normal logic and knowledge.

Something else is going on besides logic. We let the illogical slide in the interest of the punch line. Besides the sheer fun of the joke, you can even get serious (which you shouldn't do) and draw a moral lesson from it, a "truth dressed in story" kind of thing. For example, "Be careful what you wish for." So, again, take the story or the type of biblical book (genre) on its own terms, whether it's poetry, fiction, theological history, biography, etc. Don't stumble over the illogic, as we see it, from a two- or three-thousand-year perspective or a three-hundred-year scientific mindset. The acid criticisms of the Four Horsemen of New Atheism fail precisely from their lack of appreciation for genre, the subliminal mind categories that surreptitiously move us between the left and right brain hemispheres, which help us to distinguish truth, where and how it is embedded.

WHILE WE'RE ON A ROLL

Let's add some more intriguing examples from our own lives. As we walk into the United States Capitol building, we look up to the great classic dome. There, high above our heads, is a painting of George Washington, dressed in a Greek toga, looking for all the world like some Greek god on the clouds of Mt. Olympus. In fact, the painting is called the "Apotheosis of George Washington." The dictionary defines apotheosis as the elevation of a person to the rank of a god or the idealization of a human being. That is what happened to George Washington. He becomes no longer a mere fallible man who happened to be the first president of the United States. Rather, he is depicted here as founding father, more than human, idealized with overtones of divinity, riding on the clouds.

It's a famous painting like many Renaissance paintings of "Mary, Mother of God" fame. Robed in splendid silk brocade, she sits serenely in front of an Italian villa with fat little cherubs hovering around her,

Joseph, and little John the Baptist, each haloed with bright rings around their heads. Mary was not Italian. (Sorry to burst your bubble.) She never wore silk and brocade, nor lounged in an Italian villa with her prayer book at her side. There were no angels floating around, much less fat ones with shortened wings that would never get them airborne anyway. And if she, Joseph, and John wore bright halos, everyone would have had to shade their eyes when they met them— nor would you want them sitting in front of you at a movie. And the prayer book was only a symbol because Mary, like all the young girls of her time and place, could not read or write.

The artist who painted the picture knew all that. The painting is false in terms of factuality, but true in conveying a truth: To the artist and all the ancients, what he painted are symbols, metaphors, and allusions that say that an "Italian" Mary is a woman for all peoples, times, and seasons; that she is royalty where it counts most: before God. The halos are indications of the inner brightness of grace and the prayer book that she couldn't read is a symbol of her prayerfulness.

Speaking of angels, how *does* one paint an invisible spirit? One makes him or her visible. Give them wings like the god Mercury, since they are messengers between heaven and earth. They are sometimes strumming harps because music is the nearest thing to ecstasy we have. Saints wear crowns of gold since gold is the one metal that does not rust, signifying eternity. If you go visit a cemetery, you'll learn more about who's there if you can decode the symbols. Anchors, for example, mean hope; an anvil symbolizes martyrdom; a bugle, the military; a shattered urn, someone old; steps, a sign of one's ascent into heaven; and so on.

I have in mind another painting, which shows St. Jerome in his medieval study. The Bible is there because he wrote it (translated it). So is a resting lion. St. Jerome himself is dressed in a Cardinal's distinctive garb. The lion is a reference to a legend of how Jerome tamed a lion. The study is far from the cave in which Jerome lived while translating the Bible into Latin. The cardinal's robes he's wearing are an anachronism, since he lived in the sixth century and cardinals were invented in the twelfth century. Historical accuracy was not the artist's intent, and no one took it as such. The artist was simply portraying the saint as a cultured gentleman worthy of church distinction.

The point is that art has its own logic and one must know what to look for when contemplating it. If you know the code, the symbols, it tells you much and is quite intriguing, if not moving. To pick up the Bible is to enter a world of verbal art and be challenged. You need to bring the tools of art with you. For some atheists to criticize the Bible on literal grounds is like ridiculing the artist who paints angels. So, you see, I can make a good case for reading the Bible as story rather than as history.

MUSIC IN THE AIR

Let me offer another popular analogy while I'm at it. Take the movie music I referenced in the last chapter. Its genius is to go unnoticed, enhance the action, evoke an emotion, create an atmosphere, or prompt the audience in how to set its receptivity agenda. Intellectually, we have so conditioned our minds that we don't even attend to the subliminal music. We never ask ourselves, as the killer stalks the victim and the menacing music revs up from nowhere, where the music is coming from. Just like we do when someone starts a joke with a talking animal. We know dogs don't talk, but we switch genres and take the story on its own merits.

So it is with movie music. We hear it, but there's no orchestra in sight, not an instrument to be seen. Nobody says it's a fraud. Nobody questions it. We know that, in some studio somewhere, the musicians are watching the movie and adding a soundtrack. Nobody complains. In fact, nobody even notices, but the effect of background music is profound and essential to the movie. In *Casablanca*, there was no sixty-piece orchestra in the hangar or on the field as Rick and Elsa parted, but the music was meant to be a mood enhancer, a metaphor of the movement of sacrificial love.

Here's an insightful paragraph from Margaret Visser's wonderful book *The Geometry of Love*, in which she explores the hidden symbols of a church:

I set out to do the same thing now with a church: take one particular example and see what I could find out about it. Casting my net as widely as possible in order to explain it to myself, I resolved to look at history and politics, theology, anthropology, art history and technology, iconography, hagiography, and folklore; I would find out about the community of people who used the building. I would discover the meanings of symbols, consider the manner in which this building expresses temporal concepts by means of space, track down if I could both the historical background and the living connotations of each artifact. If there was a statue of a woman in a voluminous pleated garment holding her heart in one hand and a staff in the other, I would find out who she was and what she had done, what her disembodied heart was doing in her hand, why she was wearing those clothes and carrying that staff, and for what reason she came to be represented in that particular church. I would be interested in art, of course, and in the history of beautiful objects (if any) in the church I chose—but I would also want to know what that art was depicting, what it was trying to say.[1]

THE STORIES UNVEILED

Picking up the Bible is like that: What is it depicting in its stories? What is it trying to say? Why was there thunder and lightning on Mt. Sinai? Is the story of King Herod's killing of the Bethlehem babies true—there is no record of it—or an echo of another king (the Pharaoh) killing the Hebrew babies at the time of Moses? Why did Jesus take these particular three apostles into the Garden of Olives (the only ones who bragged they would never leave him)? Why did Jesus give the Beatitudes on the mountain in Matthew's version but down on the plain in Luke's? Why is Veronica not in the Gospels, but in popular lore? What are these things trying to say? The Bible is like that. It is trying to say something, but doesn't say it like we would wish: in

---

1   Margaret Visser, *The Geometry of Love: Space, Time, Mystery, and Meaning in an Ordinary Church* (New York: North Point, 2000), 2.

direct, objective discourse. No, it says it in stories that are often illogical, contradictory, inconsistent, and enormously unscientific. Still, it's filled with clues that hint at something deeper that the ancients read with ease and we with puzzlement—until we find the key.

Let's add two quotations to nail it down. The first is from Phil Christman. He writes that while we do appreciate the insights and wisdom of ancient writings like, for example, the Epic of Gilgamesh, Canaanite poetry, and other sources that the Bible often tapped, "the Bible brings a degree of attention to human interiority, and to the feelings of ordinary people, that distinguishes it from every surviving text of comparable antiquity."[2]

The second comes from that elegant writer Frederick Buechner and is helpful if you want to turn back and re-read the Matthew section in chapter 4.

> Let us assume that if we had been there that night when he was born we would have seen nothing untoward at all. Let us assume that the darkness would have looked very much like any darkness. Maybe there were a few stars, the same old stars, or the moon. . . .
>
> Maybe that is all we would have seen if we had been there because maybe that or something like that was all that really happened. . . . So a great many biblical scholars would agree with the skeptics that the great nativity stories of Luke and Matthew are simply the legendary accretions, the poetry, of a later generation, and that were we to have been present, we would have seen a birth no more or less marvelous than any other birth.
>
> But if that is the case, what do we do with the legends of the wise men and the star, the shepherds and the angels and the great hymn of joy that the angels sang? Do we dismiss them as fairy tales, the subject for pageants to sentimentalize over once a year come Christmas, the lovely dream that never came true? . . .

---

2   Phil Christman, "Poetry and Prophecy, Dust and Ashes: A Review of *The Hebrew Bible: A Translation with Commentary*, by Robert Alter," *Plough*, September 1, 2019, https://www.plough.com/en/topics/culture/literature/poetry-and-prophecy-dust-and-ashes.

> Who knows what the facts of Jesus' birth actually were? As for myself, the longer I live, the more inclined I am to believe in miracle, the more I suspect that if we had been there at the birth, we might well have seen and heard things that would be hard to reconcile with modern science. But of course that is not the point, because the Gospel writers are not really interested primarily in the facts of the birth but in the significance.... Whether there were ten million angels there or just the woman herself and her husband, when that child was born the whole course of history was changed....
>
> This is what Matthew and Luke were trying to say in the stories about how he was born, and this is the truth that no language seemed too miraculous to them to convey. This is the only truth that matters, and the wise men, the shepherds, the star are important only as ways of pointing to this truth.[3]

This lovely quotation is a primer on how to sidestep the literalism of the Bible—something not pleasing to fundamentalists, fodder for those waiting to discredit the Bible, a pause for agnostics, and an insight for believers. After all, as I have tried to show, there is more to a human being than sheer rationality. We're a complicated lot, a mix of reason and unreason, thought and emotion, mind and body, mythos and logos.

BUT WAIT...!

As the obnoxious advertisers, after promising you the world, add "But, wait! We'll throw in free shipping, three more towels, six knives, a Toyota, and the state of Vermont for free!" so, too, fence-sitter that I am, I still can't end these last three chapters without a challenging word.

Yes, you knew it wouldn't last long, so let me revert to a critical state of mind. It is this. Agreed: approaching the Bible from the point

---

[3] Frederick Buechner, *The Hungering Dark* (New York: Seabury, 1969), 52–54.

of view of storytelling, with all its metaphors and literary "lies that tell the truth," has been helpful. It has freed the Bible from a constricting literalism and given us an entrance into wisdom and the graciousness of a God who loves us. Every page of its seventy-two books carries the breath of God and the inspiration of his Spirit. Compositely, the Bible is the word of God.

Nevertheless, the old doubts keep surfacing. The Bible stories may indeed be privileged, but they are not alone in their story power. Literary critic Terry Eagleton offers these words:

> Fiction does not primarily mean a piece of writing which is not true. Truman Capote's *In Cold Blood*, Norman Mailer's *The Executioner's Song* and Frank McCourt's *Angela's Ashes* are all offered to us as true, yet they translate the truths they convey into a kind of imaginative fiction. Works of fiction can be full of factual information. You could even run a farm on the basis of what Virgil's *Georgics* has to say about agriculture, though it is doubtful that it would survive for very long. Yet texts we call literary are not written primarily to give us facts. Instead, the reader is invited to "imagine" those facts, in the sense of constructing an imaginary world out of them. A work can thus be true and imagined, factual and fictional, at the same time.... There is a difference between being true to the facts and being true to life.[4]

So, other fictions also tell the truth. Take, for example, the Grimm's fairy tales. They turn out to be profoundly religious tales from the pens of deeply religious brothers, devoted to their Calvinistic Reformed faith tradition, who drew on tales and traditions that ranged from ancient Egypt and Greece to medieval France. Wilhelm Grimm, in fact, was quite a mystic and an ecumenist who saw much value in pagan religions, in so far as they reflected the Christian faith. He took the pagan tales and "baptized" them: water crossings that symbolized baptism, Christ in the form of noble princes, helpful doves that

---

4   Terry Eagleton, *How to Read Literature* (New Haven, CT: Yale University Press, 2013), 121.

evoke the Holy Spirit, the Hansel and Gretel story being reworked by the Grimms into a classic parable of the journey of the human soul from infancy to spiritual awareness of right and wrong, the journey of human salvation.

In *Little Red Riding Hood,* the three oak trees visible from Grandmother's house bind into one image of the Christian Trinity. *Cinderella* depends for its power upon the idea of the communion of saints, in which the heroine, her deceased mother, and the doves unite in love and charity. Snow White comes back to life through the agency of a prince, Christ in camouflage. *Sleeping Beauty* contains both the harrowing of hell and the resurrection as the Christ-Prince breaks through the thorn barrier that surrounds the enchanted castle and his kiss gives life.

How about the fictional works of Dante, Shakespeare, Dostoevsky, Jane Austin, Charles Dickens, John Cheever, Graham Greene, Flannery O'Connor, Edith Wharton, J.K. Rawlings, J.R.R. Tolkien, Emily Bronte, and others? They too write the "lie that tells the truth." Robert Alter reminds us that one of the byproducts of our digital and scientism age is that we have lost our skills for reading the Bible because we have lost the ability to see through the images and ask the right questions. This applies to all fiction and art. The Bible doesn't have a monopoly on "lies that tell the truth."

THOSE STICKY POINTS

In reality, that "of" God still sticks in the craw and "about" God becomes more compelling. The truth is that the biblical stories, with their use of allegories and prophecy, their hidden agendas, are often so freewheeling, so arbitrary, so partisan that even if they tell the truth, it is "their" truth and commentators will parse it, depending on what perspective they're coming from. The truth is that nobody reads all seventy-two books equally. Nobody, even fundamentalist Christians, reads all those purity laws, much less follows them. The various biblical codes of conduct are wholly impractical and irrelevant, and few, outside of some strict Jews, even attempt to keep them.

These laws are comprehensive and minute and it's not always clear as to their reasons. To rehash: Moses could not possibly have written all those laws. For one thing, there are several collections scattered here and there; we call them the Priestly Code, the Holiness Code, the Deuteronomic Code, the Covenant Code, etc. They often repeat the very same materials. Why would they do that if they came from the hand of one author? The laws also sometimes contradict one another. For example, the burnt offering altar in one place must be made of earth and in another place of wood overlaid with gold. Remember that rule where, in one place, one must boil the Passover meat, but in another it must be not be boiled, but roasted (Exodus 12:8–9)?

Nor do the laws always make sense. Why, for example, may the Israelites eat sheep but not pigs? The purity laws seem to have more to do with taboos than with common sense. And they were often harsh: Rebellious sons must be stoned by the community (Deuteronomy 21:18–21, Exodus 21:17, Leviticus 20:9), a young woman who loses her virginity before marriage must be stoned (Deuteronomy 22:20–21), adulterous couples are to be stoned (Deuteronomy 22:22, Leviticus 20:10), and a father has absolute authority over his children and can even sell them as slaves (Exodus 21:7–11). Whether these penalties were actually applied or served as mere scare tactics to protect what were basically commercial marriage alliances, nevertheless, they are in the Bible. They are presented as direct divine commands and so, for us, divinely, eternally inspired. Still, today, we dismiss them entirely. These "words of God" are outdated and obsolete. We do pick and choose.

As already mentioned in chapter 1, evidence that the Mosaic laws were neither unique, nor from Moses' hand, came at the beginning of the twentieth century when archaeologists found other older and similar collections: for example, the codes of Lipit-Ishtar, the Hittites, and especially the Babylonian law code of Hammurabi, dated centuries before the Exodus collection. We should note that, as in the Bible, the Mesopotamian gods had similarly authorized Hammurabi to make laws. These laws had striking similarities to the Exodus list, to the point that some laws and their wording were identical. The collection of cases found in Exodus chapters 21 and 22 are derived from already existing Canaanite laws. Other materials are much later additions from outside sources. The idea of all these later additions was, of course, to imprint the aura and authority of Moses on them, much like later anonymous Christian writers would write epistles and attribute them to St. Paul. All of this obviously hands the notion of Mosaic authorship a setback.

In any case, the God who gave these laws is highly reminiscent of the God of Genesis in his compulsive demand for order. Just as Yahweh brought order out of chaos in creation, so, with exact blueprints, he brings order to the sacred space of worship in the desert. Most ritual laws, according to Jacob Neusner, are derived from the Jewish compulsion to link divinity with an imposition of order over chaos that began at creation. In other words, keeping separated what God intended to be separate—earth/sky, rain, desert, etc.—joins one with God in maintaining creation.

In any case, to put it bluntly, much of the Mosaic Law is obsolete and everyone feels perfectly at ease in dismissing this divinely inspired "word of God." Look, we know that the biblical authors did take the old sacred, oral legends and folklore common to the Near East and weave them into stories to suit their purposes. Such was their reverence that they were even hesitant, as we saw, to dismiss any revered source in their own tradition, including contradictory stories and conflicting plots. All was grist for the grand narrative of their interpretative affair with Yahweh, but—and here is the rub—we are quite aware that the sacred authors, by nature of being "sacred," had agendas. That's why they were writing in the first place. We saw that. They were not neutral, and we need not be surprised at that. We expect that, but their partisanship often led them, in telling and reimaging their mythical stories, to distort facts, sour attitudes, promote prejudice, invite revenge, demonize enemies, and leave us a legacy justifying terrible injustice and cruelty. One biblical scholar offers pertinent comments that we should read very carefully:

> Every historical narrative is composed of two basic dimensions: details of the events and a viewpoint from which those details are delivered. In the case of a Bible story, our right to survey the

details of the event, to listen to whom we wish to listen, to see what we wish to see has been usurped. The storyteller acting through the narrator in the story makes those decisions for us. Those decisions are not made thoughtlessly but strategically in a bid to influence our adoption of a specific, ideological point of view. If we follow the lead of the narrator, we do not get to cheer for Goliath, even though we may have been able to find some things in his real life to celebrate. Ultimately, we are not permitted to side with King Saul. Rather we are cajoled into celebrating the rise of David at the expense of both Goliath and Saul. The narrator is leading us to adopt this point of view.

In contrast to what some may call "fair and honest reporting," the narrator typically directs the camera and the microphone so that the reader meets only those actions and words that ultimately reinforce the intended perspective of the narrator. Thus the goal of the divine storyteller is not merely to inform about the past but to transform the future by impacting the reader's values and attitudes. It is the "re-presentation of past events for the purpose of instruction."[5]

This perspective is not easily dismissed and calls up David Brooks' observation concerning data. Data "is never raw; it's always structured according to somebody's predispositions and values. The end result looks disinterested, but, in reality, there are value choices all the way through, from construction to interpretation."[6]

These words apply to all written material, including the Bible, which is to say, concerning the Bible, no matter how you slice it, no matter how much more congenial the new interpretations are to the modern mind, all this is simply a soft way of saying that it is a matter of one's "value choices." Whether you accept them or not depends on the existence or depth of your faith. We shouldn't be surprised at this, any more than we would be in reading the official version of Russian

---

5   John Beck, *God as Storyteller: Seeking Meaning in Biblical Narrative* (St Louis: Chalice Press, 2008), 61.

6   David Brooks, "What Data Can't Do," *The New York Times,* February 19, 2013, https://www.nytimes.com/2013/02/19/opinion/brooks-what-data-cant-do.html.

history. The storyteller interprets events and bends them to his ideology "for the sake of instruction."

Even though we are told (on faith) that this is the work of a divine storyteller, his ideology has left, at times, a legacy of considerable mischief—the mischief of racism, xenophobia, sexism, superstition, and so on—and we're stuck with it since this is, after all, "the word of God." While some "metaphorical" parabolic biblical stories do leave a legacy of inspiration, challenge, comfort, and awe, others leave a bitter ideological aftertaste that, as religious history has amply shown, has spat out war, racism, witch hunts, colonialism, exploitation, and persecution. Even at best, modern interpreters leave us their faith convictions. Yes, as one scholar has said, the Bible is all "foreground," leaving subsequent authors to fill in the background—but often the background they filled in from their imaginations became foreground. Whatever the case, wherever we stand on the conservative-liberal line, consciously or unconsciously, we sort, edit, ignore, underscore, prove, and disprove according to our orthodoxy or heterodoxy.

Chapter 16

BEFRIENDING SCIENCE

> For far too long science and faith fell into the "sin of certainty" each claiming Truth only for themselves and ignoring the beautifully symbiotic relationship that exists between them.
> —Richard Rohr, OFM

> Theology cannot deny what is commonly taken as established scientific conclusions about reality and retain its credibility.
> —Roger Haight, SJ

Ok: back to our book, with a final thought about science and religion. Since the current antagonism remains between science and religion, let me end with a postscript on the subject. I have mentioned that one of the modern difficulties with faith in God or the Bible is science or scientism: the belief that science does or ultimately will explain all. "In proportion as science explains more and more, less and less is needed of God" is the accepted mantra, one enshrined in our educational institutions. As Charles Taylor put it,

> When a naturalistic materialism is not only on offer, but presents itself as the only view compatible with the most prestigious institution in the modem world, viz., science; it is quite

conceivable that one's doubts about one's own faith, about one's ability to be transformed, or one's sense of how one's own faith is indeed, childish and inadequate, could mesh with this powerful ideology, and send one off along the path of unbelief, even though with regret and nostalgia.[1]

The Four Horsemen of New Atheism, brilliant scientists, are committed to the notion of scientific reductionism, that science explains everything. Yet, as John Cornwell observes,

Reductionist Megalomania has been in retreat. Discoveries of new phenomena at successive levels in matter, living organisms and mind-brain relationships have led instead to a dynamic emergent, relational view of nature. There is a new emphasis on holism (reductionism's opposite); an appreciation of nature; complex combinations of structure and openness, law and chance, order and chaos, determinism and probabilities.[2]

Astronomer Martin Rees, in his book *Our Cosmic Habitat*, adds, "The preeminent mystery is why anything exists at all. What breathes life into the equations of physics, and actualizes them in a real cosmos? Such questions lie beyond science, however: they are the province of philosophers and theologians."[3]

So, it's time to end the war between science and religion, the "myths" of the Bible versus the facts of science. It's time to cancel condemnations of science as, we have noted, Pope John Paul II has done. It's time for science to give religion its due and religion to befriend science.

As usual, I am out of my element here, so I must fill this chapter with quotations from my scientific betters. But one thing I do know,

---

1 Charles Taylor, *A Secular Age* (Cambridge, MA: Belknap of Harvard University Press, 2007), 28.

2 John Cornwell, "The New Theism," *The Tablet*, September 12, 2018, https://www.thetablet.co.uk/features/2/14402/the-new-theism.

3 Martin Rees, *Our Cosmic Habitat* (Princeton: Princeton University Press, 2001), xi. I also suggest reading Andrew Briggs, Andrew Steane, and Hans Halvorson, *It Keeps Me Seeking: The Invitation from Science, Philosophy and Religion* (Oxford, UK: Oxford University Press, 2018).

and repeat: At this stage, science and religion must get together in mutual dialogue where religious people can talk about science and scientists can talk about spirituality.

Science might begin by admitting that scientism—the notion that science is the only source of knowledge, the only avenue of truth, the one true path to progress—is an inadmissible and indefensible ideology. The photo of a young adult wearing a T-shirt where the cross is X-ed out and the logo reads "in science we trust" has seen its day. Chastened by recent findings and the constant revelation of intractable mysteries, science needs to be humbler. Its belief system (and it is that) and its being beholden to, and sometimes in conspiracy with, the marketplace needs reexamination. Science must admit that there are other ways of knowing, that the transcendent is not lightly dismissed, that myth—a story, remember, that gives meaning—is not a retrograde word and that religious behavior has been proven to be good for mental health. William Phillips of the University of Maryland insists that science and religion are not "irreconcilable enemies." While the intelligibility and fine-tuning of the cosmos are suggestive of a Divine Being, he adds that a feeling of God's presence and God's goodness in the world is not meaningless because these aspects are not scientific.

The Church, on its part, might confess to its hostility to science and apologize for its persecution of those scientists it deemed incompatible with its truth claims. The Church, so long dominating Western culture, needs to temper its urge to pontificate and condemn, to claim special and overriding privileges bestowed by the Holy Spirit. In light of the fact that it has been proven doctrinally wrong in some issues, it needs to be more restrained in offering certitude and more respectful of other voices. Both religion and science need to be reminded that, by its very nature, our understanding of the world, our unfinished universe, is always an interpretative process at best; thus, both sides' prejudices must be left at the door. Einstein expressed it well; "Science without religion is lame. Religion without science is blind."[4]

---

4   Albert Einstein, "Science and Religion," *Ideas and Opinions* (New York: Citadel, 1956), 26.

SCIENCE AND RELIGION REVISITED

Some scientists, unfortunately, are convinced that religion impedes progress and is even hostile to it. Some take out full-page ads in the *New York Times* declaring that religion must be eradicated because it is so toxic to society. Indeed, the well-known stories of Galileo and others who suffered persecution from religion support the accusation. Then there are those scientists who offer a Darwinian account of religion, suggesting that it's an evolutionary device to promote human survival by inclining us toward group cohesion and sociality—both necessary to deal with life's everyday threats. Religion, in other words, is a biological adaptation. It basically has nothing to do with God, much less any sacred texts like the Bible purporting to reveal that God, and someday we may "evolve" out of the need for it. There is no considering the fact that religion may be a response to the sacred.

There are others today, however, who support interaction between science and religion. There are people who are trying to realign spirituality and science, to bridge the gap and set up dialogue. The tendency is to try to align revelation and evolution, to embrace science, using it to reinterpret faith, and for faith's myths (the Bible) to be seen through evolution's lens, thus challenging its claims to be the answer to all reality. Science, as some scientists have admitted, does have its blind spots, its intransigencies, its reductionist methodologies, its absolutist claims, and its tendency to become an ideology that closes itself off from other forms of knowing. Revelations such as quantum physics, black holes, and other perplexing new ideas have given science pause and show how much is unknown.

Scientists believe and rely upon a set of assertions that they do not even pretend to understand—namely, quantum theory. It's what Einstein famously called "spooky action at a distance," but an inescapable fact of the universe. Science may be more ready to listen, to reexamine its self-centered and self-absorbed stance, its beholding to capitalism and big business. The fact is, both science and religion bring prejudices to the table, but at least today, more and more, they are sitting at the same table.

Still, as I mentioned in the eleventh chapter, any dialogue will be very difficult for a Church that has made a fetish of being Spirit-guided, absolutely right, and the purveyor of eternal, unchanging truth. Having reversed itself on slavery, anti-Semitism, and no salvation outside the Church, it will have to take a humbler approach to any kind of dialogue. Anyway, it increasingly appears that science and religion are both intrinsically part of the human condition and that they must join in a common search for understanding. The proven observations of science and the truth-bearing "myths" of religion need not be antithetical. We have an unfinished universe and we need many ways to understand it.

NO LONGER EARTH-CENTERED

Up until modern times, we thought that objects moved on well-defined paths, so much so that we could predict their positions. All that was upended in the 1920s by quantum physics, which is based on a very different concept of reality, which has allowed us, through science, to gaze deep into the atom or back to the early universe. The result is that what was once thought common sense—the sun circles the earth, for example, as anyone can "plainly" see—was subverted by modern technologies.

Look at it this way. There is no way to remove the observer—us—from the perception of the world. That means our brains interpret reality, what the world is like, and from this we claim absolute truth. But that's necessarily limited. Interpreting "reality" in a different way (quantum theory) might bring another concept of what is "real." Add to this Werner Heisenberg's uncertainty principle, which shows that our very ability to measure data is limited. As Stephen Hawking put it, "Quantum physics tells us that no matter how thorough our observation of the present, the (unobserved) past, like the future, is indefinite and exists only as a spectrum of possibilities. The universe, according to quantum physics, has no single past, or history."[5]

---

5   Stephen Hawking and Leonard Mlodinow, *The Grand Design* (New York: Bantam, 2010), 82.

It's all very esoteric and I don't understand any of it, except to intuit that we are living in a new world. Religious teachers and authorities have to come to terms with these facts. As the theologian Michael Dowd reminds us, quoting Carl Sagan:

> How is it that hardly any major religion has looked at science and concluded, "This is better than we thought! The universe is much bigger than our prophets said, grander, more subtle, more elegant. God must be even greater than we dreamed."... A religion, old or new, that stressed the magnificence of the universe as revealed by modern science might be able to draw forth reserves of reverence and awe hardly tapped by the conventional faiths. Sooner or later, such a religion will emerge.

Dowd goes on to say:

> I submit that the "religion" of which Sagan spoke has been emerging for decades, largely unnoticed, at the nexus of science, inspiration, and sustainability. Rather than manifesting as a separate and competing doctrine, it is showing up as a *meta-religious* perspective (... an insight discerned by Thomas Berry). Such an evidence-based emergent can nourish any secular or religious worldview that has moved past fundamentalist allegiances to the literal word of sacred texts.[6]

And if this means putting organized religion in its place, as it were, it also applies to science—or, as I should say, scientism, meaning the near infallible teaching in nigh every university that science is the sole answer to life, the only source of truth, reality's only valid interpretation. All else is myth, mischief, and, more to the point, irrelevant, not needed. Pope Francis said that science and theology are not at odds with each other and we should "welcome new scientific

---

6   As quoted in Richard Rohr, "An Evidence-Based Emergence," *Center for Action and Contemplation*, November 5, 2019, https://cac.org/an-evidence-based-emergence-2019-11-05/.

discoveries with an attitude of humility."[7] He welcomed atheist scientist Stephen Hawking to the Vatican, saying that each mystery science explains builds a case for God. We must remember that the Vatican Observatory was established in the 1770s.

THE MARTIAN

Let me digress a bit. I don't watch much television, except in the evening, when I tune in to the six o'clock news, followed by *Jeopardy*, and then move on to PBS or Turner Classic Movies (TCM). I would like to see some other programs, but the incessant commercials drive me crazy. I would rather watch a mediocre movie on commercial-free TCM than a great program full of inane commercials.

Anyway, there are certain recurrent movies that, no matter how many times I see them, I can't help watching them again. I can almost recite the dialogue! I try to move on, but I am hooked (addicted?) to movies like *Pride and Prejudice*, the Greer Garson-Lawrence Oliver version, or Bette Davis in *Now, Voyager*, or *The Ghost and Mrs. Muir* starring Rex Harrison and Gene Tierney. The last is not only a captivating and charming movie, but the Bernard Herman music is gorgeous. Lately, I've been watching Ridley Scott's *The Martian*, starring Matt Damon. It's the story of an astronaut accidentally stranded on Mars for years and his eventual rescue. It is beautifully directed and stunningly photographed. The special effects are breathtaking and it's just a fantastic, mesmerizing story.

Above all, one is awestruck at the incredible knowledge of the scientists behind the space programs, the sophistication of the hardware, and the scientific brilliance of the lost astronaut. At every step, at every crisis, technology steps in to save the day. Matt Damon's character, a genius botanist, finds a way to grow food and survive on Mars. The earthlings at Houston Space Center are knowledgeable beyond

---

[7] Pope Francis, "Greeting of His Holiness Pope Francis to Participants at the Conference Organized by the Vatican Observatory," May 12, 2017, http://www.vatican.va/content/francesco/en/speeches/2017/may/documents/papa-francesco_20170512_specola-vaticana.html.

words. Intricate mathematics are harvested to bring him home. In short, you can't help but feel that the real star of the movie, from beginning to end, is science. And it works! God is never mentioned. No one prays—no need to. The only religious item in the movie is a small wooden crucifix left in a fellow astronaut's trunk that Matt Damon whittles to produce shavings to start a fire. The hidden message of the movie: In real life, science counts. Deity is irrelevant and—worse—useless. The Deity doesn't get the job done. Science does. That's scientism.

THE WIDER VIEW

Yet, the more responsible scientists are more measured. They have a wider view. Alan Kohler comments on the reflections of scientist Jim Baggott:

> Some of the biggest and most disputed questions in physics—string theory, the multiverse—are no more than ideas. They can only be debated theoretically; they cannot be tested experimentally, and there is no plausible argument that they will ever be testable. But if they are immune to experiment, should they still enjoy the high status of "science"? And if they *do* count as science, how can we deny the stature of "science" to other unsupported ideas, such as the claims made by religion and folk medicine?[8]

Baggott himself writes:

> Isn't science in any case about what is right and true? Surely, nobody wants to be wrong and false? Except that it isn't, and we seriously limit our ability to lift the veils of ignorance

---

8   Alan Kohler, "The Strange Australian Paradox, Santa, Mike Henry's BHP, Little Trouble in Big China, and More," *Eureka Report*, November 16, 2019, https://www.eurekareport.com.au/investment-news/the-strange-australian-paradox-santa-mike-henrys-bhp-little-trouble-in-big-ch/146406.

and change unscientific beliefs if we persist in peddling this absurdly simplistic view of what science is....

Despite appearances, science offers no certainty. Decades of progress in the philosophy of science have led us to accept that our prevailing scientific understanding is a limited-time offer, valid only until a new observation or experiment proves that it is not. It turns out to be impossible even to formulate a scientific theory without metaphysics, without first assuming some things we can't actually prove, such as the existence of an objective reality and the invisible entities we believe to exist in it.... Our best theories are full of explanatory holes. Bringing them together in a putative theory of everything has proved to be astonishingly difficult....

Do [scientists] pretend that they can think their way to real physics, ignoring Einstein's caution: "Time and again the passion for understanding has led to the illusion that man is able to comprehend the objective world rationally by pure thought without any empirical foundations—in short, by metaphysics."[9]

Then there's Ronald Dworkin, physician and political scientist, who writes:

> In the modern world, science has become the ultimate guide for describing reality.... It has ... become the unifying principle of many activities in daily life.... The scientific revolution permeates our lives, shaping our sense of reality and truth. But sometimes it does so in ways that result in sheer absurdity. This is because of flaws within the scientific method itself.[10]

He goes on to point out that Newton's method of hypothesis, experimentation, and analysis requires some assumptions that inherently limit how true the result can be because it isolated other details

---

9   Jim Baggott, "But Is It Science?" *AEON*, October 7, 2019, https://aeon.co/essays/post-empirical-science-is-an-oxymoron-and-it-is-dangerous.

10 Ronald W. Dworkin, "The Limits of Science," *National Affairs*, Winter 2019, https://www.nationalaffairs.com/publications/detail/the-limits-of-science.

not germane to the experiment. Individual isolated details make any conclusion the result of the narrowest conditions from which generalizations are made.

> Rather than use generalizations merely to organize their thoughts, they [the scientists of various disciplines] credited their abstract concepts with a positive and authoritative existence, as an actual representation of facts.... Our society's obsession with a certain idea of science has resulted in the popular prejudice that the scientific method is the mark of a thinking person, and that those who question its conclusions are "anti-science" or "deniers" of science. At the very least, people feel inclined to give the findings of neuroscience, psychology, social science, and human science the benefit of the doubt as these disciplines gain more influence over our lives. But, in the process, we neglect their limits. As humanity increasingly looks to the scientific method to understand itself, it will inevitably be disappointed by the results. The methods that work on celestial objects—bodies too distant to be knowable—can never produce truly satisfying results at the intimate level of the human. There is simply too much rich complexity to isolate our variables, or to make statements or formulas or theories that can apply to all of us."[11]

Remember, "science is only good for repeatable phenomena," as the character David Acosta says in the pilot episode of the CBS series *Evil*. There are other ways of knowing.

EVOLUTION

There is a trend today among such people as Richard Rohr, Ilia Delio, Jack Mahoney, and Daniel O'Leary to shift the focus to an evolutionary lens rather than the lens of the mythologies of the Old Testament. Richard Rohr, for example, makes a case for our evolutionary interconnectedness when he points out that, in quantum

---

11 Ibid.

physics, "one particle of any entangled pair 'knows' what is happening to another paired particle—even though there is no known means for such information to be communicated between the particles which are separated by sometimes very large distances."[12] It's the equivalent of what we call the Communion of Saints, the human entanglement of all creation, a basis for global and spiritual responsibility for all of humanity. At bottom is the evolutionary sense of unfolding, of the movement of the Spirit, and we need to shift to this context.

All this I find fascinating, even though I don't understand much of it. But I do know that we are at a crossroads and any problems with the Bible, such as the ones I have, will have to be settled within the wider context of a science-religion compromise.

I end this section with three more pertinent quotations:

> We need to understand how science is actually made; how scientists themselves think and feel and speculate. We need to explore what makes scientists creative, as well as poets or painters, or musicians.... The old rigid debates and boundaries—science versus religion, science versus the arts, science versus traditional ethics—are no longer enough. We should be impatient with them. We need a wider, more generous, more imaginative perspective.[13]

> In my view, none of our knowledge, including science, just "tells it like it is." Knowledge, even the best scientific knowledge, interprets experience through human cultural understanding and experience, and above all (just as it is for poets and preachers) metaphor is the key to the whole enterprise. As I developed my own career path, as a historian and philosopher of evolutionary biology, this insight grew and grew. Everything was

---

12   Richard Rohr, "The Field of Love," *Center for Action and Contemplation*, November 7, 2019, https://cac.org/the-field-of-love-2019-11-07/.

13   Richard Holmes, *The Age of Wonder: How the Romantic Generation Discovered the Beauty and Terror of Science* (New York: Vintage, 2008), 469.

metaphorical—struggle for existence, natural selection, division of labor, genetic code, arms races and more.[14]

Cynthia Bourgeault has expressed it this way:

Like most other critically thinking Christians, I see the Bible as a symphony (sometimes a cacophony!) of divinely inspired human voices bearing witness to an astonishing evolutionary development in our human understanding of God (or God's self-disclosure as we grow mature enough to begin to comprehend it, another way of saying the same thing).[15]

CONCLUSION

With all this being said, we have to admit that, for some, the whole biblical enterprise seems to come down to this: The Bible, in its most fundamental identity, is a certain people's national (self-serving) epic, one that, unlike others, caught on in the West because of the triumph of Christianity. It is one people's mythology among other peoples' mythologies. As such, it serves, as it is supposed to, the noble purposes of meaning, identity, and community.

"Why is this night different from any other night?" The story that is the response to that question reinforces the national epic, the national identity, and ethnic cohesion. No matter what scholars say about the Passover's origins or the blatant historical difficulties of the Exodus stories, the mythology holds fast. The myths persist, despite contradictory evidence, because the story, regardless of the facts, embodies a deeper truth that people need. So what if Marie

---

14 Michael Ruse, as quoted in Gary Cutting, "Does Evolution Explain Religious Beliefs?" *The New York Times*, July 8, 2014, https://opinionator.blogs.nytimes.com/2014/07/08/does-evolution-explain-religious-beliefs/.

15 Cynthia Bourgeault, "Final Court of Appeal," *Center for Action and Contemplation*, October 22, 2019, https://cac.org/final-court-of-appeal-2019-10-22/.

Antoinette didn't say, "Let them eat cake"—the story captured a regime that showed little concern for the public welfare. So what if George Washington didn't confess to chopping down the nonexistent cherry tree—the story captured his reputation as a man of integrity. So what if St. Francis didn't write the Prayer of St. Francis—the sentiments captured his gospel spirit. This mingling of myth and memory suffuses every epic, every saga, and the Bible is no exception.

Nobody said it better than anthropologist Bronislaw Malinowski, who, over a century ago, argued:

> Myth fulfills in primitive culture an indispensable function: it expresses, enhances, and codifies belief; it safeguards and enforces morality; it vouches for the efficiency of ritual and contains practical rules for the guidance of man. Myth is thus a vital ingredient of human civilization; it is not an idle tale, but a hard-worked active force; it is not an intellectual explanation or an artistic imagery, but a pragmatic charter of primitive faith and moral wisdom.[16]

That's an argument for the Bible and its validity, even for those who see it as a merely human work. It is precisely in its stories and the core truths those parabolic stories contain. Its worth lies in its claim to call kings to order, undermine conventional thinking, castigate injustice, and sit in judgment on capitalism and sovereign self-interest in a time when people no longer know how to describe what they are doing without the language of individualism and when unrestrained greed undermines society and the ideals it offers. In short, the Bible gives shape to history, provides a narrative, a sweep of events, a communitarian ethos (in contrast to "debauched libertarianism"[17]), a morality for people whose tendency is to be selfish and shortsighted. Its deconstruction is a loss for today, when our

---

16   Bronislaw Malinowski, *Myth in Primitive Psychology* (New York: W. W. Norton, 1926), 19.

17   David Brooks, "The Spiritual Recession," *New York Times*, June 27, 2014, https://www.nytimes.com/2014/06/27/opinion/david-brooks-is-america-losing-faith-in-universal-democracy.html.

nation is soul-sick, when everyone just goes his or her separate ways, making individual choices.

It is within this context that some seek to preserve the Bible by offering a conciliatory stance, a spiritual flavoring:

> Instead of getting bogged down by debates regarding the historical accuracy of the patriarchal narratives, of the Exodus... can we focus rather on what it means to be called, to be saved, to be a covenanted people (Genesis through Kings)? Can we learn from the prophets the importance of loyalty to God (Hosea, Jeremiah) and of living in justice (Amos, Isaiah, Micah)? Can we learn from Israel how to pray in joy and sorrow, in need and in thanksgiving (Psalms), and how to find God reflected in the world (Israel's wisdom tradition)? Can we move beyond the simplistic notion of suffering and sin as the author of Job did and as Jesus did in the New Testament?... Can we learn what it means to say God is love... prayer from psalms, loyalty from the prophets, God's presence from the wisdom tradition, what it means to be human from Jesus' life, death and Resurrection?[18]

The generous answer, of course, is yes to all of these questions, but at the same time, we can't forget the disagreements and a long history of orthodoxy-inspired persecutions and punishments that attend the Bible. We can't forget the doctrinal differences, the contradictory and mutually hostile interpretations that still exist. Mostly, even as we adopt a live-and-let-live attitude, we can't forget that consistently the biblical text still escapes us, that it has become and remains history's perennial Rorschach test.

Finally, what about the Bible's authority? By the same logic, it is secure and valid, but only for its adherents. It's the charter statement for the Jews and Christians in the same sense that the Loyal Order of Moose or the Chamber of Commerce have charter statements or mission statements, or the United States has its Constitution. These are

---

18 Pauline Viviano, "Redeeming the Bible: Can Scripture Be a Source of Unity Rather than Division?" *America*, January 22, 2015, https://www.americamagazine.org/faith/2015/01/22/redeeming-bible-can-scripture-be-source-unity-rather-division.

identity and cohesively defining ideals that are authoritative sources for its members, its adherents, its citizens—not necessarily outsiders, though its claims are universal.

Further, in regard to the Bible, we are reminded that it is a compendium that reflects how the ancients viewed reality and not necessarily how God did. The Bible, like all sacred writings, is a particular response to the ancient Israelites' and early Christians' experience of God in the particular culture in which they lived. If the Bible is sacred scripture to Jews and Christians, it's only because they themselves declared it to be so. In that sense, it is authoritative but not exclusive, not "the only way." In addition, we must keep remembering that there are two other popular claimants to being God-revealed books: the Qur'an and The Book of Mormon, which are sacred for their adherents. Like Bible believers, they too can rightly claim the books as authoritative—but not necessarily vis-à-vis the Bible—as the only word of God. In the end, they are all words "about" God, all part of the human search, the human journey.

At one time in the fourth century, St. Augustine reinterpreted Christianity within Greek categories, namely the philosophy of Plato, and changed the course of the religion. In the thirteenth century, St. Thomas Aquinas did the same when he framed Christianity within the philosophy of Aristotle and changed the course of religion. I think it is safe to say that today Christianity is being recast within the biological, cosmic, and cultural evolutions of our age.

Chapter 17

THE END: SUSPENDING BELIEF, EMBRACING FAITH

> Faith in the Bible is like having faith in Shakespeare. His plots, almost always borrowed from elsewhere, can often be both preposterous and gripping and his characters more substantial than real life people. Yet we are fascinated by him. Our experience can be partly explained by what Coleridge calls "the willing suspension of disbelief for the moment, which constitutes poetic faith." Shakespeare is an example of literature's intrinsic powers.... Faith in Shakespeare is sustained and explained only by the complex, subtle and entirely human power of poetic eloquence and dramatic performance.
>
> —Richard C. McCoy, FAITH IN SHAKESPEARE

It appears to be that way with the Bible. The characters, though also often fictional, are substantial; the plots, often historically and archaeologically preposterous, are borrowed; the intent is propaganda; and yet, for reasons cultural or intellectual, we bring a "poetic faith" to it and unconsciously suspend our disbelief. This book, no matter how hard I desire to have it otherwise, gives reasons why bringing faith, poetic or otherwise, to the Bible is not easy. However, before I run down a summary litany to demonstrate this, it might be worthwhile to reprint here the thematic words from James Kugel I cited at the end of chapter 6:

> Gradually... the historical circumstances in which a particular biblical passage might have originally been uttered were eventually forgotten or, in any case, considered irrelevant. What was important by, say, the third or second century B.C.E. (and quite possibly, even somewhat earlier) was what was thought to be the text's deeper significance, that is, how it was explained by the traditional interpretations that now accompanied it. And this traditional interpreted Bible—the Bible itself plus the traditions about what it really meant—was what was taught to successive generations of students, expounded in public assemblies and, ultimately, canonized by Judaism and Christianity as their sacred book.
>
> The way in which these traditions of interpretation came to cling to the biblical text may be difficult for people today to comprehend. We like to think that the Bible, or any other text, means "just what it says." And we act on that assumption: we simply open up a book—including the Bible—and try to make sense of it on our own. In ancient Israel and for centuries afterward, on the contrary, people looked to special interpreters to explain the meaning of a biblical text. For that reason, the explanations passed along by such interpreters quickly acquired an authority of their own. In studying this or that biblical law or prophecy or story, students would do more than simply learn the words; they would be told what the text meant—not only the peculiar way in which this or that term was to be interpreted, but how one biblical text related to another far removed from it, or the particular moral lesson that a text embodied, or how a certain passage was to be applied in everyday life. And the people who learned these things about the Bible from their teachers in turn passed on the same information to the next generation of students.
>
> And so, it was this *interpreted Bible*—not just the stories, prophecies, and laws themselves, but these texts as they had, by now, been interpreted and explained for centuries—that came to stand at the very center of Judaism and Christianity. This was

what people in both religions meant by "the Bible." Of course, Judaism and Christianity themselves differed on a great many questions, including the interpretation of some crucial scriptural passages, as well as on just what books were to be included in the Bible. Nevertheless, both religions had begun with basically the same interpreted Bible. For both inherited an earlier, common set of traditions, general principles regarding how one ought to go about reading and interpreting the Bible as well as specific traditions concerning the meaning of individual passages, verses, and words. As a result, even when later Jews or Christians added on new interpretations—sometimes directed against each other or against other groups or ideologies within the world in which they lived—the new interpretations frequently built on, and only modified, what had been the accepted wisdom until then.[1]

So, with that in your consciousness, let me summarize:

There are no autographed versions of the Bible, no original manuscripts, only copies of copies, interpretations of interpretations. The "Bible" in one era is definitely not the "Bible" in another. Detecting the eternal, stable "Word of God" in this cacophony of authors, redactors, editors, and propagandists is a lost cause.

There are opaque and difficult passages in the Bible that to this day we do not understand. It makes any notion of "revelation" an oxymoron.

From the very beginning, the Bible impinged on current orthodoxy and orthodoxy decidedly reinterpreted the Bible in a never ending, ongoing yin and yang. The Bible was never a stable beacon, but a template from which warring sides drew their metaphors. Sacraments, the priesthood, the papacy as we know them were projected back into the New Testament as were deliverance, being chosen, and land in the Old Testament. I remember, long ago, attending a lecture given by noted scripture scholar Raymond Brown, who remarked that sometimes the Church Fathers at Vatican II used scripture "rather naïvely." He meant that the Fathers bent scripture a

---

1   Kugel, *How to Read the Bible*, xix, xv; his emphasis.

bit to conform to a point they were making. That temptation is as old as the Bible itself and to this day we're not sure how to disentangle it.

We definitely read the Bible as we are, not as it is. If you bring faith, intellectual or poetic, to it, faith is what you will find, just as the old man did, hugging the Qur'an to himself and exclaiming with great emotion, "This is the Word of God!"

The Bible is not unique. It recycles the ancient myths that were its matrix. It therefore has many contemporary parallels and borrowings, sometimes whole cloth.

The Bible is radically superseded by modern sensibilities and scientific discoveries. It is unequivocally nullified today on selected points. For example, today we do not look upon Original Sin or sexuality the same way as the "Word of God" Bible does.

The scholars have figured out that the Bible's main historical books were written during the exile. The scribes raided old legends and creatively rewrote them to conform to current orthodoxy, even to the point of dissing their contemporary enemies in hindsight. They justified the present from an invented past. Propaganda is the correct word to describe the process. Partisanship lurks on every page. "Creativity" is the magic wand that orchestrates new meaning from words they never thought they possessed. So, we wind up with trains of thought like "What Moses said to the Israelites, or what the author of Exodus intended in having Moses say what he said, or what the redactor or the textual tradition of Exodus was trying to emphasize when he had Moses say what he said...."

Some books contradict others.

The prophets, more often than not, struck out.

In spite of Christian interpretations, there is no tradition in the Old Testament of a Messiah being foretold. "The idea of a suffering Messiah...is not to be found in the Old Testament or in any Jewish literature prior to or contemporaneous with the New Testament."[2]

Yahweh started out as one among many gods.

Being chosen for the Jews and being redeemed by Christ for the Christians are self-referential, in-house claims. Empirically, there

---

2   Fitzmyer, *The One Who Is to Come*, 142.

seem to be no apparent political, messianic, or "prince of peace" differences in evidence to prove this. The Second Coming, so fervently believed by St. Paul and the early Christians, has embarrassingly failed to materialize. Violence before and after Christianity has shown no abatement. The Bible in both eras has, in fact, been cited to justify it.

The "God among us" paradigm, whether by cloud, tent, or temple for the Jews or present wherever two or three gather in Christ's name for Christians, has existed more as myth than reality as a God who "suffers" with us, presides absently over perennial and massive, moral and physical pain, suffering, and violence.

In spite of verbal contortions, the One, Holy, Catholic, Apostolic, and Immovable Church has certifiably changed or reversed immutable doctrine.

"Myth" is the proper key to unlocking the Bible, but it works for other literature as well. Take your pick.

FINIS

A negative thought: If one were to apply the canons of the preceding litany with its many interpretations, reinterpretations, chameleon texts, blatant partisanship, historical inventions, failed prophecies, contradictions, verbal contortions, and creative glosses—Did I cover everything?—that make words say what the author wants them to say in service to a predetermined orthodoxy, we could almost take any piece of literature, especially sacred ones, and make it into the "Word of God." Well, maybe that's over the top, but it is arguable.

That was a bit cynical, so let me end on a more conciliatory note. Perhaps individual critiques of this book don't hold up and can be disputed, but cumulatively, there is no doubt that the Bible has not only often been misused and misunderstood, but also its official, canonical, written-in-stone interpretations by a Spirit-Guided Church have sometimes been gravely wrong, if not harmful. My contention has been that we need a wider view of the "holy" Bible, perhaps coming at it from a different perspective, where the Word of God becomes the Word about God. As that Word *about* God, the Bible elicits empathy and hopefully the discovery of what those searchers and pilgrims found: an inspiration that changed the world.

PART III:

WITNESS FOR THE ACCUSED

Chapter 18

THE APOLOGY AND THE COUNCIL

An apology is a good way to have the last word.

—Unknown

A little boy was playing with his pet turtle when, all of a sudden, the turtle flipped on its back and died. The boy was devastated and ran to his father, crying his eyes out. The father tried to console him and when he had calmed down a little, the father said, "Tell you what. Let's have a little funeral and we can bury him in the backyard. We'll get a little box. You can get some flowers from the yard for a cushion. Let's decorate the box and then we'll have a little ceremony." The boy became wide-eyed. "You can get some of your friends to come over and we'll have some balloons and some soda and some cupcakes"—the boy was smiling by this time—"and . . ." Just then, the turtle flipped himself back over and started to move. "Oh Daddy," the boy exclaimed, "Let's kill it!"

AN APOLOGY

I feel like the father. I have made such a forceful case against the Bible, God, and the Church that I may have killed the faith. Spinoza would be proud of me, John Cardinal Newman less so. A friend of mine, Fr. Victor Hoagland, who generously read and critiqued the manuscript and urged its publication, slyly noted that, after reading Part I, he was ready to turn in his baptismal certificate. I smiled, because I knew he was right.

The truth is that I have written this book with considerable apprehension. I kept ruminating about my concern that I might do possible harm and strain people's faith—as this process has done to mine. I struggled with my conscience. Back and forth I wavered. As I wrote in the Introduction, my intention was not to discredit the Bible, but to reset it for the modern mind that has lost its sense of enchantment and, to use an almost quaint word today, reverence. Yet some may think that I have profoundly betrayed that intent. Instead, in their eyes, I may have sown doubt and endangered the faith of many. They may consider the occasional cynicism and sarcasm quite misplaced and irreverent. I know that some, particularly those very conservative laity and hierarchy, will be offended by this book and write hostile reviews. I understand their anger and regret provoking it.

Still, everything in Part I is accurate. It's the stuff that's "out there" in academic and popular books and media. The Bible has always been a work in progress. The Church has changed its teachings. The theodicy question forever challenges. I wanted to put that "witness for the prosecution" out there as sharply and bluntly, and perhaps even as offensively, as I could because that is the dialogical climate today; this is what's happening. My intent was that this book should be made public in the hope that someone will offer a newer and better apologetic; that someone will bring us up to date and help us find the richness in the Bible that fundamentalism tends to obscure. The proper critique would not be just condemnation, but measured response.

Let me share this tidbit from the past, which finally urged me to publish this book.

At the beginning of the twentieth century, Pius X (Guisippe Sarto) was pope. He became pope at a time when new philological, textual, and archaeological discoveries were casting the Bible in a whole new light, as something intrinsically entwined with and reflective of ancient culture. Some literal stories like the Creation, Adam and Eve, or the Noah-flood sagas were being called into question. It was all new and considered threating to the faith, so Pius X, lumping all these developments under the vague general heading of "Modernism," issued a scathing condemnation and required all clergy to take an oath against modernism. (Later, another pope, Pius XII, reversed much of the condemnation and embraced many of the things formerly condemned.)

What interests me here, and what encouraged me to write this book, were these most sensible words of reply written by historian Meriol Trevor concerning Pius X:

> The usual defense of Pius X and his advisers is that they were acting on behalf of the "little ones" whose faith was threatened by the Modernists.... But were Loisy's exegetical studies a terrible danger to the fishermen of Brittany? [Loisy was a Roman Catholic priest whose book *The Gospel and the Church* caused quite a stir.]... If the little ones were the bourgeois capable of reading books of criticism, was a condemnation the best way of answering the questions raised? If it was necessary to crush Modernism in order to preserve the faith, what sort of faith, what sort of faithful were envisaged?... No one in authority would admit the questions, let alone provide what could have subdued Loisy's influence—better answers than his.... If Rome was willing to jettison the educated in order to preserve the faith of the simple, it was shortsighted not to realize that as more and more received education, so the problems would be revived on a wider scale and would not be less difficult to solve for the passage of time.[1]

We have a highly educated laity today. Better to surface these problems now, however provocatively, than to cling to what may become more and more unsustainable.

---

1   Meriol Trevor, *Prophets and Guardians: Renewal and Tradition in the Church* (New York: Doubleday, 1969), 80.

THE SPIRIT OF VATICAN II

While Vatican II has been weaponized and somewhat neutralized in the battle between liberal and conservative Catholics, we are still feeling its effects, if not its fulfillment. The Council was an attempt at *aggorgimento*, a renewal of the Church, bringing it up to date. The Church Fathers were well aware of the arguments in this book and tried to confront them. We must not forget the radical changes wrought by this Council that we live with today: a recognition of the discontinuities as well as the continuities of the faith, a move toward collegiality, a move from pyramid to circle as it were, the ecumenical acceptance of other faiths, a complete reversal of our official attitudes toward the Jews, an explosion of lay involvement, and the support of women. For example, Pope Francis in 2020 appointed six women to senior positions at the Vatican and made a woman Secretariat of State, the most prestigious office in the Vatican. There was a distinct effort at the Council to move the emphasis of the Church away from a strictly legalistic and triumphalist, self-congratulatory identity to a more pastoral focus of a pilgrim people centered on justice and the gospel.

To acknowledge that not all of this has been successful, fully implemented, or fully accepted is to state the obvious. My point in mentioning this is to say that the contents of this book are not novel to the Church and, while all would hardly agree with everything and even vehemently argue against it, these ideas are out there. This book stands in the tradition of Vatican II—not that it reflects the Council or is approved by it altogether, but that it stands in line with a Pilgrim Church still seeking clarity and answers—and, I would argue, this book should be judged in that context.

Many of the faithful are asking, "Am I a Christian if I don't believe everything the Church teaches?" Silently or openly, people today are frequently replying in the negative, especially numerous former Roman Catholics. The old official answers, rigidly formulated and imposed in an age with different political and philosophical backgrounds, are now, for such Christians, simply mystifying and obsolete, dreadfully out of touch.

There is no doubt that dogma, official teachings, and the meaning of the Bible need reformulation as the Church regroups after a terrible pandemic. Bausch makes no suggestion that such new approaches in teaching the faith must compromise or be tailored to fit secular dominance, but rather be reformulated in the wider context of (1) newer understandings of biblical times with their penchant for storytelling and flexibility and (2) modern epiphanies regarding artificial intelligence, black holes, other worlds, genetic manipulations, and other scientific revelations. Bausch's aim is not to discredit the Bible, but to reset it. His hope is to provoke better answers—and, as you will discover, "provoke" is the right word!

www.ingramcontent.com/pod-product-compliance
Lightning Source LLC
Chambersburg PA
CBHW071112160426
43196CB00013B/2543